Love Times Three

Love
Times Three

Our True Story
of a Polygamous Marriage

Joe, Alina, Vicki, and Valerie Darger
with Brooke Adams

HarperOne
An Imprint of HarperCollinsPublishers

HarperOne

LOVE TIMES THREE: *Our True Story of a Polygamous Marriage.*
Copyright © 2011 by Joe Darger, Alina Darger, Vicki Darger, Valerie Darger, and Brooke Adams. All rights reserved. Printed in the United States of America. No part of this book may be used or reproduced in any manner whatsoever without written permission except in the case of brief quotations embodied in critical articles and reviews. For information address HarperCollins Publishers, 10 East 53rd Street, New York, NY 10022.

HarperCollins books may be purchased for educational, business, or sales promotional use. For information please write: Special Markets Department, HarperCollins Publishers, 10 East 53rd Street, New York, NY 10022.

HarperCollins website: http://www.harpercollins.com

HarperCollins®, 📖®, and HarperOne™ are trademarks of HarperCollins Publishers

Book design by Terry McGrath

FIRST EDITION

Library of Congress Cataloging-in-Publication Data
Love times three : our true story of a polygamous marriage /
by Joe, Alina, Vicki and Valerie Darger ; and Brooke Adams.
p. cm.
ISBN 978-0-06-207404-1
1. Darger, Joe. 2. Polygamy—Utah. 3. Polygamy—Religious aspects—
Fundamentalist Church of Jesus Christ of Latter-Day Saints. I. Darger, Joe.
HQ994.L68 2011
306.84'2309792258—dc23   2011019664

11 12 13 14 15   RRD(H)   10 9 8 7 6 5 4 3 2 1

CONTENTS

v

A NOTE TO READERS

In the past, people like us who have polygamous relationships have zealously guarded their privacy and sought to stay out of the public spotlight due to this lifestyle's criminal status. We have stayed silent despite widespread misperceptions, mistreatment, and intolerance. To speak up is to risk persecution, prosecution, and, because of discrimination, economic hardship. We have carried the fragile hope that our silence will allow us to avoid unfair treatment. As a family, we have come to see that as unproductive and naive.

Real and fictional events have combined to create a public portrait of our culture that is often inaccurate and at times harmful, which has led to our decision to share our story despite the risks. We hope to correct fallacies spread through statements that typically begin, "All polygamists are . . ."—a blank filled in with "abusive," "uneducated," "oppressed," and numerous other pejorative terms. Such broad-brush swipes are no more accurate than characterizing all monogamists based on the abusive behavior of actor Charlie Sheen or the infidelity of golfer Tiger Woods.

In speaking about our lives, we do not mean to deny the voice of others who have had a bad experience in polygamy; as with monogamy, there are some plural marriages that don't work out, and there are practices in some groups that we don't agree with or believe are in keeping with the ideals of our faith. Nor do we claim to represent any other family's experience, though we know many families who, like us, have successful, faith-based plural marriages. This is simply our truth.

In telling our story, we relied on journals, family histories, our own memories, and individual interpretations of certain events. We have withheld names of some individuals to protect their privacy.

We want to be clear on one point: we are Independents—the largest category of Fundamentalist Mormons, who believe plural marriage is an essential religious tenet. Historical roots aside, we have no association whatsoever with any organized polygamous group or with the Church of Jesus Christ of Latter-day Saints (LDS). Since 1890, the LDS Church has issued numerous official declarations and statements denouncing plural marriage and has disavowed any connection with fundamentalists.

Some have asked whether polygamy is viable in our modern culture. Our answer? Yes, absolutely. Ours is an example of a family created by consenting adults for whom this lifestyle works. At its core, this is a love story about people who came together to create a family that would support, nurture, and sustain each member.

Every day, people make bonds and blend relationships in ways that are redefining what it means to be "family." Our particular redefinition is nothing new, however: polygamy is the most widespread family structure in the world, permissible in more cultures historically than any other. In choosing plural marriage, we have found purpose that goes beyond ourselves, sometimes in ways we never could have imagined as we built a family based on the most traditional of values: faith, love, loyalty, and unconditional acceptance.

—*The Dargers*

A Matter of Principle

Nothing in life is to be feared, it is only to be understood.

—MARIE CURIE

Joe

THE HOUSE WAS QUIET, the younger children finally in bed, as I made my way to the family room and turned on the television. For weeks, I had been hearing about the finale for the first season of HBO's series about polygamy, *Big Love*. That evening, as the episode began, I felt a panicky, butterflies-in-the-stomach sensation. HBO was about to showcase an event plucked from my own life.

I am a polygamist. I live in a suburb of Salt Lake City, Utah, with my three wives—Alina, Vicki, and Valerie—and our twenty-three living children. I own a business, coach Little League sports teams, and am heavily involved with my extended family. But I bet you are stuck on that first sentence. Yes, I am a polygamist.

I am what some refer to as a "Joseph Smith Mormon"—in other words, I am part of the religious movement known as Mormonism but I do not belong to any church or follow any leader.

Some people erroneously refer to me as a "polygamist" the same way someone else might be called a "Catholic" or a "Buddhist." But there is much more to my beliefs than the way I've chosen to structure my family.

Many people are surprised when they meet us and learn we are polygamists. Strangers expect my wives to be dressed in conservative clothing and have their hair in French braids—not dressed fashionably, with stylish haircuts and makeup, jobs, and children in public school. The fact is, a majority of polygamous families are just as mainstream as we are.*

Alina, Vicki, and I have been married more than twenty-one years; Valerie joined the family eleven years ago, bringing five children from her first marriage. Our lives revolve around our Fundamentalist Mormon faith and our children. And we do have a bunch of them! We have six college-age children, fourteen children in grade school, and three preschoolers, including Victoria, who at one is the newest addition to the family. We sometimes need a dolly to hold the groceries during weekly shopping trips to Costco. Sunday brunches are huge affairs that typically involve five dozen eggs, gallons of milk and juice, and too many waffles to count. My weekend Honey-Do list is often pages long, and my wives have had to become master strategists in order to keep track of who needs to be where and when. My family may be bigger than most and my relationships more complex (I have to admit I sometimes have trouble tracking whose turn it is for date night),

---

* "Polygamy" technically means multiple spouses of either gender, while the word "polygyny" refers to a man with multiple wives. When Fundamentalist Mormons use the term "polygamy," they are endorsing only multiple wives, not multiple husbands. At the back of the book, we include a brief overview of the different types of Fundamentalist Mormons.

but in reality our lives aren't much different from those of our neighbors.

I don't have time to watch much television, and, to be honest, I don't care for the content of most cable shows. If it weren't for the "P word," I wouldn't have been tuning in to HBO that night in June 2006. In fact, I was shocked when I first learned HBO was doing a series about a polygamous family, and I expected the worst. I figured the show would make us out to be a bunch of kooks. At the time, there was a lot of national media attention focused on a polygamous sect in Utah whose leader had been accused of crimes and was then in hiding.

But my curiosity about the show, and my hope that it would offer a fair treatment of my culture, increased when I learned that *Big Love* creators Mark V. Olsen and Will Scheffer drew some of their inspiration from a magazine called *Mormon Focus*. "The first cover issue shows, virtually, this family—the suburban integrated family. So it's not a concoction," Olsen told media during a publicity tour for *Big Love*.

There was only a single issue of *Mormon Focus* published (in 2003), and it featured my three wives on its cover. Two stories in the magazine, intended for a Fundamentalist Mormon audience, were about my family, though we were identified only by pseudonyms. We'd agreed to participate in the debut issue after praying about it as a family, and we were scared about the fallout. But there wasn't any, at least not as far as we could tell. When the magazine folded after that initial issue, we wondered why we'd been so strongly inspired to do it. Now, several years later, was *Big Love* our answer? There was no doubt that the show was going to bring polygamy into the public sphere, probably in ways we never could have imagined.

So I knew that the show's creators were familiar with how our family lived. But as *Big Love* rolled out in 2006, I was unnerved. With each new episode I wondered, *Who is the inside person feeding them information?* Much of what was depicted in the series about the main character and his family seemed to parallel and even mirror my life, to the extent that, no matter how strongly we denied it, many friends and relatives assumed we were secret informants for the show. No one in my family had met with or spoken to *Big Love*'s creators or any of its staff. But still the suspicion that we were involved grew, especially among fundamentalists who were uncomfortable with the show's portrayal of our lifestyle. And then came the season-one finale, titled "The Ceremony," in which the polygamous lifestyle of one wife is revealed after she is named a "Beehive Mother of the Year."

It's a true story. It happened to my mother.

In 1999, Governor Michael Leavitt and his wife, Jacalyn, paid tribute to twenty-five "Remarkable Mothers" from throughout Utah. I nominated my mother, who had started a catering business to support her family after my father, who had four wives, died in 1995. "Her daily heroism both inspires me and epitomizes the high office of motherhood," I wrote in my nomination letter. I was twenty-six—the oldest of my father's seventeen children—when he passed away. My mother had ten children, six of whom were still at home, and she was determined to take care of them without putting a burden on others.

My mother took the assets she had—great people skills, a big kitchen, and experience feeding large groups of people—and put them to work. She talked several major vendors into choosing her fledgling company as their preferred provider. Like many children,

I did not always agree with my mother's choices, but I saw her as a great example of a strong woman and of a mother who was willing to do all she could to provide for her children.

My mother was chosen as one of the state's "Remarkable Mothers" and, on the day of the awards luncheon, was featured in a full-page ad in *The Salt Lake Tribune* with the other mothers who were being recognized. That's when things blew up. A tipster alerted the governor's staff that they had picked a plural wife for recognition. I was seated with two of my siblings and our mother in a room at the governor's mansion, waiting for the luncheon ceremony to begin, when a grim-faced staff aide approached, whispered in my mother's ear, and led her away. I had a sickening feeling. What had I done? When I nominated her, I had naively hoped that polygamy wouldn't be an issue, and that my mother would be judged on her accomplishments as a businesswoman and parent.

My mother was taken to a women's restroom, where the aide asked if she was a plural wife. Moments later, another aide collected my siblings and me and took us to the same restroom. A reporter from *The Salt Lake Tribune,* sensing something newsworthy, was posted outside the door, hoping for a scoop. I had never been in a women's restroom, which added to the awkwardness.

It took just one look at my mother's ashen face to confirm that her history as a plural wife had surfaced. But no one knew what to do, apparently. The governor's staff had two equally bad options: pay tribute to a polygamist or retract the award. Either choice was sure to generate controversy. The governor—who, by the way, had polygamous ancestors—already had drawn criticism for saying that Utah was not going to prosecute polygamists aggressively for legal reasons, and that the practice of polygamy might fall under First Amendment protection. He'd then had to backtrack from those comments. Now this.

"Are you prepared to come out publicly as a plural wife? Do you realize what that would mean for your family?" the aide asked my mother.

There was silence. I quickly ran through the options in my mind.

"What if my mother declined the award and walked away?" I offered. I realized that would spare my mother embarrassment and allow the governor to avoid a media circus focused on polygamy rather than on the deserving mothers gathered in the other room.

"Would you do that?" the aide asked, relief sweeping across her face.

Moments later, my mother, siblings, and I left through a side door at the governor's mansion, with a news photographer snapping away and the reporter firing off questions as we ran to our car.

"I'm declining the award," my mother told the reporter. The only thing I could think to say was, "No comment, no comment," over and over.

The headline in *The Salt Lake Tribune* the next day read, "Polygamous Mom Slips Out Back Door of Ceremony." Other media soon picked up the story and we were inundated with requests for interviews, which terrified us. A dozen years ago, polygamy was as explosive a topic as it is today.

I don't know how *Big Love* came across the story, but there is no doubt the producers recognized its dramatic potential. Alina, Vicki, and Valerie settled in beside me on our oversize leather couch that night to watch the show's interpretation of the event. Valerie wasn't part of the family back in 1999, so while she knew the basic story, she had lots of questions as we watched: "Is that how it really happened? Who was there? What did you do; what did you say?"

It was a tense hour for me. I had tears in my eyes through most of the episode as the fears and feelings I'd experienced long ago flooded back. Vicki didn't rush around our house closing curtains the way one of the wives did in the season finale, but for a while she was sick with worry that the state might investigate us, learn we were polygamists, and take away our children. Whenever the phone rang during the days after the awards luncheon, we didn't dare answer it; we feared it might be yet another reporter calling. I was uneasy when I went to work the day after the story broke. Had my coworkers heard about my mom and the declined award? What would they think? It didn't take long for a boss to approach me and say he'd seen the news. To my great relief, he added, "That's just not right."

The *Big Love* episode captured all the things I felt at the time: hurt, fear, isolation, and tenderness for my family. It accurately showed how polygamists like me have sought to keep our lives private and have learned to smoothly change the subject or give indirect answers to questions that dig too deep. Those are the times a knot grows in your stomach, one caused by the fear of the unknown, the fear that once someone knows about your lifestyle they'll treat you differently—with revulsion and suspicion. Our consensual plural relationships are considered a crime even though we do not seek state-issued marriage licenses for them.

The "Remarkable Mothers" event was my first experience with public intolerance of polygamy as an adult, but it certainly wouldn't be my last. Indeed, just two years later, I faced a personal tragedy that was worsened by prejudicial views of my lifestyle. In March 2001, my five-month-old daughter Kyra died. Alina—her mother—and I would learn later that our daughter had undiagnosed internal birth defects that compromised her health. But we had no idea that March night why Kyra had stopped breathing. We rushed her to the hospital, in such shock that we did not realize she had already passed away. This was the beginning of our heartbreak, and also of our nightmare. What should have been a routine investigation turned into a probe of our lifestyle and insinuations that our religious beliefs played a role in our daughter's death. In the midst of our devastating loss, my family suffered the unjustified scrutiny our lifestyle often attracts. Ultimately, though, the investigation that followed Kyra's death did not divide our family or break us; instead, it started us on the road to activism to fight anti-polygamy biases.

Once *Big Love* began to air, we were further moved to action. Through its five seasons, I watched the show's take on my religion and culture with recognition, amusement, and sometimes disgust. Mostly, it sharpened my feeling that people from within the culture needed to tell their story. But it was another series of events involving a fundamentalist sect that finally solidified our desire as a family to be those people.

Those events came to a head on April 3, 2008, when law enforcement officers raided the Yearning for Zion Ranch in Eldorado, Texas, home to members of a sect known as the Fundamentalist

Church of Jesus Christ of Latter-Day Saints (FLDS). News of what was happening in the small West Texas town didn't leak out until the next morning. But it then spread like wildfire among Fundamentalist Mormons, who can be found mostly from Mexico to Canada, California to Missouri. I was already at work when my cell phone rang at 7:00 A.M. "Have you heard what's happening in Texas?" a friend asked, her voice tinged with anxiety. Details were sketchy. She knew only that hundreds of law enforcement officers and child welfare workers were at the ranch.

For many of us, it was 1953 all over again. That's when Arizona officials raided the polygamous community then known as Short Creek, which straddled the Utah/Arizona state line. Law officers removed 153 children, leaving behind those on the Utah side of the town.* Officials initially planned to separate the children from their families and place them in adoptive homes, a proposal that deflated almost as soon as it was launched because of nationwide criticism of the state's action. Still, Arizona had custody of nearly all those children, along with their mothers, for two years.

Like many other Fundamentalist Mormons, we have relatives who were swept up in the raid at Short Creek (now known as Hildale, Utah, and Colorado City, Arizona). Vicki and Valerie's mother was a child during the Short Creek Raid, and the pain is still fresh all these years later when she talks about her experiences. Her stories are a constant reminder of what can happen when you choose the polygamous lifestyle. Fifty-five years later, as events unfolded in

* There were 263 children in Short Creek at the time, but only the 153 children living on the Arizona side of the community were taken into custody, according to Martha Sonntag Bradley's book, *Kidnapped from That Land: The Government Raids on the Short Creek Polygamists* (Salt Lake City: University of Utah Press, 1993), 137.

Texas, we feared there would be simultaneous raids in Utah, Arizona, and other places that are home to Fundamentalist Mormons.

By the third day, Texas authorities had removed 439 children from the Yearning for Zion Ranch and taken them, with their mothers, forty-five miles away to San Angelo. They were initially housed at a historic military fort. After a week, the women were separated from the children, who were then sent to foster shelters across Texas, from the Panhandle to the Gulf.

As a family, we were distraught, confused, and afraid. We understood the lasting trauma the FLDS children would experience. We watched the television reports and read stories about the mothers with heavy hearts. My wives were panicked when they thought of being separated from their own children and not knowing who they were with or whether they were okay. As we gathered for family prayer at night, they were often in tears as we asked God to bring healing and comfort to the hearts of both the young ones and the now childless mothers.

We tried to keep our youngest children from watching the news and shielded them from most of our anxious conversations, but there was no escaping the tension and stress we were experiencing.

"Could this happen to us, Dad? Are you going to jail?" Ashton, my nine-year-old son, asked one day. He went to his mother almost once every hour to ask, "Did they make the brothers and sisters go away from each other to strangers' houses?" My daughter Kyley, six, asked if law officers were "doing this to everyone who has more than one mom."

We'd had little contact with our relatives in the FLDS sect over the years, though we had known them to be honorable people. But like most of the public, we knew virtually nothing about the group's current practices or its leader, Warren S. Jeffs, other than what we gleaned from media reports about arranged marriages involving minors and of exiles, some just boys, who'd left or been kicked out of the church. In the years preceding the Texas raid, the accounts we'd heard of the insular FLDS sect led us to begin talking about our lives, experiences, and beliefs publicly. As Independent Fundamentalist Mormons, our culture is vastly different, especially when it comes to marriage practices and family autonomy. Through two groups—Principle Voices, an advocacy group, and the Principle Rights Coalition, which seeks to bring the diverse universe of Fundamentalist Mormons together on common ground—my family and others had emphatically spoken against underage marriage and abuse of any kind. We'd also tried to help educate the public about the distinct differences found among Fundamentalist Mormons. That April, as every day brought a new, sensational allegation involving the FLDS (including many claims that would later prove unfounded), it appeared those efforts were unraveling. I was heartsick because it seemed such a setback of what we'd been trying to do.

In the days following the raid, I received nonstop calls from Fundamentalist Mormons who shared my family's anxiety about the news trickling out of Texas. Seeing my children and community in fear, I had one thought: *I have to* do *something*. I wanted to protect and comfort, but I also was filled with purposeful anger. As national media descended on Texas, I wanted to help reporters understand the variations in Mormon fundamentalism. At the same time, I wanted to speak out against the injustice that had occurred in the way authorities had removed all the children from their mothers based on unsubstantiated claims. I feared that if we spoke out and the claims later proved true, we would be judged as sympathetic to abusive behavior—and yet what if they *weren't* true and we did nothing?

As chairman of the Principle Rights Coalition, I called a meeting the first week of the raid. I saw fear on the face of every person in the room. As ideas were batted around about how to respond, I thought of how I had turned to writing so often in my own life to deal with confusion, hurt, and pain. I suggested a letter-writing campaign that would connect our mothers to the FLDS mothers, our children to their children.

At first, the idea was not received as warmly as I'd hoped. Some coalition members pointed out that the FLDS had rejected our past efforts to reach out to them; perhaps they would mistrust our motives now. But no one had a better proposal, so we proceeded. Writing letters at least gave us something to do and provided a way for our children to deal with their fears. One letter, written by a four-year-old, brought tears to my eyes. It said simply: "I hope the kidnappers are nice."

Several weeks after the raid, my wife Val traveled to Texas with Mary Batchelor, a cofounder of Principle Voices, bearing 420 letters of support. While in Texas, Val and Mary met with media to provide another view of the polygamous lifestyle. Their message was simple: not all polygamists are alike, and many of our families, in fact, are not much different from most monogamous families.

Those were scary times for my children, my wives, and me, but the event also finally propelled my family into making a major decision. It was, we knew, time to end our silence, and time for us to share with the world what living in a polygamous family is really like.

CHAPTER ONE

A Peculiar People

For thou art an holy people unto the Lord thy God,
and the Lord hath chosen thee to be a peculiar people unto himself,
above all the nations that are upon the earth.

—DEUTERONOMY 14:2

To say our childhoods were idyllic might be going too far. But there is no question that each of us found growing up in a big family with several moms wonderful. And "big" is definitely defined differently when it comes to plural families. Can you imagine what it's like to have thirty-nine siblings, as Vicki and Val do? One thing for sure: none of us ever felt alone or unloved as a child!

We grew up in the suburbs of Salt Lake City, attended public schools, and did just about everything other kids do. At times our parents struggled to keep us clothed and fed, but we never felt deprived. What *was* hard was dealing with prejudice about our family's lifestyle. Even so, our childhoods were great, and were a big factor in our decision to pursue the same family structure in our own lives.

Alina

I GREW UP THINKING the stars were aligned for me from the day of my birth. I was my father's seventh child, born on the seventh day of the month, in the year 1969—which seemed to have particular significance because it was mentioned so often in songs. Why bring up 1969 if there wasn't something unique about it? I was just *sure* I was really special, and nothing changed that, not even the eight siblings that came after me.

My ancestors were early converts to the Church of Jesus Christ of Latter-day Saints, and were among those who continued plural marriage when the church abandoned the practice. I was two years old when my father took my mother's sister as a second wife, so I never really experienced any other kind of family. Aunt T. had even helped come up with my name before she married my dad.

My two moms shared one house for several years before my father bought a second home for Aunt T., who would add seventeen children to my mom's fifteen. But in all of my earliest memories, Aunt T., my other mother, is there. She was the one who cooked dinner when my own mother couldn't. She was the one who, when my mother was sick one Christmas, sewed new nightgowns for all the girls in the family. She made me the beautiful plaid dress with a big bow and lots of ruffles that was inside a box I opened one Christmas morning. But I knew she wasn't my real mother.

I was helping Aunt T. put away dishes in the kitchen one day and called out, "Hey, Mom, where does this go?" My hands flew to my mouth as I looked at Aunt T. and said, "Oh, sorry, I didn't mean that."

"That's okay. I love you, Alina," she said.

My mom was elegant, reserved, and responsible. She liked to paint, wrote stories she tried to get published in *Reader's Digest,* and sang beautifully. Once when I was very young, my mom got dressed to go on a date with my dad. She had on green plaid bell-bottom pants, high-heeled boots, and matching jewelry. Her thick, curly auburn hair was down, tumbling over her shoulders. I thought she was the most beautiful thing I had ever seen as she walked out the door.

Aunt T. was lovely, too, with long, dark brown hair and bright blue eyes that sometimes turned green. She was vivacious and loved a good time. She was the one who made holidays and special occasions magical, planning the taffy pulls and other fun. She always wanted to go places and do things.

Maybe because they were so different, my two moms got along very well. I never heard them or my dad exchange cross words. My mom believed parents shouldn't involve children in adult problems. It wasn't until three days before my own marriage, at age twenty, that I heard my mom and dad argue. Even then, they were trying to hide it; they thought I was asleep.

My father had a deep, booming voice and a commanding presence that sometimes came across as gruff and intimidating. He was stocky and short, his pants dwarfed next to those of his long-legged daughters on the backyard clothesline. He loved pranks, often instigating wrestling matches and water fights that drove my moms crazy.

Money was always tight. My dad worked in construction, and there was a downturn in that industry during my childhood. When I was in first grade my mom went to work as a secretary, leaving me and the family's other young children in Aunt T.'s care. We wore hand-me-down hand-me-downs and grew a big garden each summer so that we had lots of fresh food and, in the winter, home-canned goods. Though we didn't have a lot of money, we were rich in other ways. We never lacked for companionship, and the holidays were always festive. On Thanksgiving, we would set up a big buffet, and the meal would last all day as friends and family stopped by. On Christmas Eve, we would wait anxiously for a visit from Santa—an uncle dressed in the traditional red and white costume and accompanied by three or four of our grandmas. We didn't get a lot of presents, but there were so many of us that the tree was buried in packages. It would take forever to get them all opened. Christmas was organized chaos!

In big families like mine, even the littlest children are expected to do chores. I was four when my mom taught me to wash dishes. The other kids were at school or napping when she pulled a chair up to the sink and had me stand on it as she carefully showed me how to wash a glass by rubbing a dishrag along the inside and then the rim. Sunlight slanted through the kitchen window, turning the soap bubbles into tiny iridescent rainbows. The water was warm and silky. It was so cozy and comforting to be working alongside her that the day has stayed with me all these years.

When I was in second grade, our house became too crowded and Aunt T. moved to a new home that was about fifteen minutes from our home in Millcreek, a suburb of Salt Lake City. My moms would have preferred to live closer to one another. It would have saved them a lot of time since the children were always swapping back and forth between the two homes in what seemed like a giant, never-ending slumber party. Neighborhood games really got under way once the other half of the family showed up at one house or the other. We'd take over the street or a big open field for a round of Kick the Can or Pomp, a version of touch football. On Sundays, we gathered at one of our homes for family religious services, which were always followed by a big dinner.

There was one benefit to having my moms live in different cities: Aunt T.'s children went to different schools, so we were spared having to tell classmates and teachers why we all had the same last name. But our neighbors knew we were polygamists and, while most didn't like it, the gossip about my family usually went on behind our backs. In fourth grade, I became friends with an exchange student who moved in with a family on my block. She was from the Navajo reservation. We walked to school together, talking nonstop. One day, she brought up my family.

"They say that you're polygamists," she told me.

"It's true," I said.

"Who cares?" she said, shrugging. "My uncle is, too."

But others were less accepting. One summer evening, a half dozen of my siblings and I were playing foursquare on a big cement pad in front of our house. It was dusk, and we were going hard at it in the waning light. A carload of teenagers drove by and someone leaned out the window and yelled, "Polygamists!" along with some obscenities. We stood frozen until the car disappeared down the street. No one wanted to pick up the game again, so we went inside the house. Some of the older kids were mad, calling the teens a bunch of jerks. I didn't say anything, but it bothered me more than I let on. My stomach ached all night, and the next day I was afraid to go to school. I hadn't been able to see who was in the car as it whizzed by, so I couldn't rule out my classmates. Most of my siblings shrugged it off, but from that night on I played in the backyard, where I felt less exposed.

My grandmother Nor sometimes talked about how tough things were when her husband, Louis Alma Kelsch,* went to prison for polygamy in the 1940s, and about the discrimination my mother and the other children faced. My grandfather, who had five wives and thirty-one children, had refused to give up his plural families or abstain from talking about his beliefs; as a consequence, he spent seven years in prison. Arnold Boss, my great-grandfather on my dad's side, was also in prison at the time.

Home was a safe haven for me, but school seemed like a danger zone. I was proud of my family and my heritage but believed I had to keep my background secret. I lived with the constant worry that my father might be taken to jail if the wrong people found out we were polygamists. I also feared being ridiculed and rejected by my classmates, which was why I had to develop a lot of trust before sharing anything about my family with someone at school. The friends I trusted enough to bring home had usually figured it out already and discreetly let me know they didn't care about my fam-

---

* In 1934, Louis Alma Kelsch was excommunicated from the LDS Church because of his plural marriages. During his disciplinary hearing, he asked for a copy of Doctrine and Covenants, a Mormon scripture, and read out loud the salutation on the church's 1890 declaration that it would stop polygamy. "The Manifesto says, 'To Whom It May Concern,' and it doesn't concern me a damn bit," Kelsch told the hearing panel. He then ripped out the pages with Joseph Smith's revelations regarding plural marriage and stuffed them in his pocket, saying the revelations obviously meant more to him than to the court members. *Louis Alma Kelsch* by Barbara Owen Kelsch (Salt Lake City, UT: privately printed, n.d.), 29.

ily's lifestyle. "I know you have a lot of siblings and I'm fine with that" is how my best friend in seventh grade put it to me.

But I couldn't control *every* situation that threatened my carefully knitted cocoon. That same year, I was in my homeroom class as the student-of-the-month award was announced over the school intercom. The announcer was reading a description of the student, and as soon as he said, "She has eleven siblings," I knew it was me. My face turned bright red and I slumped down in my seat. Afterward, all that my classmates wanted to talk about was the size of my family: "I can't believe there are twelve kids in your family—wow!" they told me.

My brother caught me in the hall later. "Congratulations," he said, shaking his head from side to side. "Tough luck, huh?" He was right. It was both good and bad at once.

Some of my siblings didn't care what people thought about our family. For my fourteenth birthday, one of my sisters from Aunt T. planned a surprise party at my house. She invited eight of my junior high school friends, only two of whom had been to my home previously. Another sister kept me away while they decorated the backyard with crepe paper, balloons, and a big HAPPY BIRTHDAY sign. I was definitely surprised—and mortified— when I saw all these people I kept compartmentalized in my life gathered in the backyard. The number of siblings coming and going during the party was a dead giveaway. I knew that later I would have to reveal my family to the girls who hadn't already known we were polygamists.

My sister was hurt by my obvious lack of excitement and didn't understand my embarrassment. But that's how I typically handled my family background: I tried not to draw any attention to myself even in extreme situations.

That was my approach in another junior high incident as well. A girlfriend and I were walking home from school one afternoon when a silver Mercedes-Benz sedan pulled to the curb alongside us. The male driver, dressed in a business suit, rolled down the passenger window and called to us. We could see, even without moving from the sidewalk, that he had untucked his collared shirt and pulled down his slacks to show us his erection. We both laughed in nervous disbelief and took off running to our homes. The man sped off in his fancy car.

I went straight to my bedroom without saying a word to anyone. But my friend immediately told her parents, who called the police. An officer then telephoned my house and asked to speak with me, much to my mother's surprise. She handed me the telephone and then stood listening as I did my best to downplay what had happened.

"It's not a big deal," I told the officer. "It's nothing." The last thing I wanted was for a police officer to come to my house and start asking questions that might end up with my father being hauled off to jail. When I hung up the telephone, I told my mom about the man in the Mercedes. She was upset about it and encouraged me to speak with the officer, who had given me his number in case I wanted to add any details.

"It's fine," she said. "You should talk to him. Go ahead."

I was silent. My only thought was, *Like that would ever happen!* In my mind, it was better to say nothing about the pervert who had scared my girlfriend and me than to risk publicly exposing my family.

For much of junior high, I worked to stay below the radar. I was a good student but avoided the popular crowd, which wasn't hard since I didn't have the money to keep up with the latest styles or participate in many activities. I carefully thought through everything I did at school, weighing how it might put my family in jeopardy. When I was fifteen, I wanted to try out for the newspaper and yearbook staff. I asked my mom's advice first.

"It will be fine," she said.

"But what if anybody says anything about our family?" I asked her. "What if they say, 'She's a polygamist kid'?"

"It will be fine, dear," she said again.

So I forged ahead, putting my heart and soul into creating the required sample newsletter. To my delight, I was picked as coeditor. Miss Johnson, who knew my family background, even praised my creation to the class, nodding at me with a look that said, "Good job. You did it. You took the risk." A lot of kids flaked out when it came to getting the work done, but I willingly took on extra responsibility for finishing the yearbook. The next year, as I started high school, I joined the journalism class.

Coincidentally, that's when my family hit a really rough patch. My dad was having a hard time finding jobs, so both my moms went to work. At the end of tenth grade, my parents asked me (the oldest child still at home) to switch to night school so that I could care for four younger siblings during the day. I loved school, and I was being asked to give up a lot.

"I really need your help," my mom said firmly.

"But I've been accepted to the journalism staff," I argued, urging my parents to consider other options.

My dad said only one thing: "This is what needs to be done."

So I went to night school. Despite the hardship, I did not resent my parents, their lifestyle, or our big family for this change in my life. I wasn't into the social scene at school, so that didn't feel like a loss; my best friends and the people I was most comfortable with were fundamentalists, too, and attended different schools. And I knew I would still be able to finish my education. A smaller family would have meant less sacrifice, but I wouldn't have given up a single brother or sister. I believed then, as I do now, that family sticks together, does what it takes, and works through the challenges. There was a bigger plan than just what *I* wanted.

Joe

I WAS FOUR YEARS OLD when I first experienced the power of prayer. As I said my evening prayers, I often had one special request. "Dear Heavenly Father," I would say aloud, "please help my dad quit smoking." My dad grew up rough and as a teenager developed some bad habits. As I prayed one particular night, eyes shut, my dad happened to walk by my room. He stopped to listen. Right then and there, he quit cold turkey. My dad always said it hit him so hard to see his little boy praying like that that he could never smoke another cigarette.

My parents married in 1968, when my mom was sixteen and my dad twenty. I was born a year later. It wasn't long before my first sibling came along, and there were five of us by the time I turned eight, the year I officially became a member of the Fundamentalist Mormon faith.

I was baptized on Easter Sunday at my dad's workshop, where an above-ground swimming pool had been set up and filled with tap water. Twenty-six people were baptized (including, I would later discover, Alina, Vicki, and Valerie). I didn't know what to expect when it was my turn. I walked up a little ladder and stepped into the pool. The water was so cold I thought I might freeze to death.

"I'm going to say a little prayer, and when I say 'Amen,' I'm going to dunk you under the water and then pull you up," said Jim Jessop, a respected elder who was presiding over the baptisms that day. "Okay?" he added, waiting for my confirmation.

I nodded my head. He said some words and then leaned me back so that I was completely under the icy water. Gasping for air, I broke through the surface again. I was so stunned by the cold that some men had to carry me out of the pool.

The significance of that event changed how I looked at things. Now that I was a baptized member of the faith, I knew I had a responsibility to do right at all times. I was so afraid of making the slightest misstep that my mom had to intervene.

"Joseph, baptism is a promise to seek perfection, not an expectation of perfection," she said. This came as a great relief. For one thing, I could once again stick up for myself in fights with my younger brother!

By the time I was eleven, I understood that my family was among the peculiar people who believed in polygamy and the old Mormon ways. I knew that my religious heritage went back six generations to Joseph Smith's era and the founding of Mormonism. Israel Barlow, my great-great-great-grandfather, served as Smith's bodyguard, and the Mormon church had been around for just fourteen years when James C. Owen, one of my other great-great-great-grandfathers, converted to the faith. Owen, who would become the first police chief of Ogden, Utah, was banished from his family's Pennsylvania home after joining the church in 1844 (he never practiced polygamy). Decades later, when the Church of Jesus Christ of Latter-day Saints agreed to stop practicing polygamy, my ancestors were among those who continued to engage in plural marriage.

Everyone in our middle-class neighborhood in Taylorsville, Utah, knew that my family was different because we didn't attend Sunday services at the local LDS Church. I joined the church-sponsored Boy Scout troop, though, and sometimes went to other church activities for kids. The church also occasionally sent men to our home to try to convert my parents to the mainstream faith. My dad would just explain what we believed and that was that. Some neighbors were friendly, but others refused to let their children come to our house or play with us. In time, we were no longer welcome at church functions.

Utah's construction industry was in a slump in the early 1980s (unemployment was at a historic high of 10 percent) and, even with just one family, my dad struggled to pay bills. The gas and telephone service got turned off occasionally, and we came close to being kicked out of our home too many times to count. Anonymous donors sometimes made the house payment for us. They slipped money to my mother for food, too, and made sure we had Christmas. It was hard on my dad, who didn't believe in accepting handouts.

We couldn't afford vacations; I never left the state of Utah until I was eighteen and on my own. Instead, my family went camping in the nearby canyons and made day trips to local reservoirs. Some of my cousins lived near Park City, where there was fun to be had outdoors all year long, and one grandfather owned a cabin in the mountains near Marysvale that we visited frequently. But there was a lot of financial pressure, and it fueled some loud fights between my parents. My mother called me the family peacemaker because I intervened so often in their arguments.

From an early age, my siblings and I were expected to help around the house. I weeded flowerbeds, tended my younger siblings, and deep-cleaned the kitchen. I thought making applesauce, something we did each fall, was the hardest work in the world. I often babysat for my parents and other relatives; when I was paid, I willingly handed half of what I earned to my mother to help the family.

I was thirteen when a woman expressed interest in my father and his family, and my parents began courting her. Several previous courtships hadn't worked out, so the whole family was praying this one would succeed. That summer "Aunt Mom," a term of respect I sometimes used for my dad's second wife, came into the family. My dad took two more wives after I left home, and had a total of seventeen children.

With Aunt Mom's arrival, I had to give up my large basement bedroom and was displaced in other ways, too, initially. I had figured it would be hard adjusting to a new mom, and it was. My dad had less time for me, and—a mixed blessing—Aunt Mom took over many of my responsibilities, such as getting the younger kids up for school, sometimes cooking dinner, helping my mom when she had a new baby. I wasn't the only one affected, of course. My parents argued even more than they had before. It wasn't easy for Aunt Mom, either; she had to adjust to a new, already formed family and became, in an instant, a mother. I began to understand how hard it was to live plural marriage and why it was considered one of God's higher laws.

But within three months, my two moms had begun developing a close friendship, even taking ballet classes together. And I discovered that there were pluses to having a second mother that went beyond the extra help in our home. Aunt Mom was young and vibrant. My parents didn't listen to popular music, but Aunt Mom did, and she introduced me to rock 'n' roll—Journey, ABBA, and Styx. She also brought her own family values and culture. My dad, with the added responsibility of a new wife in the family, became more consistent in holding Sunday school and in focusing on other spiritual matters.

It took a few months for our Mormon neighbors to catch on to Aunt Mom. One day, our house was plastered with tomatoes; I was sure it was because we had an "other mother." Being the oldest, I knew that my younger brothers and sisters would follow my example, so I tried not to react to such attacks. I wanted us to stay united, to be a powerful family that could not be splintered by outside forces. I prayed often that God would make me capable of withstanding persecution.

My family faced challenges even without the meddling from the neighbors. The construction industry was so depressed that we were flat-out poor despite my dad's efforts to get any work he could: he earned money as a stone mason, ditch digger, truck driver, fiberglass and marble finisher, drywall installer, framer, and—the trade he settled on and excelled at—finish carpenter. My two moms started a babysitting business to bring in extra money; some clients were polygamists, some weren't. My mothers were able to get food staples—cheese, milk, canned beans—from the federal Women, Infants, and Children Program and, for a brief time, we needed food stamps to get by.

After Aunt Mom joined our family, I was more careful about what I told school friends and whom I invited to my home. One of my favorite classes in junior high school was history, even though I cringed when my teachers talked about Mormon pioneers and plural marriage. Invariably, if the teacher didn't make derogatory statements, some of my classmates would. I sat silently as they ridiculed the "extremists" who still practiced polygamy. I didn't see my parents and relatives as extremists; I saw them as faithful. For the most part, though, my family background didn't hinder me at school.

I was big for my age and, by ninth grade, wrestled on the varsity team. In high school, I was captain of the football team. This boosted my popularity among my classmates, especially the girls. But even then my religious beliefs were beginning to shape me. Unlike some of my friends, I steered clear of cigarettes, alcohol, and drugs. I liked several girls but decided I never wanted to risk anything more than holding hands. One Halloween, I went with some friends to a haunted house in Salt Lake City. We bumped into some girls from school, including one I knew had a crush on me. I skipped the spook alley and stayed outside talking to her. Soon I was holding her hand and asking her to be my girl-friend. She said yes and we ended up kissing. Later, I was embarrassed and even ashamed, and vowed to keep myself clean for my future wife. It was okay to flirt, but I had been taught that kissing was reserved for marriage since, outside that sacred union, it might lead to further temptation. "When you're a young man, you have to learn to govern your passions," my dad told me.

Staying virtuous was just one of the goals I set for myself in junior high. I added morning prayers to my daily routine and tried to read fifteen minutes of scripture a day. I set my alarm for 5:30 A.M. to allow myself time to go on a two-mile run before school. And I had a constant no-sugar bet going with my mom, who was a health-food nut before it was trendy. Between the demands of home and school, I was learning to be a master at multitasking and time management.

Most of the time I didn't mind tending my younger siblings, even if it meant missing school occasionally. My mom gave birth to her first four children at the hospital and had the rest at home, aided by a midwife. I was there for those home births, helping out by watching my younger siblings. Later, I would proudly note each baby's time of birth and weight in a journal I kept. My mom had health problems when one of my younger brothers was eighteen months old, so for a while he slept with me at night. My mother was trying to wean him, and he would wake up crying at midnight and again at 3:00 A.M. wanting to nurse. I would have to coax him back to sleep. I was determined to keep at it until he slept through the night.

Our family went through times when Sundays were spent on formal, organized religious instruction at home, and other times when Sundays were spent visiting our grandmothers. Despite that inconsistency, I had a clear understanding of what my dad believed; he often talked to me about religion and his views on it. My mom tried to make learning the religion fun. One year, she started a Book of Mormon club: she would put money in a jar for a family activity, like a trip to an amusement park, every time we read so many pages of scripture.

When I was fourteen, I realized I was the same age Joseph Smith was when he received the revelations that led to the creation of the LDS Church. In 1820, Smith prayed for help finding the correct path to salvation. The Lord appeared to him in a vision and told Smith not to join any existing church. Three years later, in September 1823, the Angel Moroni appeared to the prophet and told him about golden plates buried in a hillside near his home in Palmyra, New York. The angel said the plates, inscribed in a hieroglyphic-like language, contained a history of the ancient peoples of America and of the Savior's work preaching the fullness of the everlasting gospel to them. Smith recovered the plates in 1827 and, with spiritual guidance, began translating into English what's known as the Book of Mormon. As early as 1829, while still involved in translating the plates, Smith received a revelation that God would, as in Old Testament times, sanction the practice of plural marriage. The prophet organized what is now known as the LDS Church on April 6, 1830. He also published the Book of Mormon that year.

Why can't I have a revelation? I wondered. I decided I would stay awake and pray all night in hopes of receiving my own heavenly visitor. But I kept dozing off as the hours ticked away. I would wake up, chide myself for having slept, and start praying again, only to nod off once more. By morning, I was disappointed that no angel had come to see me. I told my dad about it, and he chastised me harshly. "You did it only to prove something to God," he said. "He has to have a *reason* to grant prayer. You have to have a *purpose* behind your prayer."

My father was a very hard character. He was a strict disciplinarian, like his father, who had spent a lot of time on the run or in prison because of his plural marriages. My dad lived in every state in the West during his childhood, because his father had moved his seven wives and thirty-nine children from place to place to avoid prosecution. My dad and his siblings, who used the surname Brown as an alias, always kept a dime and a slip of paper with a telephone number on it tucked into the socks they wore. They were to call the number if anything happened or they became separated from their parents.

One day, as my dad was walking home from school, he saw some police officers in his front yard. His father had been charged with cohabitation again but was still living at home while awaiting trial. The officers had come to subpoena his mother as a witness in the case. As it happened, his mother was in the hospital, where she had given birth a day earlier to her tenth child, though no one answered the door to share that news with the police. My dad kept walking, bypassing the home, and went to a nearby park, which was the family's prearranged meeting place in the event of trouble.

An older sister was waiting there in the family car. He got in and she drove off; they never returned to that home.

The next day, my grandfather moved his family to an abandoned ranch in New Mexico. My grandmother had heart problems and, at age forty-two, died while they were hiding in the desert. My dad was twelve, and his life was even tougher from then on.

I idolized my dad, as a lot of kids—especially first sons—do, even though I received the brunt of his harsh treatment. I looked for every opportunity to spend time with him, even if it was just running errands, doing chores, or working with him. After completing a shared task, my dad often took me golfing or for a movie and a malt. My father had a solid moral compass: he treated people honorably and didn't pretend to be anything but what he was. Even though he never finished high school, he was a voracious reader and was always trying to improve himself. My dad was an early adopter of technology. We were the first people on our street to get a personal computer—a Leading Edge machine loaded with WordPerfect software. He had a big brick Motorola cell phone and a fax machine.

My dad loved the construction work that was his livelihood, but he always encouraged me to find a different way to make a living. "You're going to need an education in this next generation," he'd say.

Compared to many of my friends, I already understood a lot about the importance of a career, money, and what it meant not to have enough of it, especially if you had a big family. As I entered high school, I knew I was at a critical juncture. Choices I made now would have a real effect on my life. There were so many things to figure out, which is why I set new goals for myself: *study, read, and pray often.*

Valerie

MY TWIN SISTER, VICKI, and I always had lots of moms. There was our actual mother, our two other mothers, our mother's two younger sisters, and our three oldest sisters. Yes, we hit the mother lode at birth! They all showered us with love and attention.

My mother had sixteen children and we came right in the middle—numbers eight and nine. One of her sister wives, Aunt S., also had sixteen children, and the other, Auntie M., had eight. In other words, there were forty children altogether in my father's combined family.

Auntie M. lived in Midvale. My mother lived twenty minutes away, on the east side of Salt Lake County. Aunt S. lived in her own house just around the corner from my mother, which allowed them to share a car and tend each other's children. Aunt S. would often bring her sewing machine over to our house and the two moms would sew and laugh and visit for hours. They never fought, at least not in front of the children. All three families got together on Sundays. My dad would read stories from the Book of Mormon, and the moms would take turns making lunch for the crowd.

My dad would stop by each wife's house every day, regardless of where he was staying that night. My mom used to say she could set her watch by my dad's visits. As soon as he arrived, Dad would search out the children so he could give each of us a kiss on the cheek. I felt cheated if I missed mine for some reason. My dad never said much, but I always knew I had his love. He was kind and gentle; because of his example, I couldn't imagine how any man could be mean and abusive to his wives or children.

My dad worked in his brothers' cabinet-making shop, and when we were in grade school, my mother started a business called All Doll'd Up to sell handcrafted porcelain dolls and teach doll-making classes. She converted our living room into a classroom/workshop, and it was always crowded with what seemed like millions of dolls in various stages of completion. People paid top dollar for my mom's dolls. Bride dolls were her specialty, with each doll fashioned to look just like a particular customer and her wedding gown, right down to the lace and beadwork. She'd let us make our own dolls, too, patiently guiding our hands as we painted their perfect lips and eyelashes and sewed their little dresses. After a while, my mother went into partnership with her mother and Aunt S., who sewed and knitted doll dresses and booties, and moved the business into a shop in Salt Lake City. My mom had a house full of children and her own business, yet she always found time to take us on picnics and on trips to the lake or to the mountains for campouts.

With so many children, money was always tight, but my dad was very frugal and we got by. As he went around the house giving out kisses, he also turned off every unneeded light. He could repair any appliance that broke down and didn't let anything go to waste, from food to clothing to electricity. He once removed the knob from our television set so that we had to unplug it, rather than just turn it off, to save power. We probably qualified for all kinds of assistance, but it was against Dad's values to accept aid. Instead, we were the recycling kings and queens of the world; every piece of clothing went through three or four kids until it had to be tossed because it was finally too holey or stained. My dad once brought home a carton full of shoes—an assortment of boots, tennis shoes, and loafers—in every size up to 13. He had purchased them at the bargain rate of two or three dollars a pair at Kmart during some special sale, grabbing a pair of everything on the shelf and throwing it in his basket. He figured he either had a kid who could use a particular size now or would eventually. It was two decades before the last pairs were claimed, when Converse shoes finally came back in style! My mom sewed many of our outfits, which cut costs, too. When we were in first grade, she sewed Vicki and me cute plaid wool coats. At least, *we* thought they were cute. The first time we wore them, the school nurse, who knew there were a lot of kids in our family, called to ask our mother if we needed money to buy winter coats.

My dad loved to fish, and he would often take his children who were old enough with him on these day trips. Sometimes we all went along—females, too—but mostly these were father-and-son outings. Since my dad is Mr. Equal, he also made sure he spent special time with his daughters. He loved Chinese food, and would sometimes take all his girls to the Ming, a buffet-style restaurant. The servers would have to put a couple of long tables together to seat Dad and as many as a dozen daughters. I wasn't very fond of Chinese food, but I never missed one of these daddy-daughter dates.

I loved having my extra brothers and sisters so close by. Aunt S. had two daughters, one younger and one older than Vicki and

34

me. We were a little foursome, constantly moving between the two homes for playtime and sleepovers. We'd play house and make believe we were married to the Beatles. Paul was always the first one we put dibs on as a husband; George, always the last. Our favorite activity was making up skits and performing them for our parents. My dad liked country singer Slim Whitman, whose version of "Una Paloma Blanca" was a favorite, so we once made up a play about that song. One of us even dressed as a bird, wings flapping, as we sang: "Una paloma blanca, I'm just a bird in the sky. Una paloma blanca, over the mountains I fly. No one can take my freedom away." My dad loved our little show.

Our elementary school had a policy of putting twins in different classes. Our mom went along with it, but she later regretted that decision. Vicki and I ended up having different friends and teachers, and probably missed out on a lot of fun "twin" experiences and pranks! Aunt S.'s children went to the same school we did, so I always had siblings in the grades ahead of and behind me. We all had the same last name, of course, which led some of my more sensitive siblings to tell classmates we were cousins. My dad, in his gentle way, let it be known that he didn't approve: the truth was, we were all brothers and sisters, and he thought we should be proud of it.

My parents never sat me down and said, "Now, honey, you're not going to tell anybody about Dad, right?" so I never thought to keep my family secret. When I was in fifth grade, though, I heard two of my sisters from different mothers talking about whether certain people knew about our family.

"They probably do," one sister said. "*Everybody* knows."

"How do they know? I never tell anybody. I never tell a soul," the other sister said.

A classmate had just asked me if my parents were polygamists and, without any hesitation, I had given her the details, from how many mothers I had to how we lived in separate houses. But I kept my mouth shut about that earlier conversation as I listened to my sisters talk. Sensing trouble, I realized it was best not to be so forthcoming about my family.

In grade school, I attended religion classes at the local LDS Church, which was always very welcoming to my family even though we were not members. My parents thought the exposure was harmless, since most teachings were in line with our own beliefs. I loved learning all the primary-level songs: "I Am a Child of God," "Jesus Wants Me for a Sunbeam," "Popcorn Popping on the Apricot Tree." I'm sure most of our neighbors knew about my family's lifestyle. They could see us going back and forth between the two houses and knew we didn't attend services on Sundays. They were polite but kept their distance.

But as I got older I found it easier, and safer, to make friends with people who lived farther away. I wanted my friends to know me as a person first, before I told them about my family or invited them to my house. Although my moms lived in different houses, there were always so many kids coming and going that there was no way to hide our connection. But breaking the news wasn't easy.

"I have something to tell you about my family," I told a friend one day.

"What is it?" she asked.

"It's kind of hard to say, so I'm going to write it down on a piece of paper," I told her. I then handed her the slip.

She sounded out the key word: "Poli-gam-ous. What's that?"

"Well, my dad has more than one wife, and there are lots and lots of kids in our family," I said.

She didn't care about my family, as it turned out. Neither did my best friend, Mindy, who was Catholic. She and her mother had moved to a mostly Mormon neighborhood after her parents divorced. The neighbors welcomed them with cakes and pies at first, but shunned Mindy and her mom after learning they weren't Mormon. With this sort of discrimination as a common bond between us, Mindy was very accepting of my family.

But there were times I was directly confronted with the distaste some people had for our lifestyle. I had moved away from home when someone spray-painted the words "Polygamist Bitches" on the driveway of my parents' home and even fouler words all over a car parked there. My mom wanted to report the vandalism to the police, but my dad said no. He got some gray cement paint and, with the help of one of my younger sisters, scrubbed at and painted over the graffiti. We never talked about it again.

Our high school had so many students and such a diverse population that Vicki and I just blended in. I got a job working at a taco restaurant in a nearby mall and then, during the summers, at a medical supply company. My dad's rule was that if you didn't have a job, you did chores at home to contribute to the family; if you worked, you gave some of your paycheck—$40 or half of the sum, whichever was less—to your mom. It was his way of preparing us to be responsible and self-sufficient. We all did it, and none of us resented it. I still had plenty of money left to spend on clothes and hairstyling and fun activities. I was into the "new wave" style, à la singer Cyndi Lauper and the band Flock of Seagulls. I wore wild clothes and always had a different hairstyle, once cutting my hair short and bleaching it with hydrogen peroxide so that it turned an orangey blonde. Vicki didn't go as crazy as I did.

Vicki and I loved going to dances put on by one of the organized fundamentalist churches. The dances often went until midnight, but for us, being teenagers, that was usually not the end of the night. One evening after a dance, we headed back to our friend Michelle's house to change from our dresses into jeans before going to a late-night restaurant to get something to eat. Vicki was driving our mom's station wagon along a windy gravel road that skirted a canal and then sharply veered as it crossed over the water. The road was hard to see in the dark, and Vicki realized too late that we were at the curve. She swerved and the station wagon slid. In an instant, the car was upside down in the canal, with just the back end, undercarriage, and tires poking out of the water. None of us was wearing a seatbelt, which in that instance was probably fortunate. As I tried to orient myself, I could feel the water rising. I also could hear Michelle screaming and Vicki calling out, "Don't panic, don't panic!" The water covered my face and I began to flail my arms. My hand brushed the door handle, allowing me to get my bearings, and the next thing I knew the door was open. Gratefully, I slipped through it.

Vicki had climbed out her window—it had been open when we crashed—and was standing next to the car, calling Michelle's name. I had no idea how many minutes had passed. All I could think was that Michelle had been trapped in the car and had drowned. Suddenly Vicki asked, "Did you hear that?" A sound like the mewing of a cat was coming from the back of the station wagon. We waded through the chest-deep water, holding on to the car for balance. As we reached the back, we finally made out the sound: it was Michelle calling, "Help, help!" The back hatch had flipped open and we could see Michelle's head poking out above the water. We pulled her free and climbed up the canal bank to the road. Michelle was in shock and wasn't sure which way led to her house, so we just started walking. We were soaked and shoeless, the high heels we had worn to the dance lost in the chaos.

We walked for a few minutes before we spotted a house illuminated by its porch light. Safe! We were so happy. But Michelle cried out, "No, no, no—we don't want to go to *that* house. They aren't nice to polygamists."

Vicki and I were bewildered. We needed help and couldn't imagine that our family background mattered at that moment. We couldn't tell if Michelle's fear was real or due to shock, so we kept walking. (She was right about the family, we learned later.)

Finally, another house emerged out of the darkness. We knocked at the door and an older couple answered. They ushered us inside, wrapped us in blankets, and let us call our parents. The loss of the car may have been a hardship, but my parents never chewed us out. They were just relieved we hadn't been hurt.

The woman who helped us turned out to be a collector of porcelain dolls, which she displayed in her front room. A week or so after the accident, my mom paid the couple a visit and, as a thank-you for their kindness that night, gave the woman a doll she had made.

The fact that we survived the accident—we weren't even cut or bruised—seemed miraculous to me. I could not have opened that car door under my own power, given the force of the water pressing against it. My guardian angel was there, protecting me, and I felt that I had been spared for a reason. Life was such a blessing, and I was determined to get mine on the right track and find my greater purpose.

Vicki

WHEN WE WERE VERY YOUNG, Valerie and I shared a bedroom with an older sister, who used her big-sister status to always make us clean it up! But I didn't care. I never wished for my own bedroom. I loved having sisters to help decorate our room and to talk to as we drifted off to sleep at night. Most of my friends had their own rooms and everything else they wanted, but no one to share it with. That didn't seem like much fun to me.

When I first heard the term "latch-key kids" in elementary school, I had to have it explained to me. It broke my heart to imagine some of my classmates going home to an empty house day after day. My mom mostly worked from home, so either she or my older siblings were there when we returned from school. Our house was rarely empty, and I never felt alone or bored. I was so excited each time my mom or one of my other two mothers had a new baby that I could sit for hours holding my newest sibling. I loved babysitting for my moms, too. When my baby brother was two, I begged my mom to have another one, but after sixteen children she was done.

As the only twins in the family at the time, Val and I were quite the novelty. She and I loved to sing, and it drove everyone else crazy because we sang everything we heard—television jingles, the *Brady Bunch* theme song, children's church songs. Our siblings called us by the same nickname, Twinner. But by junior high, our distinct personalities really took shape, and I didn't like being referred to as if we were part of a single person. Val and I were very competitive with each other, though my mother did her best to help us be close.

My family didn't have a lot of money, but we had plenty of homespun good times. In the summer, running through the sprinklers or "swimming" in fifty-five-gallon drums filled with water from the garden hose was as much fun as a trip to the public pool. Birthdays were the same for every child, every year. Our parents would give us a five-dollar bill and let us choose what flavor of homemade ice cream to make in the hand-cranked freezer. Val and I would collaborate so that we got a double variety of flavors. My picks were usually strawberry-banana, orange-pineapple, or chocolate–Oreo cookie. It was awkward when friends would ask what I got for my birthday. "That's all?" they'd say when I told them. But I thought it was plenty.

My dad hated to travel, but that didn't stop my mom from taking us on trips. When I was seven, she saved enough money to take us to southern Utah to see our cousins in Short Creek and then on to the Grand Canyon. My mother also took us to Lava Hot Springs in Idaho for a reunion with my maternal grandmother's side of the family. Ours was the only polygamous family in attendance, but we still were welcomed. It took time for me to realize my family was different.

In fourth grade, our lesson on Utah history included an explanation of polygamy, and my teacher, Mrs. Smith, didn't make it sound like such a bad thing. I didn't yet understand the need to be discreet when talking about my family. So I raised my hand. "My grandpa was a polygamist," I said proudly when Mrs. Smith called on me. She smiled, nodded her head, and kept on with the lesson. No one seemed alarmed. Mrs. Smith said a few more things that, to me, made polygamy sound pretty good. So I raised my hand again. I was going to tell her my dad was a polygamist. This time, Mrs. Smith, who knew about my family, wisely ignored me!

By the next year, my family background wasn't anything I wanted to admit to at school, let alone publicize. One day at recess, a boy asked me about my family.

"Are you a polygamist?" he asked.

"No," I said. True, I wasn't.

"Is your dad a polygamist?" he then asked.

This made me nervous. "No," I lied.

We went on playing, but I felt guilty about that fib for years. I bumped into this classmate at my twentieth high school reunion and apologized for lying about my dad. He didn't remember our playground exchange, but it felt good to get that lie off my conscience!

For our fourteenth birthday, Val and I planned a big party with our family, friends who were Fundamentalist Mormons, and some of our classmates. It turned out to be a very awkward gathering: we hadn't realized how hard it would be for the groups to mix, or for us to split our time between them.

My parents didn't really care who knew about our family and never pressured us about religion. They gave us a lot of freedom when it came to making decisions, from music to clothes, and later, marriage. My mom let my brothers grow their hair long and deflected criticism from her sisters by telling them, "I let my boys wear their hair however they want because pretty soon it will be gone. Enjoy it while you've got it!"

But even with all that freedom, my parents still had a way of letting me know when I'd made a bad decision. One day, I was running late for school when my dad called me to join the family's morning prayers.

"I don't have time!" I shouted back, irritated.

My dad gave me a look that was a perfect mixture of disappointment and sorrow.

"We'll say a prayer for you," he said quietly.

I've never forgotten the shame I felt in that moment, or his message.

I was a sober child and, I admit, a goody-goody. I would constantly tattle on my siblings, so much so that my mother actually got after me for it. I always wanted to do what was right, and I wanted everyone else to live up to my standards. My parents were good and faithful people, and I admired them for it. I was shocked as a teenager to learn that not all my siblings and friends felt the same way about our culture and upbringing. I loved everything about my parents and their lifestyle.

By high school, I was studying, meditating, and praying a lot about the kind of life I wanted. A big family? Definitely! Plural marriage? Yes! I knew in my heart and soul that the right opportunity would come along. I only had to wait.

CHAPTER TWO

Our Path to Plural Marriage

*In the celestial glory there are three heavens or degrees;
and in order to obtain the highest, a man must enter into this order
of the priesthood [meaning the new and everlasting covenant
of marriage]; and if he does not, he cannot obtain it.*

—DOCTRINE AND COVENANTS 131:1–3

As we fell in love, it often seemed like the rest of the world was against us. Ours is an unusual love story, even within the Fundamentalist Mormon culture. It is not typical for a man to court, and then marry, two women at once. But despite the naysayers among our family and friends, it felt right to us from the start.

We had to learn to deal with jealousy and insecurity, which doom some plural marriages, as we dated. We quickly figured out that for our marriage to succeed we had to trust each other completely and talk openly and honestly, all the time, about everything. Prayer, along with advice from our parents and the teachings of early Mormon leaders, helped us find our way.

Like a triangle, our love story has three seamlessly connected points of view about why and how we came together to create a family. It all began with Vicki and Alina.

Vicki

I WAS ELEVEN WHEN I first got a crush on Joe. My sister was married to his uncle, and I saw Joe occasionally at family get-togethers, but I was too shy to talk to him. I got butterflies just writing his name. By junior high, I had scrawled "Joe Darger" all over the inside of my school locker. When I was fifteen, Joe asked me to go to the homecoming dance at his high school. At last! I had wanted to get to know Joe for a long time, and I hoped this was my chance to get him interested in me, too.

I agonized over what to wear for days, trying on at least twenty different outfits before settling on a dress that belonged to my twin sister, Val. I spent the entire day getting ready, wanting to look perfect. Unfortunately, the date was ruined before it even began.

At the last minute, one of Joe's football teammates asked to double-date. I didn't know the guy or his date, who happened to be model-beautiful. I was already nervous because I wanted to make a good impression on Joe, but now I felt even more self-conscious and shy. I was practically mute all night, and I made things even more awkward by spilling chicken on my lap at dinner. It wasn't exactly the night I had been dreaming about for years.

I stewed about the date for days, alternating between hurt and embarrassment, and finally decided to talk to Val. Joe had gone on a date with Val weeks before taking me to his school dance. I figured, after my disaster of a date, he must like her better.

"Val, if you want to pursue Joe, go ahead," I told her. "I don't think this is going anywhere for me."

"I'm not sure I want to," she said. "I don't know if I'm ready to date seriously."

As it turned out, neither of us heard from Joe again.

In high school, I went on lots of dates, some with boys who were, like Joe, Fundamentalist Mormons, and some with boys who were not. I also attended a lot of LDS Church youth dances and activities. The idea of belonging to a church really appealed to me; I liked the structure, organization, and sense of community. As a young teen, I would ride my bicycle by an LDS meetinghouse in our neighborhood and think, *Maybe someday*. But my mother's oft-repeated saying—"Where you date is where you marry"—was always in my thoughts. I tried to focus on guys from my own culture, but the truth was, I didn't have any serious prospects. Many of the Independent Fundamentalist Mormon guys I knew drank and partied and didn't seem to have a clue where they were headed in life.

In eleventh grade, Val joined an organized fundamentalist group called the Apostolic United Brethren (AUB). I was attending a lot of AUB activities, too, hoping to meet other young people who shared my standards. While my family gathered frequently with other Independent Fundamentalist Mormons for barbecues and dances, the AUB did far more to reach out to its youth with dances, mountain hikes, and religion classes. One of my older sisters had married a man in the AUB and some of my mom's relatives were AUB members, and they all encouraged my interest and made me feel welcome.

During this time, I met a girl who told me about a promise she had made to herself: she had vowed not to kiss a guy unless he was the one she was going to marry. I'd kissed a few boys already, but as I listened to my friend her promise resonated deeply with me, and I instantly made the same commitment. Even sharing a kiss with someone was giving away too much intimacy, I decided, unless I knew that person was going to be part of my future. I was willing to wait because I had faith that I would find the right man someday.

I began dating a guy from the AUB, and after four months, he asked if he could kiss me. I told him no and explained the promise I had made to myself. He was a perfect gentleman about it. "It's a good promise," he told me that night, giving me a hug instead. When we broke up a month later, he was really upset, but I knew he wasn't the one for me.

Just before starting my last year of high school, I reconnected with Joe during a camping trip that involved both our families (and many others), and I realized I was still interested in him despite the fact he'd never called after that homecoming dance. After having dated other guys, I could appreciate him even more. Joe was smart, confident, grounded, and spiritual, and he was putting together concrete plans for his future.

Joe, Val, and I spent a lot time sitting around the campfire that weekend, sharing our views on everything from religion to the families we hoped to have someday. Once the trip was over, I couldn't get Joe out of my head. My feelings for him were stronger than ever, and I decided that *this* time I wasn't going to let it drop.

Luckily, Joe's mom, whom I had known for years, apparently liked me. Joe's parents were compiling a family guide to raising children based on scripture and early LDS Church leaders' sermons, and Joe's mom asked me to help. Other Fundamentalist Mormons I knew had published pamphlets on faith principles, sharing them with family and friends. But this was a much more comprehensive undertaking. I thought it was a great project and jumped at the opportunity. Of course, it also was a good way to get my foot in Joe's door! I began going to his home after school to type additions to the manuscript, and Joe's mother often invited me to stay for dinner. I was growing really fond of the whole family, even though I wasn't getting many chances to interact with Joe himself. Joe was friendly, but it was obvious that he was keeping his distance, and I wasn't sure why. But my mind was made up: I wanted to be part of his life, and I wasn't going to go away. Joe's mother made me feel comfortable in their home, and without directly talking about it kept me encouraged even when Joe avoided me.

I was seventeen and in my last year of high school by this point, so I was thinking a lot about my future. I had briefly considered becoming a teacher, but what I really wanted in life was to be a wife and mother, and I thought Joe was the perfect guy for me. There was one complication, though: my cousin Alina always seemed to be at the Dargers' house when I was there. Her sister had married into the family, which got Alina involved, but I could tell by the things she said and the way she looked at him that Alina was interested in Joe, too.

It was tough enough for an introvert like me to keep up the pursuit, but when I realized I had competition, it brought out all my insecurities. Alina was very outgoing, and I began to worry that Joe might like her more than me. I decided I had to up my game: I pushed myself to be interesting and engaging, and I made sure I looked great when I was around Joe.

Several months went by without anyone talking about the fact that Alina and I were both hanging around a lot. Finally, Joe's mom got straight to the point one day while I was working alone with her. "I know you have an interest in Joe, and so does Alina," she said. "What do you think about pursuing Joe together?"

Since childhood, I'd been drawn to the plural lifestyle, and when envisioning my future family, I could hardly imagine that it included just my husband and our children. I was taught that while some people are not prepared or able to "live the Principle"— that is, practice plural marriage, also known as celestial marriage— that alone wouldn't keep them from heaven; in fact, among the fundamentalists I knew best, there was complete acceptance for each other's choices.* But I saw benefits and blessings in the lifestyle. My mothers made having a plural family look appealing and easy, and my father was loving, kind, and dedicated to all his families. I had already engaged in my own soul-searching, study, and prayer about whether I was capable of living the Principle and sharing a man I loved, and I thought the answer was yes.

Among Independents, a young woman has to decide first whether she wants to pursue the fundamentalist faith and second

---

* In 1843, Joseph Smith received two revelations that were eventually recorded as Sections 131 and 132 of the Doctrine and Covenants, a Mormon scripture. Most historians, however, believe that Smith had earlier revelations on the subject, and that he entered plural marriage in the early 1830s. The revelations introduced plural marriage as "the New and Everlasting Covenant of Marriage," binding on earth and through eternity. The church publicly announced the doctrine in 1852. Early Mormons referred to plural marriage as celestial marriage, the Principle, patriarchal marriage, and the Law of Abraham, terms now also used by Fundamentalist Mormons.

what kind of marriage she wants: Does she want a strictly monogamous marriage? Want to have a monogamous period before a second wife enters the family? Or join a family as a plural wife? A woman's thoughts about marriage often change as she assesses her ability to live plural marriage and as she considers possible partners. Depending on which man catches her interest, he may be single or married. If a woman is interested in a man who is already married, it's a package deal!

One of my nieces, for example, was adamant from the time she was an adolescent that she would never, ever be a plural wife. There was one guy she really liked but never got a chance to date before he married someone else. About a year later, that guy and his wife approached my niece about joining their family, and she agreed. Another woman I know had planned since childhood to have a plural family. Then she met and married Joe's brother and discovered she didn't want to share him. That was that.

I had never heard of any simultaneous courtships, but the idea didn't strike me as odd when Joe's mom suggested it. Her words spoke to my heart, and I just knew it was the right thing to do. I asked myself, *If that's what I have to do to get Joe, why not?* In fact, the thought had already crossed my mind that Alina and I might both be Joe's wives some day. She had the same tenacity I did about pursuing Joe, and she seemed to fit in with his family. But I had not shared that thought with anyone.

My conversation with Joe's mom happened just before his family threw a New Year's Eve party in 1988. Alina and I were both at that event, and we stayed up all night talking. We began hanging out together, and I discovered that Alina and I had a lot in common. We really enjoyed each other's company, liked the same activities, and had similar views on faith and family. For Fundamentalist Mormons, marriage is meant to be binding on earth through time and in heaven through eternity—which means you'd better really love your husband and his other wives or you are going to be miserable for a long time! As I got to know Alina, I realized she was the type of sister wife I could live with eternally.

Alina and I did not talk openly about our feelings for Joe, but the issue hovered between us and over everything we did. We were aware that Joe's mom had talked to both of us, and that we were each considering a dual courtship. Clearly, neither of us was willing to bow out! That winter, as we worked on the guidebook—Joe's mom had gotten her involved, too—Alina and I began searching church history for examples of dual courtships, and I was surprised and encouraged when we found some.

There was one problem: we were waiting for Joe to make a move, and nothing was happening. That April, Alina and I were at Joe's home working on the book when he finally asked to speak to us together, privately. He was very nervous, which only made me like him more.

"It's obvious that you're both interested in me," he said, stammering a bit. "I think you're both amazing girls and I'd like to get to know both of you if you are willing." It was all I could do to keep my excitement from bursting forth. Of *course* I was willing! But I waited until Alina said yes, and then I happily agreed, too.

We knew we were taking on a huge challenge and responsibility. Friends and family were concerned about our plan. Some told me, "You need a seasoned man." Others warned, "You are in over your heads." The accepted pattern in our culture was for a couple (and especially the man) to prove themselves first in a monogamous marriage before taking on the challenges of a second wife. One of Joe's aunts, who had heard about the dual courtship, walked up to me at a family party and said, with a sneer, "You should tell Joe he needs to learn to walk before he can run." I was annoyed by her comment but kept my mouth shut and just nodded before walking away. I understood why people were upset. I listened to everyone's advice and concerns, but I had prayed about this matter and had received my own answer that this was the right path for me.

From the beginning, Joe, Alina, and I decided to mostly go out together, since that would, if everything worked out, be the basis of our family. Joe's parents were always putting together fun activities, which provided public settings for us to get to know each other. At these family gatherings, everyone scrutinized our behavior. Those who hadn't lived plural marriage were openly curious. Plural wives would often watch to see how I reacted when Joe sat close to Alina, and vice versa. Did either of us avert our eyes or appear uncomfortable? This scrutiny added to the pressure we were already feeling.

The three of us also went on traditional dates together. For one of our first dates, Joe prepared chicken, potato salad, and his famous cinnamon rolls and took us on a picnic in Farmington Canyon. We hiked to Francis Peak, where there is a spectacular view of the Salt Lake Valley, and then ate the delicious meal he'd made for us. At times like these, we talked and talked and talked, really getting to know one another. Was it strange to do these romantic things with three people? In a word, yes. But Joe made each of us feel special. We'd take turns sitting in the front seat of his car; on the rare occasions when Alina wasn't there, I sat a little closer, massaged his neck a little more freely! When we were at his house, we'd sit together on the couch and Joe would put an arm around both of us. There were times I wished it was just Joe and me, but I also knew that the way we were getting to know one another was an important framework for our future.

We had been dating for several months when Joe took us on a picnic in East Canyon, just outside Salt Lake City. That afternoon, Joe asked us to date exclusively and commit to growing our love for each other. I had been prepared to take this step for a long time, so my heart pounded with excitement as he spoke. We were no longer just casually getting to know each other. It wasn't yet an engagement, but it felt like one to me, and I knew we were finally on the path that might lead to marriage.

Our dates became more serious. We spent a lot of time talking about and preparing to live in a plural marriage. We often ended up at Joe's house on Saturday nights, where we would read and discuss scripture passages and pray together for the strength and wisdom to overcome the jealousies we were already experiencing. For me, the bad feelings often arose when I made comparisons. For instance, that year Joe gave me an outfit for my birthday. But he gave Alina an outfit *and* a necklace on her birthday. I was hurt and wondered if Joe had stronger feelings for her. Finally, it occurred to me that Alina's birthday had come six months after mine, at a point when our relationships were becoming deeper and it was natural to give and receive more meaningful gifts. I reminded myself that I needed to think things through and not jump to conclusions.

Since Alina didn't have a car and I did, I would often drive her home at the end of an evening spent at Joe's house. Before we left, Joe always took time to visit alone with each of us so that our individual relationships continued to grow. If we went out on a date, Joe would drive and would alternate which one he took home first to make sure we had equal amounts of time with him. Sometimes, after dropping off Alina, Joe and I would take long walks through the neighborhood or sit in his car for several more hours, getting to know one another. I cherished these moments, since it was easier to open up when it was just the two of us. At the start of our courtship I knew I liked Joe, but I quickly found myself completely in love with him.

Romance is important to any marriage, but it isn't the only focus in Fundamentalist Mormon courtships, since many men already have families, making prolonged dating inappropriate. I had romantic moments with Joe, but that certainly wasn't my sole concern in our relationship. I was never preoccupied with whether he treated me like a princess, or with having a big wedding and a perfect day that was all about me. What mattered was finding the person who was right for me, who shared my faith, values, and goals for a family, and with whom I was compatible; everything else, I trusted, would fall into place.

But I still had worries: Did Joe think Alina was more interesting than I was? Did he consider her more attractive? Was she more fun to be with on their dates? I knew that most of my fears were irrational—and I might have experienced similar insecurities even if Joe and I were dating only each other—but that didn't stop me from having them.

I often couldn't eat because of the stress, and I dropped to ninety-five pounds. I had to learn to control my negative feelings and not get carried away by emotion. I took solace in seeing how my own relationship with Joe was growing. When Joe was on a date with Alina, I would immerse myself in other activities or surround myself with people, especially the women in my life who understood what I was experiencing. Joe's mom would often tell me, "It's hard when this happens, right? But it's okay. Your feelings are normal and you don't have to bury them. Instead, try to understand what's at the root of those feelings."

My own mother was uneasy about what we were doing. My mom always said she knew when her children had found the perfect person to marry because they had stars in their eyes. "Do I?" I asked her once. She was silent for a moment and then said, "With Alina." We laughed, but I knew why she was concerned. She understood how hard it was as she watched me being courted by a man who at the same time was also courting another woman.

Not long after we began dating, I went on a short trip to Mesquite, Nevada, with one of my sisters. I hated every minute of being away. All I could think about was that Alina had Joe to herself. Sure enough, when I came back it seemed they had grown closer. I poured my heart out to Joe's mom. A great listener, she told me something that continues to guide me today.

"A man who loves you always has a place in his heart for you," she said. "Just because he loves other people, that doesn't mean his love diminishes for you. It's the same capacity a mother has for her different children."

I was filled with peace at thinking about our love in that way. Her comment came at a crucial point, when I needed strength to keep going because my feelings for Joe were growing more intense, making sharing him even more difficult.

Alina and I had to work as hard at our relationship as we did at our relationships with Joe. We spent a lot of time together typing and editing the family guidebook, but we also often went to the movies or out shopping. We were definitely best friends. We started to pray together for strength to overcome the insecurities and jealousies that inevitably crop up and that we knew were barriers to spiritual growth. I had to work at being respectful of Alina and her relationship with Joe, allowing them the same space that I wanted in *my* relationship with Joe.

After graduating from high school, I began working full-time at a medical products company, and in August 1988 Alina got a job there, too. We sat next to each other for eight hours a day, packaging pipette tips. Sometimes those hours passed in nonstop chatter; sometimes, when misunderstandings got the best of us, the workday passed in awkward, brooding silence. I would shut down when I felt left out, felt hurt, or was raging inside, which only created more problems. Joe had reminded us early on that communication, trust, and respect would have to be the keys to our relationship if we wanted our marriage to succeed. I really had to force myself to communicate, especially at times when I thought Alina was dismissing my opinions. Joe encouraged us to get our feelings out and deal with them.

I also learned that being selfish always seemed to have a karmic backlash. One time, Alina's dad wouldn't let her go over to Joe's house so I went alone, excited that I was going to have his complete attention. Joe ended up having to work with his dad, foiling my plan. A few days later when Joe was unexpectedly free, I was busy helping my mother bottle peaches, and Alina ended up getting alone time with him! Little lessons like this taught me never to wish for something at Alina's expense.

I knew nothing was going to change until I could truly trust that Joe could love us both to the same degree, and believe that beginning a family together meant no one was "first" and no one was "second." My relationship with Joe couldn't be my only focus, or I would be failing Alina. I had to trust Alina's intentions as well if we were ever going to make it as sister wives. It was easier to become more trusting, frankly, after Joe let me know he intended to marry me.

Alina and I were spending a lot of time at the Dargers working on the guidebook that first summer after high school. One day, she left before I did, and I was able to spend another hour alone with Joe. I didn't want to leave at all that night, but finally I had to and Joe walked out with me. It was a beautiful evening, and we could see the moon just beginning to peek over the Wasatch Mountains. Joe took me to the side of his house, the most private part of the yard, and we sat under a peach tree to watch the moon rise. We talked quietly, enjoying the warm night, the smell, and the view, and then Joe took my hand.

"Vicki, I've had more than a romantic feeling for you for a long time," Joe said. "I am in love with you."

I had waited so long to hear those words! "I have always loved you," I said, grinning.

Joe leaned over and softly kissed me on the lips once, and then once more. He knew about the vow I had made to myself not to kiss a man unless he was the one I was going to marry. It was just a kiss, but it meant much more than that to both of us. It was a promise.

But we still didn't rush into marriage. We continued to date, and it wasn't until the following summer, after courting for eighteen months, that Alina, Joe, and I decided we were ready for marriage. Joe went to our fathers to ask permission to marry us, and my dad agreed to it. Alina's father, however, said no!

Alina and I were at Joe's when he came home that evening. He pulled us into a quiet room, still visibly upset as he filled us in on the heated conversation he'd had earlier with Alina's father. I just kept shaking my head, overcome with disappointment and frustration. I would be getting married if it weren't for that man! We'd been trying to do everything the right way, so his refusal seemed unreasonable. I felt bad for Alina, too, because she was embarrassed about it.

But we were determined to move forward together since we had started out together, and it was important to all of us to have the consent of Alina's dad. We decided to keep dating and working on our relationship, focusing on what God wanted us to learn through this delay. When it was time, I knew the way would open for us. And when it did six months later, everything happened quickly.

Joe came to my house to pick up my furniture to move to a trailer he had fixed up for the three of us to live in. We married days later, in ceremonies that followed one after the other. In our culture, age is given a lot of respect. Alina, like Joe, was twenty and I was nineteen, so Alina's marriage took place first. She also is Joe's legal wife. I was the witness at their civil ceremony, which took place weeks later before a judge.

Did I resent not being chosen as the legal wife? Not at all. People who do not belong to this faith put more emphasis on the notion of who's first and legal than we do. The women I knew who had come into established families had as much love and clout as the first wife, and that was what mattered. This was a necessary legality, but nothing more. It didn't signify that Joe loved Alina more than me, or mean much at all in the scheme of our lives. Alina went out of her way to make sure I was included and comfortable, which I thought showed a lot of character on her part.

I was so thrilled to finally be married and to start this new chapter in my life. My long-laid plans and much-awaited dreams were being fulfilled. People had told me that things would get tough after we married. "Get ready for the bomb to hit," they'd say. Every marriage has its challenges, so I shored myself, getting ready for that bomb, but it didn't hit. At least not right away.

Joe

I DIDN'T GROW UP assuming I would be a polygamist someday. It wasn't until I was a senior in high school that I really considered what kind of intimate relationships I wanted to have in my life. I had become infatuated with a girl in my class, and we spent a lot of time together after school and on weekends. Despite all the time together, we never talked about religion. She was LDS and, like most of my friends, assumed I was Mormon, too. Halfway through the year, though, I began to think more seriously about my life, my future, and how this relationship fit in with my plans.

I was heavily involved in sports, especially football. I played running back and was the captain of our high school football team.

I was weighing whether to go out for football at a junior college the next year, which was probably as far as my NFL dreams could go, or give up sports and concentrate on academics. I loved American history, especially Mormon and Native American history. With a degree in education, I could become a high school teacher/coach and combine two interests: history and football. But a business degree, I knew, was more likely to provide the lucrative income I would need to support a big family. I wanted lots of children, but wasn't sure I was capable of living plural marriage.

These were my questions as, relying on the teachings I had received all of my life, I turned to God for guidance. After a period of prayerful searching, I gained a better understanding of myself, how important my religion was to me, and what kind of relationship I wanted with God. I also reflected a lot on my family. I hoped to live up to the example set by my ancestors, whose faith, sacrifice, and dedication to their children I admired. They were hardworking, God-fearing people who'd striven to be the best in every aspect of their lives.

My grandfathers, with whom I had been close, had strong convictions about their faith and about plural marriage, with no fear or regret despite years of persecution. Grandpa Dave (David Brigham Darger) often shared the story of his marriage in 1926 to Eliza Aldora McDaniel, which took place in the LDS Church's Salt Lake Temple when he was twenty-three and she was twenty-one. More than two decades earlier, the LDS Church had made its second pronouncement prohibiting plural marriage. But my Grandpa Dave said that immediately after their ceremony, Apostle George F. Richards, the president of the temple, asked them to pledge to live plural marriage if they ever got the chance. He and Aldora promised to do so if the opportunity came. Grandpa Dave later made a covenant with God to practice plural marriage even if it caused him to be shunned, or cost him his freedom or his life. Ten years after his first marriage, Grandpa Dave took a plural wife: Aldora's sister Beth, my grandmother. Grandpa Dave eventually had six wives. As it turned out, Aldora and one other wife were unable to have children. Fortunately, they were still able to be mothers within the large family. Grandpa Dave had thirty-three children of his own; he also raised another seven brought into the family through marriage, including six children of a brother who had been killed in an automobile accident. To me, Grandpa Dave was a great example of a man of faith and family.

I also soon discerned what qualities I wanted in a wife and mother for my children. I wanted someone who shared my fundamentalist beliefs and who put her faith first. Given her beliefs, I knew that the girl I was dating was not part of that future, so I ended the relationship.

As I graduated from high school in 1987, I finally had a few things figured out. I would pursue a business degree and give up my dream of playing college football. I threw my energy into earning money to pay for my studies at the University of Utah. I had my own lawn care business and also went to work on a construction crew. I didn't have time for another serious relationship. Or so I thought.

That August, I went camping with my extended family at a nearby reservoir. This "family" gathering brought together about two hundred people, including Val and Vicki. Their older sister had married my uncle, and their older brother and I were friends. But I had not seen the twins since going on a date with each girl two years earlier. Neither date had been hugely successful. I laughed to myself as I remembered what had happened. As is customary in my culture, I'd had to ask the twins' father for permission to date them. My dad had counseled me about what to say, but I was still nervous.

When I arrived at the twins' home, their father answered the door and joined me on the porch. "Step into my office," he said, leading me to a Chevy Nova parked in the driveway. We got in. I was so stressed I could hardly speak.

"I've been getting to know the twins and would like to get to know them more. I would appreciate your permission to take them out," I said.

"Both of them?" he asked, surprised.

"Yes. I don't know that I would take them out at the same time, but I'd like to know each a little better to see if there's any interest," I said.

He said he'd check with their mother and the girls and let me know. A few days later, he called and told me I could date his daughters. "Keep their mother informed about where you're going and what you're doing," he cautioned.

Since I was interested in both girls, I flipped a coin to decide which one to take out first. Val won the toss, which led to the most humiliating date of my life. At the time, I worked after school on a cleaning crew at O. C. Tanner, a jewelry manufacturing company. I decided to take Val to the annual company party at Snowbird Resort in Little Cottonwood Canyon. It was my first real date in high school, and I wanted to make a good impression. I borrowed my uncle's station wagon, which was a lot nicer than my dad's car. Once Val and I got to the party, I realized I didn't know anyone. We were the youngest people there and drew a lot of "Oh, aren't they cute!" stares, especially when we danced.

We left before the party ended so I could get Val home by her curfew. Once in the station wagon, I found that I couldn't turn the steering wheel or get the car to shift into reverse. I had been driving for only a couple months and had no idea what was wrong. It was 11:00 P.M., which meant I had one hour to get Val home, and we'd come a long way. Nothing I tried worked: we were stuck. We went back inside the building, and I called my dad, who had already gone to bed. He arrived in our ratty car about thirty minutes later. He jumped in the station wagon, tugged on the steering wheel, put the car in reverse, and backed it up perfectly. He chuckled as he got out. "Sometimes you just have to pull on the wheel when you park on an incline," he said. I was so humiliated that I didn't even say a proper good-bye when I dropped Val off at her home.

A few weeks later, I took Vicki to the homecoming dance at my school, and that didn't go much better. The day of the dance, a junior on the football team asked to double-date with us; I was a sophomore and really looked up to him, so I agreed. Neither Vicki nor I knew how to answer the other couple's questions about how we'd met. That would have required revealing more information about our backgrounds than we wanted them to know. There were lots of awkward silences. The date was so strained that I waited a year before I gave Vicki the formal photos taken that night.

I didn't take either Vicki or Val on a second date, and not just because the dates had gone badly: I felt too much pressure about having to pick one over the other. Dating two girls at once seemed complicated, especially twin sisters who looked and acted so much alike. I feared I might mix them up. And what if they compared notes about our dates and about me? I left it alone, despite my interest.

But here they were again, out at the campground that August, and they were as cute as I remembered. I knew Val had recently been rebaptized as a member of the Apostolic United Brethren, a Fundamentalist Mormon group, and Vicki was checking out the AUB, too. The twins had been raised as Independents, and I was curious about their new beliefs and reasons for getting involved with an organized group. That weekend, we had long talks around the campfire about religious doctrine, faith, family, and even plural marriage. There weren't many girls—or people, for that matter—with whom I could talk about those subjects. I was intrigued by Val and Vicki, and really enjoyed our conversations. But at the same time, I wasn't interested in starting up a relationship. For one thing, I faced the same dilemma I had years earlier: How was I supposed to choose between them? I didn't want to hurt either girl's feelings. And I didn't think I was mature enough to date both at once.

A month later, there was another huge camp gathering, and a third girl piqued my interest: Alina, one of Aunt Mom's younger sisters. I was friends with Alina's brother and had known who she was for years, but I'd never paid much attention to her until that camping trip. My interest started during one of the many fast-paced, competitive volleyball games that took place that weekend.

Unlike the twins, Alina wasn't athletic. In fact, she was downright clumsy. When serving, she would toss the volleyball in the air, swing at it, and miss. She finally began simply throwing the ball over the net when it was her turn to serve. Despite her lack of coordination, she didn't give up, and she met every wisecrack about her inability to serve with a witty comeback.

"Come on, Alina, you're supposed to *hit* the ball, not *throw* it," I teased her.

"You better watch it, or it will be you I'm hitting and not the ball!" she countered.

Her reply made me laugh. I liked Alina's spunk and her character.

That fall, Vicki and Alina always seemed to be turning up at our social gatherings and coming to my house to visit my family. I was friendly but, to be honest, I tried to avoid the girls. I was busy with my college classes and work. Besides, I didn't want to consider another relationship until I had resolved, on my own, the questions and doubts I had about my religion. So I ignored the attention they were giving me. My mom really liked Alina and Vicki—that much was obvious—and was constantly asking what I thought about them, which made me bristle. I didn't want my parents involved in my dating life. I didn't like the pressure or being made to feel guilty because I didn't want to deal with them. But that didn't stop my siblings from teasing me every time Alina or Vicki came around.

It went on like this for months. One day, my dad and I were cleaning the carport together and he nonchalantly commented on the two girls' frequent visits.

"You can't just leave them hanging forever," he said. "You either have to tell them to move on with their lives or you've got to act. A man is under certain obligations to find out what God wants of him. You need to make a study of praying and fasting about it. That's how you get answers."

My dad was suggesting that I take the time—intellectually, emotionally, and spiritually—to figure out how to respond to Alina and Vicki. Fasting, a common practice in our religion of going without food for one or more days to achieve the proper spirit of humility and contemplation, would help me get answers to the serious questions before me.

That conversation with my dad scared me. I didn't want to have to face the fact that no matter what answer I got, I would have to act on it. But I put my faith in God and let go of my own will, trusting that prayer would bring the insight I needed to know what to do. I got my answer when I least expected it.

Alina and some other friends were at my house, and the group of us stayed up late into the night visiting. I was sitting across the room, listening to and watching Alina talk. All of a sudden it was as though my eyes blinked open and I saw her for the first time— her heart, her soul, the person she was and would be. I had never experienced anything like it, and it was a life-changing moment for me. In that instant, I fell in love with Alina, and I knew she would be my wife.

But I faced a dilemma: What about Vicki? I had been attracted to Vicki since that homecoming date in high school. My connection to her seemed timeless somehow, and I knew I had strong feelings for her. She had a firm faith, revealed a good and loving character, and would be an excellent wife and mother. She was exactly the sort of woman I wanted to marry.

As I thought through my situation, I realized that as much as I might have wanted to run from the truth and the responsibilities it would entail, deep down I wanted to live all the principles of my faith—including, if possible, plural marriage. But could I pursue relationships with both Alina and Vicki? I began to let down my guard and spend time with both of them. I found that they were always together and had become best friends. I could tell, too, that they knew of each other's interest in me, but weren't threatened by it. By their actions, they let me know that I could get to know them both, without choosing one over the other.

My dad was compiling a family guidebook at the time, and my mother, brother, and I were all working on the project. My mom invited Vicki and Alina to help. One March day when we were proofreading, Vicki randomly selected an excerpt from a sermon by Brigham Young, a former LDS Church president, for me to read aloud:

This is for you young women who want to get husbands. Now, girls, court up the boys, it is leap year. Give them to understand in some way that it is all right. You are ready, and you want to help them to make a good home, to form a nucleus around which to gather the blessings and comforts of life, a place to rally to. . . . Tell the boys what to do, and you sisters of experience, ye mothers in Israel, go to and get up your societies, and teach these girls what to do, and how to get the boys to come and marry them.

By the time I finished reading, I was beet red. My mother, brother, and the two girls burst out laughing.

A month later, I went to Vicki's and Alina's fathers to ask permission to formally begin dating. It is not common in our culture for a man to date two women at once, and Alina's dad was worried, especially because we don't believe in casual dating.

"You're taking on too much, too soon," he told me when I met with him.

"I'm not asking permission to *marry* Alina," I said, "just to get to know her better."

He didn't like it but he didn't say no, nor did Vicki's dad, so I moved forward with what would turn out to be a two-year courtship. But now that I had the permission I needed, I was overwhelmed. How was I supposed to go about courting two girls? How was I going to get to know two girls who were already better friends with each other than with me? There wasn't exactly a rulebook for such matters. I prayed about it, asked my parents for advice, and scoured scripture for how to build two strong, interconnected, spiritually grounded relationships. I decided that since Alina and Vicki were close friends and were interested in pursuing me together, the best thing I could do was to nurture that combined friendship. It would have been easier for me to pursue separate, distinct relationships with each girl, but I saw that as setting up a competitive trap that would likely never be overcome. I was attracted to both girls and knew that individual relationships would develop in time. The most important task now was to develop a unity as a potential family.

After dating for several months, I asked Alina and Vicki to commit exclusively, and even more seriously, to pursuing a life together. I told them that communication, trust, and respect—what I referred to as CTR—would need to be the cornerstone of our relationship if we were to have any chance at success. These values, important to *all* relationships, are especially critical for a successful plural marriage.

With those values guiding us, we continued on in typical dating fashion: movies, ballroom dancing lessons (yes, I had to drag my younger brother along as a fourth), picnics and hikes, long canyon drives, and family barbecues and camping trips. For my nineteenth birthday, Alina and Vicki prepared a spectacular candlelight dinner, served on my mother's china. We also often met to read scriptures together, sessions that were always followed by long discussions about doctrine and faith that focused on the hows and whys of the path we were pursuing. Marriage, whether monogamous or plural, is not taken lightly in our culture, and these conversations helped us think through the commitment we were contemplating.

Each relationship had its own ebb and flow. Once, we took my little sister to an amusement park near Salt Lake City. I had a terrible time. Alina and Vicki shunned me most of the day. It is tough when one woman treats you with indifference; when two do it in concert, it's powerful! I learned later they had been working through some jealousy issues and needed to focus on each other, not me.

The obstacles thrown up by Alina's family were also hard to take. Alina worked for a dentist who was a Fundamentalist Mormon and followed what I referred to as the "Short Creek

Doctrine" (the religious philosophy of what became the FLDS Church). Alina and the dentist's son had once liked each other, and some of Alina's sisters were unhappy that she was dating me; they were constantly nagging Alina to drop me and date the son again.

Alina's dad caused even bigger problems. He was a short, barrel-chested man with slicked-back hair and a Brigham Young–style beard that hung from the rim of his jaw to his chest. He was a very intimidating character. He made his displeasure about our courtship known by going into another room or out the back door of their home if he saw me coming. Although Alina was nearly nineteen, he monitored our telephone calls, for a time he limited our dates to once a week, and he often set outrageous curfews. I picked Alina up one night at six o'clock, only to learn she had to be home by eight! Months after telling me I could court Alina, he claimed he had given permission only for a few dates. The more Alina's dad or others tried to interfere, the more determined we were to succeed.

At times, my emotions were all over the place: I was attracted to Alina and Vicki but I was cautious; excited but fearful; confident but unsure. My goal was to be honorable and not let passion or lust rule our relationships. Truthfully, it wasn't always possible to balance my feelings between them. The relationships progressed in different ways and at different speeds. The girls had very different personalities. Vicki was quiet, reserved, and tentative, but very affectionate. Alina was bright, outspoken, and spontaneous, but reticent when it came to expressing affection.

I had a different view of appropriate dating behavior from that of most guys my age. I drew the line at kissing, and unequivocally considered premarital sex unacceptable. But I had not seriously dated anyone before courting Alina and Vicki, and I discovered it was much harder than I'd thought not to let desire overtake me. Everything hinged on my not acting selfishly, since Alina and Vicki were relying on my moral character to guide the development of our relationship. One way I avoided temptation was by limiting our one-on-one dates. That helped, but it still wasn't easy.

One night, we spread blankets in my parents' backyard to stargaze and talk. Alina fell asleep, and Vicki and I ended up making out. We both felt terrible for days. It wasn't the first time we'd kissed, but it was absolutely inappropriate in that setting. If Alina had woken up and found Vicki and me kissing, it would have been horrible for all of us. I went to Alina later, confessed what had happened, and offered an apology for violating her trust and being disrespectful toward her. I apologized to Vicki, too. I wanted Vicki to know I considered my behavior inappropriate; otherwise, she might easily have thought I was doing the same thing behind her back with Alina. That experience provided powerful motivation for me to stick to my principles.

After dating for eighteen months, we were firmly committed to each other. We shared the same beliefs, the same hopes for the future, and the same goals for a family. After fasting and praying about it, we set a goal of marrying by summer. At the end of May 1989, I sought out each girl's father to ask permission to marry his daughter.

If Vicki's dad had any concerns, he didn't voice them, which was in keeping with his strong feelings about the importance of freely making your own decisions and then taking responsibility for them. In his view, Vicki was old enough to make a choice and live with its consequences. He gave his approval.

Alina's father was a different story. He didn't return any of my telephone calls and managed never to be around when I stopped by either of his two homes. Days passed before I hunted him down at his mother's house, where he was working in the garage. I spent an hour making small talk until some other men who were there left. Then I got to the point.

"I'd like your permission to marry Alina," I said to her father.

"What if I tell you no and ask you to back off?" he said sharply.

"Well, that's your right, but I disagree with it," I said.

"Damn right it's my right," he said.

Alina's father then asked if I'd had a revelation—which, in his view, meant a personal visitation from a heavenly messenger—informing me that Alina was to be my wife. It was an unusual, irrational, and, in his family, unprecedented demand, and he knew it. It seemed like the only thing he could come up with to justify telling me no: I was a good kid, came from a solid family, shared his fundamentalist faith—and Alina and I loved each other.

I told Alina's father I had a strong belief that she was the right person for me, the same kind of belief he must have had when he married Alina's mother.

"Belief and knowledge are two different things," he said. "You need to *know*."

"Let's say I get a revelation that she's right for me, and come and ask you for permission. How will you know I'm telling the truth?" I asked.

"What makes you so great that you would get a revelation and not I?" Alina's father asked. That was the kicker: apparently, in his view, he would need to get the same revelation from the same heavenly messenger.

"Let's just say that for whatever reason I got it and you did not—are you saying I would have to wait for you to get it also?" I pressed.

"Yes."

The conversation went on like that for an hour. I left angry, disappointed, and frustrated. I was still upset hours later when I told Alina and Vicki about it. It was an unrealistic requirement; I had no expectation of satisfying his demand since I did not believe a heavenly messenger would make an appearance for such a purpose. I wanted to be married, and nothing was going as I hoped.

We were adults and could have gone ahead with the marriage if we'd wanted. But I did not want to marry Alina without her father's permission, and I did not want to marry Vicki without also marrying Alina. I had faith that, with the Lord's help, the path would open if our marriages were meant to be. In the meantime, I vowed to learn whatever lessons I could from the situation. So we waited.

I spent a lot of time fixing up a trailer house I had moved onto some land my family owned. The thought that this would be our first home helped me stay positive and focused. Six months passed. At the end of 1989, Alina's dad told us he would give us an answer about marriage in two months, after fasting and praying about it. In mid-February, I went to Alina's dad again and asked him to go on a three-day fast with us, while we prayed for an answer.

He agreed at first, but later told Alina he had changed his mind and wouldn't join us. We went ahead anyway, and as we began the fast, Alina's father finally told her to just go ahead with the marriage if she wanted.

At the end of the third day of our fast, I went to Alina's home and asked for her father.

"I am here for Alina," I told him. We had waited two years, and my attitude was, *Parents, be done. Get out of the way.* Alina's father was resigned to our marriage at that point and didn't say much. He stepped aside as Alina came to join me.

Alina, Vicki, and I were married that same day in a ceremony patterned after the sacred marriage ordinance performed in LDS Church temples. Our weddings took place in a private home and were witnessed by a few members of my family. My father rarely expressed his feelings, but afterward he gave me, Alina, and Vicki each a warm embrace and said how much he loved us.

"You're my daughters, too, now," he told my wives. Tears welled in my eyes, and I suspected that though he would not have admitted it, behind my father's tinted glasses there were tears in his eyes as well.

We did not have a reception. Public announcement of a marriage to anyone but the most trusted friends and family has always been a risky endeavor, given the illegal status and historical persecution associated with plural marriage. But that night we celebrated with a small group at the Red Flame Restaurant, a steakhouse that also had a ballroom dance floor. All those dancing lessons paid off that night. I also gained new insight as I experienced my own twinge of jealousy.

As I danced with Vicki, a single guy spotted Alina and asked her to dance. He didn't know she was "taken," and Alina was too polite to turn him down. When he asked Alina for a second dance, I intervened. We had a good laugh about it later, but it gave me a small glimpse into what Alina and Vicki had to endure every day.

That night, I felt both relief and apprehension—relief because our life together was finally beginning, apprehension because of the unknowns ahead. I wondered if, despite all my efforts, I was adequately prepared for my new life. I had grown so close to Alina and Vicki during our courtship. But now, after putting it off for so long, I faced the reality of having multiple intimate relationships. I was proud to be their husband, but humbled by what that commitment actually meant.

Alina

FOR A TIME AS A TEENAGER, I had one thing on my mind, and it sure wasn't marriage! My "P word"? Not "polygamy" but "party"! I was wild, hanging out with my older siblings and other kids who were into drinking and smoking and carrying on without a care in the world. I finally came to my senses in my last year of high school, when I realized I was headed for nothing but trouble. As I started thinking about what kind of life I wanted for myself, one guy stood out because he was already moving in the direction I wanted to go. That guy was Joe.

I knew Joe because my older sister, with whom I was very close, had married his father, and I would see him occasionally at family gatherings. In junior high, I had an encounter with Joe that left a lasting impression. I had gone with my sister to pick up Joe after football practice. There were groceries in the backseat of her

Monte Carlo, so Joe had to sit in the front, next to me. As Joe slid into the seat, our bodies brushed against each other, and in that instant it felt to me like a magnetic force fell over us, pulling us together. The feeling flashed powerfully but briefly and then was gone, and I didn't know what to make of it. I'd certainly never experienced anything like that sensation with guys I'd dated.

In high school, I heard lots of talk about Joe because he was quite popular and many girls were after him. He had good values and was really grounded, yet he was willing to think outside the box and already had a lot of plans for his life. I decided to check Joe out again: when his football team played my school, I went to the game to watch him. Joe was the captain of the team, and I could see that he played with a lot of heart, passion, and energy. Everything I knew about Joe made me want to know more, but it was a year before I made a move.

In the fall of 1987, I began going by the Dargers' home more often to visit my sister and always accepted any invitations to family get-togethers. I found that I really liked Joe, but I kept my feelings for him secret. Joe had started college and had a lot going on, so I saw him only once in a while. But I was getting to know his family, especially Joe's mom, quite well. Joe's family was always doing fun things: hiking, going to aerobics classes, painting, camping, playing volleyball, having barbecues, and going on long bike rides.

My cousins Vicki and Val were often at Joe's house, too. I knew that Vicki had liked Joe for a long time, but I figured she was still trying to make up her mind about him, as I was. I kept hoping someone else would catch Vicki's interest! And if that didn't happen, I figured Joe would just have to decide between the two of us. But Joe's mom, who knew that Vicki and I both were interested in Joe, had a different idea.

She brought it up one day after I called her to ask what I could bring to a New Year's Eve party the family was hosting. The conversation turned serious.

"You like Joe and Vicki likes Joe," she said. "Instead of competing for him, why don't you just get together and date him?"

"I don't know if I could do that," I said. In fact, I wasn't sure if I even wanted to *consider* it. In the days leading up to the party, where I knew I would see Vicki, a million thoughts filled my head.

I thought of all the things I would be giving up, according to the standards of the world, if I agreed to a dual courtship—mainly, the luxury of a one-on-one relationship where I wouldn't have to think of anyone else as I fell in love. I would have to build two relationships, not just one, from scratch, at the same time, and to the same depth. I wasn't sure I was capable of that. I knew it would take a huge amount of openness and honesty. *Was I ready and willing to trust that deeply? Was Vicki? Was Joe mature enough to handle the emotions and feelings of two women sensitively and fairly?*

But all those concerns collapsed under my belief in the law of celestial marriage as an essential aspect of my deepening faith. Despite the way my family's secret lifestyle had sometimes made me feel as a child, I really liked growing up in a plural family, and I admired both my mothers. Although as a teenager I spent time partying and dating guys who weren't into that lifestyle, I'd decided I believed in plural marriage and hoped to live it someday, if I found the right person. And I wasn't set on having a special period alone with a husband as a monogamous first wife. In fact, I saw a benefit in being the second or third wife: I would have the opportunity to observe how a man treated his other wives and children, and how the women interacted with each other and the husband's children, before committing myself. As I spent more time thinking about what Joe's mom had suggested, I realized there were advantages to starting married life immediately with a sister wife. We would be able to create a family culture together, and I would be spared having to adjust later if another woman entered the family.

I decided to proceed cautiously and get to know Vicki better before making up my mind. At the New Year's Eve party, Vicki and I stayed up all night talking. I found that, while our personalities were very different, we had a lot in common. About two weeks into the new year, I was looking for something to do one day and decided to invite Vicki and Val ice-skating. To my surprise, they accepted, and we had a great time. From that point on, Vicki and I were fast friends, always together—and Joe wasn't even in the picture!

Vicki, I discovered, was very accepting and good-natured. A creative and talented person, she easily picked up everything she tried, from learning the piano to playing tennis. More important, she was deeply committed to doing what she felt was right. Her faith was strong and, like me, she hoped to create a very close family someday. I could see that if we became sister wives, she had qualities that would make it possible to work through the challenges. And even if it didn't work out with Joe, I knew she would always be my good friend.

Vicki and I never sat down and had a heart-to-heart talk about our mutual interest in Joe. We didn't have to; we just knew we were in it together. But we did joke about it. Joe had been interested in a girl named Sandy in high school and, before Joe ever acknowledged our interest, Vicki and I congratulated each other on the special two-for-one deal we were offering him! Another time, the Jefferson Starship song "Nothing's Gonna Stop Us Now" came on the radio, and we changed the words in the second line to fit us: "And we can build this dream together; Sandy's gone forever; nothing's gonna stop us now!"

Joe finally came to us one day and asked if it would be all right if he spoke to our fathers about getting to know us better. I had already let my dad know that Vicki and I both wanted to date Joe, and he was concerned. He didn't think we were mature enough to deal with the feelings and complications that would come with a three-way relationship at such a young age. I think my dad expected our efforts to fail of their own accord, without his intervention, so he gave Joe permission to get to know me.

Our decision to date mostly together created some interesting exchanges. On one early date, we went on the Heber Creeper, a historic train that takes passengers on a scenic ride through Provo Canyon. Afterward, we went on a horseback trail-ride, and the guide cooked our group a meal. He tried to engage the various couples and families in friendly talk around the campfire. He was clearly puzzled by us.

"Are you all related? Family?" he asked.

"Friends," Joe quickly answered, as Vicki and I exchanged smiles.

It was a question we got often over the months of our courtship. We rarely held hands or displayed affection in public, but once in a while people figured us out. For my birthday, we went to Park City to ride the Alpine Slide. Afterward, we had lunch and then window-shopped along Main Street. A storeowner was sweeping the walkway outside his business as we passed by. He stared, sizing up the situation.

"Two, huh? Hardly seems fair!" he said, shaking his head as he went back inside the store.

We often went camping with our families, and one evening Joe, Vicki, and I stayed up late talking with my parents and other relatives. Finally, we said our goodnights and headed off to our separate tents. As I slipped into my tent, I overheard an exchange between my dad and his brother-in-law, who were still seated next to the campfire.

"Are they dating each other?" my dad's brother-in-law asked, gesturing in the direction Joe and Vicki had gone.

My dad threw his hands in the air and, in an exasperated voice, said, "Yes, and you don't know the half of it. Literally, you don't know the half of it!"

When my dad saw how serious we were and realized that the "problem" wasn't going to go away, he tried to derail the relationship by making it difficult for me to see Joe. Sometimes, my dad wouldn't let me go out at all. He'd never thrown up such hurdles for my siblings.

Meanwhile, Vicki had the freedom to see Joe as much as she wanted. As a result, she developed a closeness and ease around him sooner than I did. One semester, Joe took a large class load. He was working part-time, too. As finals approached, he was under a lot of stress and got sick. He had a high fever and chills, and could barely get out of bed. Vicki and I went to Joe's house to help care for him. Vicki seemed to slip naturally into the role of comforter, while I felt like a third wheel. I just seemed to be in the way, which left me feeling hurt and jealous.

It wasn't as easy for me to show Joe attention and affection, especially around Vicki. I was more focused on building a spiritual foundation for our relationship, and so I didn't let my guard down as fast with Joe. Vicki and Joe kissed first, which bothered me. It wasn't that I didn't expect them to be intimate, and *one* of us had to be kissed first. But it made me wonder whether Joe liked Vicki more than me. I felt, too, that my dad was holding me back.

In my culture, parents are to be respected, so for a long time I went along with the rules my dad set. I was an adult and could have made my own decisions, but I was determined to show my dad that I was going about things honorably. When he finally got totally unreasonable, though, I stopped asking permission to see Joe and just let my parents know where I was going and when I would be home.

Even though we were young and inexperienced at relationships, Joe understood the sacrifices Vicki and I were making as we considered sharing a life together. He tried to be respectful of our feelings and worked hard at learning what was important to Vicki in a relationship, and what mattered to me.

But we still encountered challenges, some made more difficult by our own insecurities. Vicki couldn't eat when she got stressed, but I turned to food for comfort. I grew up with five older sisters who were always worried about their weight, which had never been a problem for me until I turned sixteen and puberty hit like a hurricane. I went from a size 3 to a size 9 in less than six months, and had a hard time accepting the changes in my body. I saw myself as fat and had a very negative self-image. Joe had unwittingly already made me feel self-conscious about it, too. Before he knew I liked him, I was at his house with a bunch of other people. Joe told everyone he was really good at guessing people's weight, and started going around the room, picking out people and estimating how much each person weighed. He was within a few pounds every time. I was horrified! I got up and slipped out of the room before he got to me.

A year later, after Vicki and I had started dating Joe, my self-image took another hit. As my feelings for Joe grew stronger, issues that would rarely come up in a "normal" relationship became a challenge. It was hard to have to think about and talk through every detail: What was the proper way to show affection to Joe in front of each other? Who sat next to him in the car? When was it okay to hold his hand? To kiss? Where were the boundaries? What did we need to do to show respect for each other? Under the pressure, food became my guilty pleasure. While Vicki lost weight, I gained it, swinging up to 145 pounds. This exacerbated my feelings of insecurity—especially since Joe was lean and well built and considered fitness a big deal. Unhappy with my appearance, I frequently closed myself off emotionally. Joe had no idea what was going on or what triggered my emotional shutdowns.

For one of our first dates, we decided to see a play at the Hale Centre Theatre in Salt Lake City and then go to dinner. I spent hours at the mall shopping for the right outfit to wear, thinking that something new might boost my confidence, and then realized

I'd cut it too close and had to rush home. When Joe and Vicki arrived to pick me up, right on time, I was still getting ready. I finally went out and climbed into the backseat; Vicki, of course, was already sitting next to Joe in the front. I apologized, and said I had gotten home late after shopping for new clothes.

"We won't get in until intermission now, but at least you have some cute clothes," Joe said, his voice tinged with irritation and sarcasm. When they both laughed at that, I sank down in my seat, feeling hurt, humiliated, and angry.

Afterward, Joe dropped me off at my Aunt T.'s house. It was late and the house was quiet. I slipped into the kitchen, which was illuminated only by a nightlight. I grabbed a carton of burnt-almond-fudge ice cream from the freezer and a loaf of homemade bread and began eating. By the time I'd finished, half the carton was gone and nearly all the bread, and I hadn't tasted any of it. All I could think about was how silly and shallow I must have seemed to Joe earlier that evening. I finally crawled into the bed I shared with a younger sister, who was still awake.

"How was the date?" she asked.

"Okay, but I'm not sure I'm going to fit in with them after all," I said.

"Why?" she asked.

"It's a lot harder than I thought it would be," I said. "I'm really discouraged. I just want to go to sleep."

"Don't give up too fast," she said. "You three seem great together."

That night, I would learn later, Joe talked to his mother about our date. He told her we had missed the first half of the play because of my shopping trip and added that I had been very quiet all evening. Joe's mom knew I was sensitive about my appearance and immediately filled in the nuances Joe had missed. The next day, Joe called and asked if he could meet with me.

As we sat in his truck, Joe apologized for his rude comments the night before.

"You looked really good last night—you always do—and I'm sorry if I hurt you," he said. "I didn't mean to. I just got really frustrated because we had made arrangements."

"I *shouldn't* have been late," I agreed. "I kept hoping to find an outfit that made me look slim, and there weren't any!"

"I like how you look," he said. Then he added, "But if you want, we could go on a diet and exercise program together."

To me, this showed that Joe recognized the sensitivity I felt and wanted to help me deal with it in a positive way. It also let me know my weight wasn't an issue for him. I was grateful for Joe's offer, and the three of us later began what would be the first of many health-boosting programs.

That summer, I got a job at the same medical supply company where Vicki worked, and we usually sat side by side so we could visit. There were times, though, that I kept my distance, choosing a booth as far away from Vicki as possible so I could sort through raw feelings in silence. Sometimes I jumped to conclusions—often the *wrong* conclusions, which resulted in misunderstandings. I figured, for example, that when Joe took me home first, it meant he wanted extra time with Vicki because he liked her more. It was a while before I realized that Joe rotated which girl he took home first!

And sometimes the hurts were real. One evening, Vicki and I were at Joe's house. We had spent the day together just hanging out. Vicki's mom called and told her to come home; she thought Vicki was spending too much time with Joe. I offered to wait at Joe's house while he drove Vicki home. I thought this would be a good opportunity for Joe and me to get some time to work on our relationship.

It should have taken Joe thirty minutes, but he was gone for several hours and seemed distraught when he returned. I thought maybe he and Vicki had had a fight. "Are you okay?" I asked. Joe hesitated, then took my hand. "Let's drive over to the park and talk," he said.

We were both silent as we got in the car. As Joe began driving, I noticed that the Subaru's windows were fogged up. And just like that I knew why it had taken Joe so long to return home. I was sick inside, and couldn't believe Joe was so oblivious to the telltale sign they'd left behind. I knew that Vicki and I each had our own personal relationships with Joe, but it was hard to have it staring me in the face this way. I wanted to open the car door and run away as fast as I could. Instead, I just sat there in silence, and so did Joe. After a few minutes, I noticed a tear running down Joe's cheek.

"This is the hardest thing I've ever tried to do in my life," he said. "I don't want to hurt you. I feel so weak. I don't know if I'm worthy to live this principle."

I was hurting, too, but listening to him express feelings of remorse about his behavior made me realize what a seemingly impossible situation he was in, and what this would truly require

In 1945, fifteen men—including five of the Dargers' relatives—were convicted of unlawful cohabitation because of their plural marriages. The men are shown outside the Utah State Prison before beginning their sentences. *Front row (left to right):* Joseph White Musser, Joseph Lyman Jessop, Charles Frederick Zitting, Heber Kimball Cleveland, Arnold Boss (Alina's great-grandfather), David B. Darger (Joe's grandfather), Oswald Brainich. *Back row (left to right):* Morris Quincey Kunz, Rulon Clark Allred, Alma Adelbert Timpson, Edmund F. Barlow, John Y. Barlow, Louis Alma Kelsch (Alina, Vicki, and Val's grandfather), Ianthus W. Barlow (Joe's great-grandfather), Albert Edmund Barlow (Joe's grandfather).

Joe, Alina, and Vicki *(left to right)* posed for this portrait in November 1989, several months before their marriage. And yes, the photographer wondered what was going on!

Vicki, Joe, and Alina were married on February 18, 1990, in a private ceremony attended by close family.

Vicki, Kyra, Alina, and Joe after Kyra's birth on October 12, 2000.

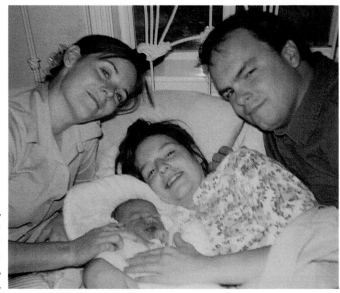

Joe and Val's engagement photo, taken on June 17, 2000.

Alina *(left)* and Vicki *(right)* participated in the ceremony as Val married Joe on October 14, 2000.

MormonFOCUS

EXPLORING THE DIVERSITY OF MORMON CULTURE

Premier Issue 2003

It's All About Family
An Inside Look at Today's Plural Marriages

Successful Home Schooling
The quest to educate our children

A Paradise Lost
The choice between church and family

Your Choice, Faith or Fear
How to deal with trials and adversity in your life

Premier Issue - USA $6.95
ISSN 1545-1909
09

This is the 2003 cover of *Mormon Focus* magazine, featuring Val, Alina, and Vicki *(left to right)*, that creators of HBO's series *Big Love* say was part of their inspiration for the show.

A water trough makes a perfect swimming pool on a hot summer day in 2006 for Maddie, Logan, Sabrina, Tavish, and Kyley.

Alina and Joe during a family outing at Murray Park in 2004.

Each child receives a modest number of gifts, but add them up and you have this: a Christmas tree nearly buried beneath the presents (2009)!

Alina, Val, and Vicki at a Christmas party in 2006.

Laura, Val, and Amanda on Thanksgiving 2008.

Joe takes Vicki, who likes adventurous dates, for a spin on his motorcycle in 2009.

The Darger children and several cousins playing on pumpkins outside their home in October 2010.

The Darger family in 2009 (two children, Sam and Victoria, not shown).

of me—of all of us. The challenge of balancing three relationships was hitting home more than ever. At that moment, I grasped how hard it would be to develop an unselfish love, not only for Joe, but for Vicki, too.

We talked for hours. Joe told me how hard it was to manage the physical side of the two relationships. He told me he would work harder at being more respectful in his choices, and at strengthening the spiritual basis of our relationships. He told me he was amazed, grateful, and humbled by my willingness to work through the challenges.

When we finally parted, I knew that Joe respected and loved me, not just out of passion, but also for who I was and who we were together. That night, we forged a bond that was deeper than ever. I realized that at my weakest moment I had found my greatest strength.

I was staying at Aunt T.'s house that weekend, and she was sitting at the kitchen table when I came in. She asked how my evening had gone. "Good," I told her. But she could read the truth on my face. Cheerful and perceptive despite the late—or rather, early—hour, Aunt T. asked me to sit and share a piece of pie with her.

"You know, things get easier," Aunt T. said. "As time goes by, you come into your own. It's your faith that gets you through."

As we talked, I was amazed by how well she understood what I was experiencing.

"In the early days, I would get jealous and angry," she said. "I would think, Why am I upset? Why do I care? He's not so special. He's just a man—nothing so great!"

We laughed so hard our stomachs hurt.

"Then I realized it was about so much more than that, about a bigger picture," Aunt T. said. "What we created was real, a family."

It felt good to be able to share my feelings with Aunt T., and to realize I was becoming part of an exclusive club of women who had gone through these experiences and remained strong, independent individuals who loved, believed in, and found happiness in plural marriage.

But learning to handle the misunderstandings, hurts, and jealousies was, I found, an ongoing process. One night after a date, Joe dropped me off before Vicki. The next day at work, Vicki kept falling asleep at her workstation. I realized they had stayed out late together, and I was really ticked off. I was still feeling ornery when Joe met us for lunch. Sensing that I was upset, he gave me a hug and was very attentive. My defensive shell began to crack. As we sat on the lawn eating, Joe told some jokes and Vicki started laughing. I began laughing, too. I looked at Vicki and thought, *What's the big deal? Does it take anything away from my relationship for them to have one as well?* In that moment, I realized how much I cared about Vicki. I tried to envision my life without her in it, and was flooded with thoughts of how much God cared for each of our souls and how he wanted us to care just as lovingly for each other. My perspective shifted. I knew there would still be hard moments ahead, but I was able to go forward, truly wanting the best for Vicki.

During our courtship, Vicki and I spoke to a lot of women who were in plural marriages, seeking advice on how to make our relationships work. These conversations solidified our conviction

CHAPTER THREE

Losing Faith

*There is a grand opportunity to improve ourselves, and the lessons
learned in a few years are worth the experience of a lifetime, for this
reason, that you are better prepared to make a home happy.*

—LUCY WALKER, PLURAL WIFE OF JOSEPH SMITH

Valerie

I WAS THE FIRST to get married, but not to Joe. A week after graduating from high school, at age eighteen, I became the fifth wife of a man who was forty-four. Like any starry-eyed bride, I had no doubts at the time about my feelings for my husband. I was sure this was a marriage that would last forever. The truth is, as with monogamy, not every plural marriage is perfect and, despite all the hopes and dreams, relationships fall apart.

I knew from an early age that I wanted a plural marriage—one that would create a family filled with the warmth, love, and attention I'd had as a child. As a girl, I had once seen a television commercial for an antidepressant that showed a woman curled in a fetal position as a voice intoned, "No one has to be alone." I didn't understand it. How could *anyone* be alone? I was growing up surrounded by people who loved, cared, protected, and valued me, and I thought everyone had the same loving support.

When I began dating, I went out with boys who had grown up in plural families—including Joe—as well as guys who were not Fundamentalist Mormons. My parents never pushed us to follow their religious convictions; half of my siblings chose not to follow the Fundamentalist Mormon faith. But midway through high school, I realized that I wanted faith at the center of my life and believed strongly that plural marriage was a true principle that would provide the kind of family structure I wanted for my children.

With that in mind, I wasn't Cinderella looking for a handsome prince who would sweep me off my feet and dedicate his life to making me happy. I was looking for the right mate, someone capable of caring for a large family and loving several women in addition to loving me. I thought I'd found him when I met the man I'll call Donald.

Donald had been raised in the LDS Church. He had gotten married and had five children before he converted to fundamentalism after studying scripture and Joseph Smith's original teachings. Donald's first wife left him when he joined the Apostolic United Brethren, based in the Salt Lake Valley, but Donald had since remarried and begun living the Principle. One of my older sisters had married a man in the AUB, and she often invited me along to Sunday meetings, dances, and other social activities. Donald led the Sunday school class I attended.

I was seventeen when I met Donald. His family seemed to have qualities that I was looking for in a plural marriage. He had four wives, two of whom were expecting, and eight children, including three from one wife's previous marriage. Donald's five children from his first marriage also spent time with him. The four wives, who ranged in age from twenty-one to thirty, were close to one another, dedicated to making the family work, and committed to their religious beliefs. For the most part, the women seemed happy, to an outsider anyway, in their relationships with Donald. It was a big, blended family and the children were well cared for and got along nicely. And Donald, despite being twenty-six years older than I was, had an air of youthfulness about him and was humorous and upbeat. I viewed his age as a plus.

In my culture, younger women sometimes marry older men for the very same reasons that lead women everywhere to make similar choices: status, power, and prestige. We all know about famous May-December romances in Hollywood, from actress Lauren Bacall, who was twenty when she became the wife of forty-five-year-old actor Humphrey Bogart, to Catherine Zeta-Jones, who was thirty-one when she married fifty-six-year-old Michael Douglas. But outside Tinseltown, age is no barrier to love, either. Cathleen Heffernan was twenty-three when she wed serial monogamist William O. Douglas, sixty-seven, the longest-serving jurist on the U.S. Supreme Court (she was his fourth wife); Nancy Janice Moore was twenty-two when she became the second wife of Senator Strom Thurmond, sixty-six.

To me, an older man seemed like a good option because he would already be an experienced husband, father, and provider.

In addition, in Fundamentalist Mormon culture, older men are often viewed as being more spiritually developed. But despite this fact, my sisters and friends were concerned about the age difference between Donald and me, and pushed me to reconsider whether this was a relationship I really wanted to pursue. With all the self-assuredness of youth, I thought it was.

Until I met Donald, I had never dated a man who already had a family. I knew I didn't want to begin a relationship with a married man unless I had a feeling that joining his family was a strong possibility. If it didn't work out, it was not just *his* heart I'd break, but also those of the other wives and children. With that in mind, I initially got to know Donald's family through interactions in public, social settings.

After I'd spent about six months observing from a distance, my interest in Donald and his family was definitely piqued. It continued to grow over the next six months, and by then it was clear the interest was mutual. At that point, Donald met with my dad to ask for permission to court me. The day after their meeting, my dad pulled me aside. My father was only slightly acquainted with Donald and seemed surprised by his request. "Do you know a guy named Donald?" he asked.

I knew there was only reason my dad would ask me that question: Donald had obviously been to see him. I smiled and told my dad that yes, I knew Donald and his family. "Well, he came to ask me for permission to court you. What do you think?" my father asked.

I didn't hesitate at all before giving my answer. "I'd like to get to know him," I said.

I learned only later how my father really felt. He had told my mother, "I don't want anyone to discourage her. But I don't want her necessarily encouraged, either."

For our first date, Donald took me on a picnic at Liberty Park in Salt Lake City. He brought a basket full of food he'd made himself, which seemed very romantic. We spread out a blanket and spent the afternoon in carefree conversation, absorbed in each other and taking little notice of anything else in the crowded park.

The next week, our courtship was announced to the world when I sat next to Donald at church. Afterward, Donald invited me to his home in Mapleton, more than an hour south of Salt Lake City, for Sunday dinner. It was my first time there, and as we pulled into the sweeping, tree-lined driveway that led to the home, I was impressed. The brick rambler was on two and a half acres nestled in the foothills of Maple Mountain. A manicured lawn skirted the front of the house, which was bordered on one side by a large garden and on the other by a thick grove of trees. We entered through a side door that led to the kitchen, and as I crossed the threshold the reality hit me that this might soon be my home, too. By the end of the evening I saw myself easily fitting into the family.

I saw Donald often. He took me to his favorite restaurants and I took him to Baskin-Robbins—about the best I could afford. Some Saturdays, I went to Donald's house and joined the other wives in whatever they were doing—yard work, meal preparation, caring for the babies. Every Sunday after church, I always went to Donald's for dinner.

As I grew closer to his family, I realized that the relationship between Donald and one wife was unraveling. I was bothered by the way he ridiculed her in front of others and was often disrespectful of her feelings. *Would he ever act like that toward me?* I wondered. But I thought she deserved some blame, too, because she sometimes treated Donald poorly, which is why I dismissed those uneasy stirrings as I fell in love.

Donald and I courted for three months and then, with the consent and participation of his other wives, were married in a religious ceremony. Donald was a fireworks salesman and it was the height of his busy season, which meant he had time only for a brief honeymoon. We drove to a motel about an hour away and celebrated our first night together with a picnic in our room, with food Donald bought at a nearby grocery store. I figured it was the best he could do under the circumstances and really didn't care. I was too excited about finally joining his family and getting on with my life to stress over what kind of honeymoon we had.

I began my marriage with an open heart and a fierce determination to make it work. The various wives took on different responsibilities within the family, with some working and others caring for the children. I helped at home at first and then got a job at a medical supply company—the same one Vicki and Alina previously worked at. At home, I spent hours chatting away in the big craft room with the other wives. Once a month we had a girls' night out for dinner or a movie while Donald stayed home with the kids. We had a great time blending our different family traditions at holidays, weaving our lives together on these special occasions just as we were trying to do on a daily basis. Meanwhile, the family kept growing: four years after my marriage to Donald, a sixth wife joined us. I had my first child two years after marrying Donald, and by our sixth anniversary, I'd had two more. Altogether, there were now twenty children in our family.

By then, Donald and a few friends had come up with the idea of moving to Pleasant Valley, Nevada, to form a self-sufficient community based on the kind of cooperative effort that Joseph Smith had promoted as an original tenet of Mormonism. Among the wives, there was little excitement about leaving our beautiful home, our families, and city life to move to Pleasant Valley. I was worried, too, because the honeymoon stage of my relationship with Donald had ended; he was becoming increasingly irritated and sharp with me, and I was beginning to see faults in him I hadn't noticed before. But we all went along with the plan.

Pleasant Valley was a tiny, isolated, hardscrabble community in the West Desert region four hours from Salt Lake City and near the Utah border. Our small enclave, set up at the end of a seventy-mile stretch of dirt road, consisted of seventeen trailer homes and an old log cabin. Eight families, four of them polygamous, settled there, and I don't think any of us realized how much harder our lives would be.

After living together as a blended family, I now had my own separate trailer home, as did Donald's other five wives. It was a pioneer's life of isolation and domestic toil. Donald spent the week working in Salt Lake City, taking our only car and coming home just on weekends. Alternating among us, one wife and her younger children would accompany him for the week, leaving the rest of us on our own. He was spread pretty thin at home, too, given how little time he had with us in Nevada. Sometimes, two weeks or more would pass before it was my turn to spend time with Donald during his trips home.

There are nice spots in Pleasant Valley, which sits between low rolling hills, but our homes were located in an area with little natural vegetation and rock-hard ground that defied all efforts at landscaping. Summer brought its own challenges, but winter was the worst. The area was cold and windy, without the benefit of snow to give us, even for a moment, a pretty and playful winter wonderland. I had to heat my trailer with logs I split myself, even late into pregnancy, and fed into a wood-burning stove. Often the water pipes froze and, while I waited for them to be fixed, I'd have to borrow water from the neighbors or a sister wife for cooking, drinking, and bathing. My home had the family's only telephone, which meant that when a call came for one of the other five wives I had to go fetch her. I had a washer but, for most of that time, no dryer. I hung our clothes on a line outside and relied on the wind to dry them even in the winter, when they became stiff with ice. I learned to be handy at repairs as I scrambled to keep home and family going, but it was really due to the skills of one particular sister wife that we were able to manage. She could do anything—fix a flat tire, thaw frozen water pipes, repair a broken washer, install new electrical wiring—and had a knack for turning other people's junk into treasure.

One of my grandmothers had moved to the community of Short Creek during its humble beginnings, where she'd lived in a tent. She worried now about my life in the West Desert and would say, "Val, I already went to live in the desert and be like a pioneer, so you don't have to!" Despite these hardships, I kept up a good front. Our family continued to grow, too: I had three more children with Donald while living in Pleasant Valley. But our living circumstances were only a symptom of larger problems.

We scrounged to get by, especially once Donald began frequenting the gambling casinos in Wendover, Nevada, on his way to and from the Salt Lake Valley. He would drop whichever wife and her children who were with him at a park or grocery store, where they were expected to occupy themselves for a few hours. I eventually gave up my turn to go to the city with him because I hated those stops so much. Donald visited the casinos often enough that it got to the point we could call the poker room and ask for him by name. He once told us that the men he knew from the poker tables were his best friends. Donald claimed that his gambling junkets were a way to make money for us. But back in the desert, our bills were going unpaid.

It was too much for one of my sister wives—the one whose relationship I had suspected was in trouble when I first married into the family. She lasted three years in our desert enclave before getting fed up, long before the rest of us did, with Donald's inability to provide for his families. I hadn't managed to get very close to her, though I cared for her eight children and was sad to see them leave. But honestly, I was preoccupied with my own children's survival.

Occasionally, other fundamentalist neighbors would pitch in to help cover our expenses, such as power bills. In addition, my family back in Utah knew I was struggling financially and my mother would sometimes send me things she knew I needed, from household items to baby clothes and money. But my family became aware of the extent of my dire straits only after I moved into my former sister wife's newly vacated trailer—it was bigger than the one the kids and I had been living in—and asked for help making what was little more than a metal shell livable. Some of my brothers came to help me fix up the place. Joe and Vicki, by then in a plural marriage of their own, also came out to Pleasant Valley to help me paint and wallpaper the trailer. I could tell they were worried.

At first, Donald's other wives and I kept silent about our family troubles, sharing only with each other our concerns and ideas for getting our husband to keep his commitments and put the family back on the right track. I felt humiliated that I was married to a man who couldn't, who *wouldn't,* support his family. My lowest point came when, desperate to provide for my children, I went on food stamps. One by one, my sister wives and I went to our religious leaders and asked for help. Owen Allred, then the president of the AUB, spoke to Donald, who subsequently stood one Sunday during services in our community's meetinghouse and apologized publicly for his behavior. Donald promised to do better going forward, but he soon returned to the gaming tables.

Back at the trailer, he grew even more verbally abusive toward me. It seemed I could do nothing right. We would be sitting at the table eating as a family and he would suddenly glare at me and ask, "Do you have to chew your food so loudly?" After I got up to use the bathroom one night, he snarled that it sounded like "a herd of elephants in here." I tried to avoid his needling criticism by not doing anything that might set him off, but I could never be sure what the trigger might be. As for intimacy, I felt powerless to tell him no, especially early in our marriage. I once tried to tell him that I needed to be able to say no to sex and have him respect my feelings, but he dismissed my request as something I'd "just read out of a book." If I got up the courage to decline his overtures, he would later ignore me as punishment. All his wives witnessed the verbal barbs he threw around and chastised him for those comments, but intimacy between a man and each woman in a plural marriage is private; we didn't share what was going on behind closed doors, so I thought I alone was being sexually manipulated.

As my marital problems increased, I started confiding in one of my older sisters. She was supportive, but it was a random telephone conversation with my husband's brother that finally forced me to take a cold, hard look at my situation and my future. He asked to speak with Donald when he called, and I explained that he was away. For once unable to keep silent, I added that he was gambling. That revelation led to more questions, and bit by bit I spilled out the facts about our failing family. My brother-in-law asked me point-blank why I stayed. I told him I had made a commitment and wanted to live up to it.

He chuckled. "Valerie, if I make a business agreement with someone and he doesn't keep his end of the deal, all bets are off; I'm not required to keep the agreement." His words struck me like a thunderbolt: my husband had failed to keep his commitments and that freed me from my own. Suddenly, I had a clear vision of what lay ahead if I stayed. My boys were going to grow up and treat women the way I was being treated, and my daughters were going to accept it, just as I was.

Weeks passed, and despite that realization I remained para-
lyzed by indecision. I prayed often and rather desperately, and all
of us wives tried once again to persuade Donald to quit gambling,
stop his abusive behavior, and work with us to hold our family
together. When that failed, we again sought help from our church
leaders. This time, they reprimanded Donald. But any remorse
Donald felt faded fast as he slipped yet again into his old ways. I
lost hope for lasting change.

My conversation with my brother-in-law replayed over and
over in my thoughts. As I stood alone in the kitchen washing the
supper dishes one night, a powerful feeling swept through me, an
internal earthquake that in an instant changed everything. I
stopped, dried my hands on a towel, and went into my bedroom
to pull out my journal. I wrote: "I don't know what this feeling
is—but it feels so right, like a *knowing*." The decision was made:
the marriage was over, and I was going to take my kids and leave.
I called a sister who lived in an AUB community in Montana and
asked if she and her husband would mind if I went to live with
them for a while.

"We'd love you to come and stay," she said, not needing any
explanation for what was happening.

On the day I finally left my marriage, I stood in the kitchen
again, looking out a window in my double-wide mobile home. I
had kept my promise to Donald for twelve years. Now I was going
to break it and leave him, leave my sister wives and their children,
whom I had grown to love. Beyond the window, I could see a
group of kids riding bicycles and playing basketball and then,
farther out, dust rising from the dirt road leading to our remote
community. Two trucks were headed our way. I alone knew it was

my family, coming to help me pack and move away with my five children, who were then between the ages of nine and nine months. I gathered my older children to me then and told them we were going away for a while, but not why or for how long or what it meant.

The dirt cloud rose like a smoke signal, instantly setting off curiosity and concern in the tiny outpost. No one came down this road unless they lived here, knew someone who did, or had a specific purpose in mind. The nearest gas station was an hour away, the grocery store two hours distant. I had told one person about my decision to leave: Donald. He deserved that, at least. I had sat down with him and calmly told him I would be moving to Montana. He asked if there was anything he could do or say to get me to change my mind. "Nothing," I told him. Despite that, I think he figured I'd be back in a month or two.

The trucks finally pulled to a stop in front of my home, and it took just seconds before one of my sister wives made her way to my trailer to find out what was happening. It hurt to see the look of concern and confusion on her face. Beyond the ties of faith and marriage, the isolation and hardships of living in our tiny community had brought us even closer together. I felt a responsibility to the other wives, and to their children. I considered myself to be *their* mother, too. I had invested so much time in teaching, caring for, and loving them. Leaving the children was probably the hardest part of it all.

But now I led my sister wife into my bedroom, shut the door, and attempted to explain my decision to leave. Just two weeks earlier, as we had tried to figure out what to do about our husband, I had been adamant about my intention to make our plural marriage work. At the time, we both thought *she* would be the one to eventually leave and I would be the one who stayed, no matter what.

My parents had taught me by word and example that celestial marriage required a deeper commitment than was typical of most monogamous marriages. A celestial marriage was supposed to be binding for time here on earth and then for eternity in heaven. I believed that, and had passionately urged my sister wives to stay united and work together on our problems. Now all I could say was that my heart had changed.

"I just have a strong feeling this is what I need to do," I told her, referring to the epiphany I'd had. "It's hard for me to leave you and the other sister wives, but it's what I need to do."

She stared at me for a moment, and then said, "What can I do to help?"

A neighbor came by next, and as we stood on the lawn, I offered the same bare explanation. She also did not push too hard; she had observed my family's difficulties firsthand. She offered to make dinner for us, something I hadn't even thought about.

By sunset, the trucks were loaded with appliances and furniture, clothing, and other household items. I left some things I knew my sister wives and neighbors could use, and others that I might reclaim if I returned. A sliver of hope remained even then, deep inside me, that my marriage could be salvaged. I had decided to leave but had not figured out if this was really the end, or simply what came next. In making my decision, I left my marriage in the same way most monogamous women do: I called upon family for help. There was no need for an escape, just a lot of heartache, personal contemplation, and tough choices.

I took one last look around the empty trailer, stepped outside, and shut the door, scanning the nearby homes of my sister wives. The thoughts that had nagged me in the months leading to this moment returned. I felt like a failure and worried that my family, especially my dad, would be disappointed in me. I was the first of my father's daughters to have a plural marriage collapse.

Had I been wrong about my ability to live my faith, my convictions? Or had I chosen wrong? Was this an experience I was destined to have for some greater purpose? Were there any truths left for me to hold on to, or were my beliefs shattering, leaving me spiritually adrift? I was lost and bewildered, questioning everything. I felt like I was walking through a graveyard, stopping occasionally to pick something up and then asking myself, "Is this going to turn into dust and blow away, or be something strong and solid I can hold on to?"

I had kept my marital troubles from my children because they were so young—the explanation I'd given the day of our departure was very general—but when we stopped for a few nights at my parents' home, I told them what was happening. They were like a pack of howling wolves. They cried and cried, and their confusion and hurt broke my heart. "Will we ever go back?" my oldest son wanted to know. "I don't want to be without my brothers."

I was determined to create a better life for myself, and for them. I tried to hang on to that thought as I comforted them. But at that moment, I could not have predicted that the plural marriage I had dreamed of and hoped for as a young woman still awaited me.

CHAPTER FOUR

And One Makes Three

*This is my commandment, that ye love one another,
as I have loved you. Greater love hath no man than this,
that a man lay down his life for his friends.*

—JOHN 15:12–13

In our family, adding another wife is nothing like what you've
seen on *Big Love* or heard about in some polygamous sects. Not
that he would ever consider it, but Joe would be out on his rear if
he pursued an underage girl or did any courting without our
knowledge and consent! Joe was, in fact, initially hesitant about
courting Val. There was a lot to consider, for us and for Val. That's
why none of us expected their courtship to unfold the way it did.

Valerie

I KNEW IN MY HEART that God had released me from my covenant
with Donald, but I wanted the AUB to give me an official release—

that's the word Fundamentalist Mormons use to describe a divorce in a religious, nonlegal marriage. So four months after I moved to Montana, I returned to Utah to attend a church disciplinary council where my request would be heard. Two of my former sister wives who still lived in Pleasant Valley also planned to ask the council to end their marriages to Donald, and I wanted to be there for them. I wasn't sure what our church leaders would do, given their disapproval of divorce except in the most extreme circumstances.

Like the other women, I brought supporters: my sister Bonnie and another woman who was highly respected in the AUB. But I was still really nervous as I walked into the hearing room, where a handful of men were already seated at a conference table. Donald wasn't there yet, and we had to wait for him to arrive, accompanied by his one remaining wife. The meeting proved more difficult than I'd expected. Donald grew increasingly defensive as the other wives and I shared our stories, refusing to acknowledge the grievances we had or take any responsibility for the collapse of our marriages.

I left the meeting with hope, but also a heavy heart. Everyone in the room now had heard my full story and finally knew the truth, which lightened my load. But it had not been easy to share so many deeply personal things.

I went to my sister Vicki's house, where my children and I planned to spend the night before returning to Montana. Since leaving Donald, I had spoken to Vicki on the telephone often, and had shared some of what had happened in my marriage. She was, to my surprise, understanding and supportive. I knew that Vicki,

Joe, and Alina strongly opposed divorce. I was afraid they would see me as spiritually weak and criticize my decision to leave, especially since I had always emphasized Donald's good qualities to others, glossing over our troubles.

Vicki, Alina, and I were in the playroom with the children when Joe came home from work that night. Joe said hello to the others, and then our eyes locked across the room. In that moment, I felt an energy bounce between us. The exchange lasted only seconds, but it was real and it was profound. *What was that?* I asked myself. I hadn't had any feelings whatsoever for Joe since marrying Donald, so I was taken by surprise. This wasn't a jolt of mere physical attraction, either; it was something else, but I didn't know what to make of it.

After the children were in bed, Joe, Alina, Vicki, and I talked late into the night. Finally feeling safe and secure enough to speak openly, I began to reveal the heartache, deprivation, and manipulation I had experienced in my marriage. We laughed at some of the stories, and cried together at others. As a general rule, my mother and sisters and I never spoke openly about sex, so I cringed with embarrassment as I disclosed our most private problems.

But talking was cathartic, and I realized how much support I could have received from them over the years if I had not been so reluctant to open up. As the hours passed, both Vicki and Alina fell asleep on the couch, but Joe and I continued talking. I told him of my worry that, as a divorced woman, I would carry a stigma that would keep any good man from considering me as a wife. Joe said that a divorce alone would not stop him from marrying a woman if he felt spiritually connected to her.

As I drove back to Montana the next day, I was relieved and revived. The hearing was over (I later received the release), and if divorce wasn't an obstacle to Joe, perhaps there were other good men who felt the same way. I was far from being ready to seriously consider another relationship, but the thought that I might eventually fit into another family was reassuring.

After months of emotional upheaval, I was finally beginning to resolve doubts and questions about my life, my faith, and my future. Had my marriage been all bad? No. Was I was a better, stronger, and more aware woman than I would have been without the experience with Donald? Yes. People, not religion, were to blame when a marriage failed, I realized; there were examples of *good* plural marriages all around me. Seeing men who were living the Principle the proper way confirmed my belief that plural marriage often brought a greater spiritual awareness. But there were still fractures in my faith, and I was not sure I would ever find a man I could trust again. Going forward, I wanted to leave myself open to God's direction, and I prayed that he'd guide me to a better life. I also wrote a letter in my journal to the faceless, nameless partner I hoped to find someday. It was both a prayer and an expression of faith in what God had in mind for me:

> *To my future companion:*
>
> *Thank you for loving me, for loving my children. Thank you for being genuine and sincere. Thank you for being patient. Thank you for being willing to take on the responsibility of me and my five children. For being generous enough to raise someone else's children. Thank you*

for being so kind that my children love you as much as their own father. Thank you for waiting for me and providing for me. Thank you for loving the Lord. Thank you for protecting me and believing in me. For caring. Thank you for providing me with a home. Thank you for trusting in God. Thank you for being such a cool person! For letting me be a part of your life. Thank you for treating me like an equal. Thank you for making my opinion count. Thank you for respecting me and considering me. Thank you for helping me. Thank you for taking as long as it takes. Thank you for being a good and honorable man. Thank you for being you—whoever you are.

Over the next several months, Vicki and Alina called often to chat. I also received a letter from Joe, who offered encouragement and even sent a little money to help me make ends meet. I wrote back, and soon we struck up a correspondence. My children were struggling with the upheaval in their lives, and Joe gave me advice about how to help them process their hurt and anger. After exchanging several letters, Joe called me late one night and, for the first time, told me about a strong feeling he'd had months earlier when our eyes met across the room at their home. "Did you feel something in that moment?" he asked. "*I did, and it's not something I can just ignore.*"

I didn't answer immediately, grateful that the house was dark and quiet around me. It had been easy to put aside what I experienced that evening because it had happened so fast and I wasn't sure what it was or whether Joe had felt it, too. Now, my thoughts raced. *What should I say? If I tell the truth, I'll be opening a door that I'm not sure I'm ready to walk through.*

I chose my words carefully. "Yes, I felt something, an energy," I conceded, "but I don't know what it means, and my impression may not have been the same as yours."

I appreciated Joe's courage in speaking up and raising the possibility of a relationship, something I knew he wouldn't have done without the support of Vicki and Alina. I found it amazingly easy to talk with Joe about my life and my children, but my guard was still up, and I'm sure he heard the hesitation in my voice as I agreed to consider whether there might be something between us. The idea of getting into another relationship frightened me. I knew I needed more time to figure out who I was, what I needed, and what I wanted in my life.

Hours later, as I tried to fall asleep, the conversation played over and over in my mind: *What is Joe thinking? What am I feeling? I'm not ready, not ready, not ready.*

At the end of May, Joe, Alina, Vicki, and their children came to Montana for a visit over a long weekend. I was still living in the basement of my sister's home and had a part-time housekeeping job at the Stock Farm, a local resort. Any free time I had was focused on my children, who were having difficulty adjusting to the many changes in their lives.

On the last day of their visit, Joe happened to come by as my oldest son stormed through the house after a telephone conversation with his father. Of all my children, he was the one who found my divorce most difficult, and I was powerless to buffer him from the pain and anger he was experiencing. I stood there, staring after my son, helpless. Joe, seeing the look on my face, walked over and gave me a huge hug. With that true, selfless, caring embrace, I felt as though someone had thrown me a lifeline. In twelve years of marriage, I had never been hugged like that, and I realized how much tenderness I had missed out on during my years with Donald.

That afternoon, Joe and I went for a long drive together. We talked a lot about my children. I had shielded them from my marriage problems to such an extent that I didn't know how to help them understand what had happened or why. Joe gave me a lot of good advice, even encouraging me to avoid destroying their dad in their eyes.

Just as we got back to my sister's house, it started to rain and I headed straight for the trampoline. Jumping in the rain is one of my favorite things to do, and by the time I stopped I was soaking wet. I went inside to change, and Vicki followed me into my bedroom. We had been in there a while, talking, when Alina and Joe asked if they could join us.

Joe began by telling me they'd had a great visit. I started to reply, but he interrupted me. "Wait," he said. "We don't want to leave without talking about the possibility of you coming into our family. We've talked about it and prayed about it as a family, and we'd like you to consider it."

It was the first time we'd all talked openly, and my heart was beating so hard I thought I might faint. Joe asked me if I was okay.

"Yeah, just overwhelmed," I said, attempting a smile.

Joe reminded me of the worry I had expressed months earlier that no good man or family would be interested in me. "*We* are," he said.

"We want what's best for you," Vicki added. "We know you've been through a lot, but I want you to know how much we care for you."

We parted that evening with a commitment to continue praying about whether this was the right step for all of us. I had a lot to think about. I didn't feel ready to begin a relationship with anyone, but at the same time, I couldn't dismiss either the growing interest I had in Joe or their feelings for me. I wanted to keep an open mind and heart despite my tentativeness. And I was humbled that Vicki and Alina would want me in their family. They were such good women, so dedicated to their children and devoted to living up to the ideals of the Fundamentalist Mormon faith. I knew they would not have approached Joe or me about their feelings unless they were truly open to having another sister wife in their lives.

The fact that Joe was married to Vicki, my twin, didn't bother me at all. I took it as a sign that he would be as good a husband for me as he was for her. It seemed natural to me. As teenagers, Vicki and I had at times liked some of the same guys, Joe among them. When I first began contemplating marriage, I thought it might even be good if we married the same man. Like many twins, Vicki and I had always had a special bond, and I was really touched that she was willing to share her husband and her life with me. I couldn't have asked for better references on Joe than the love, trust, and respect he and Vicki showed each other. Joe fit all the characteristics I had listed months earlier in the thank-you note I had written to my future husband. I admired the way he was able to talk about the hard things with tenderness and concern. I also liked the way he valued his wives' opinions and encouraged their interests. But frankly, I was less concerned with figuring out who Joe was or how he might live up to my hopes and expectations; the thing that mattered to me was to know what direction God wanted me to take.

Several weeks later, I went to Utah to visit family and continue investigating my feelings for Joe. He had agreed to help me look for a car, and we spent half a day scouting the options at dealerships around the Salt Lake Valley. Afterward, we went to a park to talk. Joe opened his heart, telling me stories about his life, his faith, and what he saw in his future. He also asked me a lot of probing questions—questions that forced me to process my buried feelings. At one point in the conversation, all the emotions I had kept bottled up over the past few months bubbled over, and I started to weep.

"I don't know why I'm crying," I told Joe. "I thought I was past all that."

"It's because your heart was broken, and now it's healing," he said.

In that moment, my feelings and thoughts crystallized, and I was keenly aware of God's hand in bringing us together. I suddenly knew I would marry Joe. When we finally left the park, we drove to a nearby Jamba Juice store. We got out of the car and, as we stood in front of the building, Joe pulled me close, told me he loved me, and gave me a tender kiss.

That kiss was the question—Will you marry me?—and my answer all at once.

In a way, I couldn't believe what was happening. I had left my husband just eight months earlier. But there was no escaping the feeling that I belonged with Joe. He suggested that we go to a mall and get our picture taken, knowing we'd just made a life-changing decision. The photographer asked what the occasion was, and Joe said, "We're engaged."

"Congratulations!" the photographer said. "How long have you been dating?"

I looked at Joe as I answered: "A thousand years."

From there, we went back to Joe's house to tell Vicki and Alina the news. I was nervous. Would they understand how quickly Joe and I had reached this decision? I smiled awkwardly while Joe described what had happened, but Vicki and Alina eased my discomfort. They actually seemed to be expecting the news.

Within a month, I moved from Montana to Utah, settling with my children into a trailer behind the main family house. I told my children I planned to marry Joe, but I don't think it really sank in at first. With the decision to marry now made, I was eager to move forward, but our children—not just mine, but *all* of them—needed time to adjust to the idea of becoming one family. We set a date in October and, over the next three months, began to blend our lives together.

Two days before our marriage ceremony, Alina gave birth to her fifth child, Kyra. During our courtship, Alina had never made me feel I was taking Joe or anything else away from her, and she even invited me to attend the birth. I was thrilled to be able to share in this beautiful moment. I felt so connected to this little baby; we were both beginning a new life, entering this family together.

The wedding was a joyful celebration of commitment, love, and faith as we united as one family. Alina and Vicki stood beside me as I became Joe's wife. I was grateful for the sacrifice they were making to shake up their comfortable lives and accept me, with five children in tow, into their family. I felt completely surrounded by love.

Joe and I spent our first night together as a married couple in the trailer, but not alone. All the little children wanted to spend the night there with us. And in the morning, Vicki's youngest daughter climbed into bed to snuggle with her dad. Not your typical wedding night, but I took it all in stride!

Several weeks later, Joe and I went on a honeymoon. I had never been on a romantic vacation, and to feel so loved and special was an amazing experience. I appreciated that Joe was willing to take time for the two of us so that we could build a good foundation for our new life together. Our closeness would have come without a honeymoon, I'm sure—but far more slowly, since in the normal course of life I'd be alone with Joe only every third night.

I had been naive when I first entered a plural marriage; this time, I knew the range of challenges I would encounter and trusted my ability to conquer them. I was a stronger person and more attuned to my faith. I also had sister wives and a husband who were united in their views, and who were dedicated to putting the family first. I felt valued and empowered, and I sensed that I had finally found a perfect place for me.

Joe

WHEN DONALD AND VAL first married, the family lived in a large, well-kept house in Mapleton, and Donald, as far as I knew, was quite successful. I had no clue how greatly Val's situation had changed with their move. In fact, I was shocked the first time I visited Val in Pleasant Valley and saw the poverty she was living in. It was like taking a trip to a remote and isolated Third World country. Their family had joined with several others in trying to start a Fundamentalist Mormon cooperative, but it did not appear to be going well.* Val had a deep sense of responsibility for her choices—so deep that on the few occasions when Alina, Vicki, and I saw her at family gatherings over the years, she never said a word about the hardships she'd had to endure after moving to the enclave.

Val was barely hanging on financially, which made us all feel guilty, and she obviously missed Vicki tremendously. I encouraged Vicki to keep in close contact with her sister. I also offered Donald rent-free use of our trailer home during his trips to Salt Lake City, which meant we'd see Val a little more frequently. In return, I asked that he keep the trailer and its yard in good condition and pay the utilities. He took me up on it, but within two months he had let down his end of the bargain, and when I approached him about our deal, I learned firsthand that he didn't have much integrity when it came to his commitments. He responded by moving out, and once again Val seemed to vanish. We had only intermittent contact for

* Such cooperatives are known as United Order efforts and are based on a revelation Joseph Smith received in 1831 about the Law of Consecration. The law calls for group members to pool their assets and labor to achieve self-sufficiency and income equality and to eliminate poverty.

several years, and then we heard surprising news: Val had decided to leave Donald and move in with a sister in Montana.

We knew so little about Val's marriage that my first concern was whether she was making the right choice. In my view, except in the most awful circumstances the breakup of a family is a tragedy for everyone involved. I had no sense of the depth and breadth of the abuse Val had experienced, because she had never talked about it.

Several months after moving to Montana, Val came back to Utah to ask her church's priesthood council to officially free her from her marriage. Up to that point, I had advised Vicki to be cautious in her conversations with Val, because I did not want my family to be involved in encouraging her to break sacred commitments without good cause. After her meeting, Val planned to spend the night at our house before traveling back to Montana. I got home that night just as everyone gathered for evening prayer in the playroom. I put down my work satchel and walked into the room, where I saw Val kneeling with the rest of my family. As I looked at her, I heard a voice from deep within me say, *She is to be your wife!* Simultaneously, I felt as if I'd received an electric shock. I turned away quickly so no one would see the stunned look on my face and ask what was wrong with me.

My religion teaches us to listen to the "still small voice" of the Holy Ghost. I believe inspiration comes in the space between our thoughts, and I have found direction in my life by listening in that space, where there is deep and abiding peace. But this was an uncomfortable thought for numerous reasons, and at that moment I did my best to ignore it.

The last thing on my mind was taking on another wife. At age thirty, I was just leaving a management position in an established company to start my own business providing cafeteria services for large corporations. And after ten years of marriage, I still had a lot of work to do to be a better husband. My marriage to Vicki had hit a rough patch a year or so earlier, and we were still working through it. Vicki, who is an amazingly detail-oriented, analytical person, had taken a job as an accountant at our family-owned catering business. As she asserted more independence, I felt pushed away, and we'd lost a lot of closeness. Overall, our commitment to each other was unbreakable, but we'd had to work through some hurtful experiences.

That night, after the children were in bed, Alina, Vicki, Val, and I sat down together in the family room. Val was comfortable enough to reveal what she had gone through with Donald—the sexual manipulation, the emotional disconnection, the gambling and financial problems.

As Val shared her story, I couldn't help but think about the message I'd heard when I first saw her earlier that evening, and wonder if God would require me to take on more responsibility. But how could I do more? In addition to the career shift and my changing relationship with Vicki, I had just learned Alina was expecting. And I was feeling financially strained because I was supporting some members of my father's family.

It also was hard to imagine Val considering a plural marriage again any time soon, given her experience. She seemed embittered about men, marriage, and even our religion. I had been interested in Val way back in high school, but her life had gone in a different direction from mine. Until that night, I'd never had the slightest feeling that Val was meant to marry me. I also had never had any indication that Val was interested in our family. I kept my thoughts to myself, however, choosing to leave the spiritual prompting I'd received about Val in God's hands. If it was meant to be, he would make it so.

Val returned to Montana, and I focused on my family and my new business, putting Val out of my mind. Weeks later, to my surprise Alina and Vicki each approached me separately about her.

Alina came to me first. She told me she had felt strongly for some time that we should consider Val for our family. My reaction? "Don't bring it up! I have enough to deal with," I said, closing off the discussion.

Then, a few days later, Vicki came to me and made an impassioned plea, listing all the reasons *she* thought Val belonged in our family. I was caught off-guard because of what Vicki and I had recently gone through; I wouldn't have imagined her wanting any more stress in our relationship. But Vicki looked into my eyes and said, "I really feel that Val should be in our family. I want her to feel the same love I do and be blessed with what I've had."

I was deeply moved by Vicki's conviction about Val. Despite our recent difficulties, she considered our marriage a blessing that she wanted her sister to share! It took unselfishness and charity for Vicki to love her sister that much, knowing the sacrifice it would take. To me, she was living up to the Savior's teaching that laying down one's life for another is the greatest act of love.

There had been times during our marriage when Alina, Vicki, and I had discussed women who seemed to show an interest in our family. Nothing had come of those overtures, however. Now they both had a strong feeling about Val, and, given my own spiritual prompting, I had to consider it. I shared with Alina and Vicki the experience I'd had concerning Val when she came to town for her release hearing. We began praying about the matter together, which brought the three of us closer than ever, and once we were united in our feelings, we decided to move ahead, guided by our faith.

Over the next few months, Alina and Vicki visited Val in Montana several times. I mostly stayed out of the picture to avoid putting any pressure on Val and to let my wives forge a bond with her first. Socially, it was awkward, since people in Val's Montana community speculated that a courtship was in the works every time they saw her speaking to a married man or his wives. Although I was drawn to Val and wanted to get to know her, dating a single woman with five children was new and unfamiliar territory for me.

I kept in touch with Val through letters and phone calls, however, and as I got to know her better I was impressed. She had a sweet nature, an inherent goodness, and a real desire to do right. After a while, I decided it was time to be more open with my feelings. I called Val one night and told her about the strong prompting I'd had months earlier. I didn't go into too many of the specifics; that seemed like something I needed to share with her in person. But I said enough to let her know it had been a powerful moment, for all of us, and had led us to pray about whether she belonged in our family.

"It wasn't just nothing, Val; it was something," I said. "We all felt it. And when an experience like that happens, I have to look at it, investigate it."

Val admitted she'd felt something, too, though her impression was much less clear than mine. Understandably, Val still had her guard up, but she agreed to think about joining our family and to pray along with us for more guidance.

The next time I saw Val was when I took the whole family to Montana for the Memorial Day weekend. We had a great time, despite my uncertainty about how to approach Val and express my interest in her. Our conversations didn't stray far from safe, general topics—religion, family problems, and financial concerns. She was struggling as a single mom to govern and provide for her five children. On the last day, the four of us finally talked openly about our feelings, and we agreed again to keep praying and searching for an answer.

We also told Val that if she decided to move back to Utah, which she was already considering, we'd help her with a job and a place to live. Our trailer was empty, and there was plenty of work at the family business. We'd be able to help with her children; furthermore, it would give us a chance to continue exploring the possibility of her joining our family. Val was noncommittal and still guarded, but agreed to think about it.

Several weeks later, Val came to Salt Lake City to visit family and shop for a new car. I offered to help her and she readily accepted, which I took as a sign she'd not been put off by our conversation. I thought it would take some time for Val to feel ready for marriage again, but I was encouraged. I had no idea that that day would end as it did.

Val and I visited several dealerships before finding a suitable car: a silver Chevy Astro van. Val hated it at first; it was the color her ex-husband had preferred. But the van was the right price and the right size. We made the deal.

We then went to a park and, over several hours, talked about her marriage, her current views on religion and plural marriage, and what she was looking for in a husband and father for her children. I'd expected Val to be reserved, but instead it was as though there had been no fifteen-year gap between our first date and that afternoon. Our conversation flowed easily and openly. As we talked, I could feel the barriers coming down and sensed that Val was ready to move forward with her life. Val was so warm and accepting that I could tell her anything and everything, all my deepest thoughts. In some moments, as I listened to Val, my heart ached for what she'd been through, and I wanted to give her all the love and protection she'd never had.

We kept moving around the park, sitting in one spot for a while and then walking a bit and finding a new place to sit. Each time, we sat closer to one another, and at one point in our conversation I wrapped my arms around Val as she let go and cried.

We finally left the park and drove to a juice store to get drinks. As we got out of the car, I took Val into my arms and, for the first time, told her the full story of the moment months earlier when our eyes had locked and I'd received a spiritual prompting that she was to be my wife. It seemed to me, I explained, that when I put our situation in God's hands, he opened the way for us.

"I didn't expect to reach this moment so soon," I said, "but I know you belong in my family." I bent toward Val and she leaned in to meet me, and without another word we kissed.

We walked to a nearby mall in a daze. Val was glued to me, not wanting to release my hand for a second. When we returned to the car, I called home and told Vicki and Alina we were on our way and to meet us in the living room because we had exciting news. I practically bounded into the house and didn't even bother to sit down before I started talking. I launched into an explanation of the day's events before breaking off to get to the point.

"Val's accepted us. We're going to get married," I announced. "Now we just need to figure out how to make this happen in the best way possible for the children."

Since we had assumed that it would take much longer for Val to realize she belonged in our family, the sudden announcement caught Alina and Vicki by surprise. It was clear, however, that they were thrilled; they felt the same way I did about Val.

Next, we visited Val's parents. We didn't need their permission at this point in our lives, but out of respect I wanted them to know my intentions. Val's father spoke without hesitation: "Good on you," he said, smiling. "I can't think of a better man for her."

Many people advised me to wait a while before marrying Val. Even close friends and family did not understand how we could have made this decision so quickly. Some thought it was a mistake for me to take another wife when we already had such a great family. But Alina, Vicki, Val, and I knew it was right, and we were ready. A long courtship, in my view, is inappropriate when a man is already married—particularly once a woman has agreed to join a family. The dating stage of my relationship with Val was hard for Vicki and Alina. They were giving up time with me, trusting it would work out with Val. And since Val was not yet part of the family, she couldn't be included fully in the family routine. It was awkward to go on a nice date with Val, and then return home to whichever wife I was supposed to be with that night.

There was an important reason, however, for us to wait: we wanted to give the children in both families time to adjust to each other. Val's children, who had always known me as Uncle Joe, also needed to get used to the idea of me as their father.

When Val and her children moved into the trailer behind our house, we continued courting, both as a couple and as a family. There were still moments when I questioned my ability to take on this new responsibility. I literally broke down and cried at one point. I'd just spent a few hours visiting with Val. I came into our house and collapsed on the living room couch in a daze, barely able to breathe. When Vicki and Alina asked if I was okay, I lost it.

"I don't know if I can do this," I said. "I don't know if I have it in me to do what I know marrying another wife is going to take. How am I going to support everyone financially? How am I going to provide all the emotional support everyone will need? How am I going to be a father to Val's kids?" At times like that I really needed the support of my wives and the comfort of my prayers.

We set a wedding date for September, three months out, but couldn't make it work. Between Alina's due date and my company's opening a new cafeteria at Intel's corporate office in Utah, we had too much going on. So we moved the wedding date to mid-October. I opened the new cafeteria on October 6. Alina went past her due date, but finally delivered our baby girl Kyra at home, with the help of a midwife, on October 12. Two days later, Val and I were married in a ceremony that took place in our living room, with Alina and Vicki standing beside us as we exchanged sacred vows before close family members. The four of us celebrated at a restaurant that night, and that weekend, we rented a hall and threw a party for more than a hundred people in our extended families. We were honoring a marriage, but also a new stage in our growth as a family.

Several weeks later, Val and I went on a ten-day honeymoon to the Napa Valley and Hawaii. It was hard to leave the rest of the family behind, but I knew, as did Alina and Vicki, that Val and I needed this sweet, romantic time together. Val had never had a full, deep relationship built on trust, respect, and caring, so our love was a new experience for her.

It was an exciting time for me, too, though it seemed strange, after years of marriage, to be experiencing the short-lived, all-consuming passion that comes in the initial stage of an intimate relationship. I felt out of balance. It would take time, I knew, for my relationship with Val to match the depth and substance of my relationships with Alina and Vicki. And it wasn't as though I could forget I was in love with them, or not wonder about the children waiting for me at home. As it turned out, we ended the honeymoon a day early because we both missed the family so much.

CHAPTER FIVE

A New Marriage

True we practice plural marriage, not, however, because we are
compelled to, but because we are convinced that it is a divine
revelation, and we find in this principle a satisfaction, contentment
and more happiness than we can obtain in any other relationship.

—ELLIS R. SHIPP, PLURAL WIFE

AND EARLY-TWENTIETH-CENTURY OBSTETRICIAN

Alina

BEFORE VICKI and I married Joe, I hoped there would be more
than two wives in our family. Vicki and I had even joked about
Joe eventually having ten wives, with ten kids each. I had a dreamy
vision of us getting along nicely and having fun making cookies
with our dozens of children. Although I was a little naive about
the realities of this lifestyle, I knew that expanding our family
would bring richer textures and layers to our relationships, and
increase our opportunities for personal growth.

In the years since we'd married, I'd thought a lot about the perfect sister wife. She had to have values that aligned with ours. She couldn't be interested only in Joe and want a separate, distinct life with him. After ten years of marriage, we had really put our motto—communication, trust, respect—into practice, and our life together flowed without too much effort. We'd had ups and downs in our individual marriages, but we had been able to work through them. In fact, a friend had warned me that another woman would never be able to fit into our family because it worked so well and because Vicki and I were so close. In any case, despite my youthful hopes for more sister wives, over the years we never had a serious interest in anyone until Val.

Vicki and I had tried to keep in contact with Val after we married. We stayed overnight at her home in Mapleton a time or two and always had great fun, talking into the wee hours of the night. As far as I could tell, things seemed to be going well for her. Life was not without its challenges, but that was to be expected; she was adjusting to a new family.

Once Val moved to Pleasant Valley, we saw much less of her. Soon, though, the family network began to buzz about problems. Val's mother was very worried and would sometimes drop comments about how Donald was doing this or that—taking karate lessons, for example—while his families were barely surviving. I knew that Vicki's mom sometimes worried needlessly about her, so I suspected that she was being overly protective of Val. My policy was never to listen to gossip, especially when the talk contradicted what I personally knew. From what I knew of Donald, he was funny and charming. And Val had never said anything negative to me about her husband.

One day, I had lunch with several of Vicki and Val's sisters. Val had confided in her sister Bonnie about Donald's gambling problems and the family's financial straits. I found the stories hard to believe, and said so. But Bonnie insisted they were true; Val just didn't want to impose on her family, Bonnie said. That got me thinking, and in looking back I could see signs of trouble, such as the way Donald didn't seem able to keep a job.

It wasn't long after that luncheon that Val left Donald and moved to Montana to live with another sister. Obviously, I had been wrong. Val was a very loyal person, and I knew she would not have left her marriage unless she felt it was the only option.

I finally had a chance to speak directly with Val when she came to Salt Lake City to visit family. I sat down with her, trying to communicate how stunned and sad I was, and how I hated to see her family break up. "Why didn't you tell us what was going on?" I asked. "I heard things but didn't want to listen to rumors."

"I covered for Donald, but I'm done doing that," Val said. "You know, for a long time, our marriage problems felt like a reflection on *me*. And I know how you feel about divorce being a last resort. I didn't think you'd be supportive."

"I would never be your judge," I said. "I'm sorry I wasn't there more for you."

I didn't see Val again until she came back to Utah for her release hearing and stayed with us for a night. Val had lost weight by then, had a new haircut, and seemed to have a new lease on life. We were getting the children ready for bed when Joe came home that evening. He walked into the room, and I saw this thing, this connection, pass between him and Val. It happened in the blink of an eye, but I knew I hadn't imagined it. In all the times we'd been around Val, I had never witnessed anything like that moment, and it really surprised me.

That night, we stayed up late talking and Val opened up about what she'd been through. As I listened and watched her, I kept thinking, *Whoa, maybe there is something here.* In the days that followed, I asked God to help me know if Val belonged in our family. *And if it's not the right thing, then let it close and go away,* I prayed.

But the feeling didn't go away. It grew stronger, and I soon discovered that Vicki shared it. I went to Joe finally and told him how I felt. "I was thinking maybe Val could marry you," I said.

Joe stared at me and then told me to drop it.

"Well, okay," I said, "but you'll want to think about it, because it's probably going to happen."

Joe eventually told Vicki and me that he'd received a spiritual prompting about Val, and we began praying together for confirmation of our feelings. I became more convinced that we belonged together with each passing day. I was excited about the prospect of Val becoming part of our family. I had a genuine love and concern for her, and wanted her to be the happiest she possibly could be. I thought Val would fit into our family well and add vibrancy to our lives, just as I had always hoped when I thought about the perfect sister wife. I figured it would take a while for Val's heart to be opened, though, and for her to be ready to consider our family. I definitely wasn't expecting what happened the next time she came to Utah to visit us and look for a car.

Joe offered to help her with the car search, and they were gone all day. I knew what was up the minute they came back to the house late that afternoon, both of them wearing rather odd expressions.

"Well, did you find a car?" I asked them.

Joe had a big grin, but Val looked a bit uncomfortable.

"I've got something to tell you," he said, calling Vicki to join us.

Joe described the amazing experience they'd had that day and then circled back to the main point. "And we're engaged," Joe said.

I knew that Val and Joe had had several long talks and that she frequently called him for advice. But I didn't think her view of Joe had shifted yet from friend to husband. I looked at Vicki. "Did I miss something here? I thought they went to buy a car," I said, "and they come home engaged?"

We all started laughing. I found the situation almost comical because it had developed so quickly. They showed us their engagement photographs, including one with their faces close, staring into each other's eyes, noses nuzzled together. My mind reeled as I tried to process the giant leap they'd taken. Vicki and I had been the first to suggest the idea, but now a new marriage was really going to happen. Was I ready?

I had an underlying peace that carried me, over the next months, through the tough moments of watching my husband court a new wife. After ten years of marriage, Joe and I had the love, trust, and appreciation for each other that come with time. As in most marriages, time also brings out a lot of little annoyances. Val and Joe, on the other hand, were in that dreamy state where shortcomings and flaws don't exist.

While they were courting, Joe said to me, "Val appreciates me for who I am. She's just so grateful for *everything*." My immediate thought? *Give it time, and it will become very real!* But the comment also made me think about my relationship with Joe in a new way. I could see there were things that could be improved, things I had begun taking for granted. Their courtship revitalized my marriage.

After Joe and Val became engaged, our discussions turned to moving Val to Utah and helping the children adjust. I expected that accepting Val into the family would be a smoother experience for me emotionally than when Vicki and I both dated and married Joe, and I was right. I was older, more confident, and experienced in dealing with the natural feelings that come with sharing your husband.

At the time Joe courted Val, I was pregnant with my fifth child. In fact, we planned their wedding so it would take place after the birth—which it did, just barely, when I went past my due date! I had already experienced times in our marriage when I was pregnant and Vicki was not, leaving her free to do more things than I could. I knew that having Joe court and marry a new wife would present the same challenge, whether or not I was pregnant. In fact, Joe and I were particularly close during this pregnancy. He went overboard in letting me know how integral our relationship was to what he was developing with Val. I never felt that Joe was out looking for a replacement for me, his pregnant wife, or off having a good time while I was home miserable. His heart was sincere.

When the time finally came for me to deliver, Val was there, as was Vicki. After Kyra's birth, I felt as I always do: euphoric and ready to start anew! It was an ideal time to be welcoming my new sister wife into our family.

But I underestimated the work and introspection it would take to transition my relationship with Val from friends to sister wives. Val's ideas about the correct way to live the Principle were different from ours. Vicki and I had agreed from the start that we wanted to live in the same house so that Joe could be with our children every night. I assumed Val would feel the same way. But she did not—at least not until she'd been part of our family for several years. Val initially wanted to live separately, which she thought would allow for more individuality in her relationship with Joe. That was difficult for me. It threatened my dream of a big, close family. Would this divide us? It took a lot for me to support Val with unconditional acceptance of her choices. Just because I chose to live with Vicki didn't mean that was Val's ideal. I had to take a hard look at myself, which brought me back to the reasons I wanted to live this lifestyle in the first place.

Vicki

WHEN VAL and I were teenagers, I was quite competitive with her and was always trying to establish my own, separate identity. I kept my own group of friends and tried not to date the same guys Val did. While we had both gone on dates with Joe in high school, I never imagined us both marrying him—or any other guy, for that matter. I loved Val, but I didn't want us to always be "the Twinners." I did think it might be cool if we were married to brothers, always double-dating and hanging out together, even going on family trips. But one husband? I wasn't ready to consider anything like that back then.

Once Val married Donald, we didn't see a lot of each other since we didn't live in the same city and moved in different social circles. Val was busy with her new family; I was working full-time and was spending every free moment with Joe and Alina. Val and I would catch up on each other's lives occasionally at family gatherings, and her marriage seemed all right to me, though there were hints it was more challenging than my own.

Val and I would talk to each other on our birthday, and I would ask how she'd celebrated it or what presents she'd received. She would say "Nothing" with a light laugh, as if it didn't mean anything, and quickly change the subject, asking me instead about my day. Joe always made a big deal of birthdays, showering me with gifts of clothes and jewelry, and planning special dates or get-togethers with friends. I would downplay to Val how wonderful my birthday had been, feeling almost guilty since for her there was no comparable celebration. But I figured it was because money was tight in their household. I noticed, too, that she and her sister wives didn't seem as close as Alina and I were. Mostly, though, we were both too busy with our growing families to keep in close contact with one another.

By our seventh anniversary, I'd had three children and was expecting my fourth; Alina also had three. I began working part-time as a bookkeeper in our family-owned catering business to help out financially. Alina worked some, too, on the events side of the business. Soon, I was working full-time and, as the company grew, gradually took on more duties. I enjoyed interacting with clients, and my organizational skills made me a good office manager, which boosted my confidence at work and in my personal life.

At home, I began to want more independence in my relationship with Joe. I thought I was relying on him too much in some ways—spiritually, emotionally—for my happiness. Now that I had a good job, I also wanted more say in our spending and didn't want to have to explain every purchase I made. Joe and I began fighting about money. I am frugal by nature, but it began to bother me that I was still shopping at thrift stores and fretting over every penny while neither Joe nor Alina seemed worried about their spending. We would go shopping and I would head straight for the bargain racks, only to watch as Alina snapped up the more expensive clothes.

My frustration boiled over one day after I went on a shopping spree and bought a beautiful new bedspread. I came home, excited to show it off, and found Joe at his desk, going over our bills. He was upset that I had made such a purchase without talking it over with him first, and began questioning what I had done.

"If there's money for you to go out to dinner, why isn't there money for me to buy a new bedspread?" I demanded.

Joe threw a handful of paperwork at me and said, "*You* do the bills, then."

"That's not the point!" I yelled. "I'll just take it back."

As I stormed out of the room, Joe shouted that he didn't want me to return the bedspread, but it was too late. I was so steamed that I knew I'd never be able to enjoy it now. Back it went.

For months, our relationship was tense and raw as we continued to have flare-ups, mostly over money. We finally began to mend our relationship after we started reading books by Stephen Covey and other relationship experts, and were able to move toward interdependence, that midway point between dependence and independence. Joe and I were just getting our relationship back on track when we heard that Val's marriage had collapsed. Given our recent battles, I don't think either of us anticipated what lay ahead.

After years of not being close to Val, I wanted to reconnect with her. Once she moved to Montana, I was able to telephone her frequently, and finally began to hear about how terrible her marriage had been.

As I listened to Val talk about her marriage one day, a strong feeling—one that was both protective and spiritual—came over me that she belonged in our family. I try to be tuned in to these feelings of *knowingness,* the intuition that comes when God opens your mind and fills it with understanding. The test comes after, when you have to show God what you're willing to do with the information, opportunity, or challenge he provides. The moments when I experience God's presence in my life always fill me with warmth, love, and joy. That's what I felt in that moment: I wanted Val to have everything I had, and I knew Joe could be to Val all that he was to me. I had long ago gotten over any need to compete with Val or to have a completely different life than hers. I understood what it was to love a sister wife, and knew I could have that love for Val. I also knew that our family could provide the support needed by her five children, whom I already cared about as though they were my own. After ten years of marriage, Joe, Alina, and I had reached a comfortable trust and, despite my recent challenges, I felt our marriage was strong enough to handle the addition of a new wife.

At first, I kept my thoughts to myself, searching through prayer for confirmation that this was the right path. When Val returned to Utah to formalize her separation from Donald, she opened up more to me about her marital problems. It was difficult for me to listen as Val shared her experiences for two reasons: I felt so blessed in my own relationships, and I had been so blind to what was going on in her life. Why had I not been able to see it? Why hadn't I been there for Val?

Val came to our house after her meeting with her church leaders, and we had just gathered the family for evening prayer when Joe came home. As he entered the room, he and Val exchanged looks and I witnessed a spark of energy between them. It was my confirmation: at that moment, I knew Val would marry Joe.

Some days later, I spoke to Alina and learned that she'd had the same feeling about Val. Alina and I had never expected to be the only two women in Joe's life. He was a good man, and I knew he had a greater capacity to love. Like me, Alina thought Val would be a great sister wife for our family, but we decided to discuss it separately with Joe. When I went to talk to my husband, he wasn't too excited about the idea.

"Oh, I don't know," Joe told me. "I want to see her happy, but my plate is pretty full right now."

It is no small matter to ask your husband to take on the emotional and material responsibility for another woman and her children. But I asked Joe not to dismiss the possibility out of hand, and—respecting my strong feelings and those of Alina—he agreed to consider it. Some time later, Joe came to us and shared the strong impression he'd received during Val's last visit to our home—the sense that she would be his wife. We prayed for confirmation of our feelings, and then for guidance as we began to explore how Val felt about us.

Over the next several months, Alina and I made several trips to Montana to visit Val and her children. During my conversations with Val, I never brought up marriage—to Joe or anyone else. I knew Val needed time to heal, and she was still deciding whether or not she even believed in plural marriage anymore. Val needed to reach her own conclusions about her future, a position we stuck to even after we openly approached Val about coming into our family.

It was definitely difficult at times to watch my spouse fall in love with someone else. But they were fleeting hurts, feelings that I'd already learned to process during my own courtship and marriage. Mostly, I was excited, because I understood how this new relationship would expand our family's love and bring positive changes to our lives. I never felt displaced by Val, and I trusted Joe's integrity and love for me completely. During their courtship, my relationship with Joe grew in ways I'd never anticipated.

Once Joe and Val opened themselves to the idea, things progressed quickly. I think what sealed it for Val was seeing how Joe embraced her children. She knew she couldn't marry a man unless he wanted to build—and was capable of building—a relationship with each of them. That fall, we accepted Val into our family in a small ceremony attended by close family.

While I didn't grow up thinking my twin sister and I would be married to the same man, it did not seem weird to me in any way when it happened. I know that some people are uncomfortable at the thought of two sisters sharing a husband, but I felt that God had a hand in it. The Old Testament offers examples of sisters who shared a husband, as does Mormon history and the experiences of our families and friends. This form of polygamy is found in other cultures around the world, and is even preferred in some.* Because of a common family background and (hopefully!) existing closeness, sisters often make perfect plural marriage companions. There's a good chance that if a husband is compatible with one sister, he'll be well matched with another. Outside of polygamy, it was not uncommon in past generations for a man who lost his wife to then marry her sister. And today you hear stories all the time about siblings from one family who marry siblings from another family.

But the situation can create interesting dynamics, too. What happens if the sisters don't get along, or one relationship collapses? I know of mothers who've had to listen to differing tales told by two daughters who shared a husband, and then felt like they had to pick sides when one daughter eventually left that marriage. In our case, I was confident that Val and I could work through any difficulties. And there *were* some, almost immediately.

If there is a tricky aspect to plural marriage, it's making sure that everyone's motives are clear, united, and based on trust. Val and Joe were in her trailer home talking not long after she came into our family, and I needed to ask Joe about plans for a family picnic. When I knocked on her door, they both came out.

"That's sister wives for you—always vying for their husband's attention!" Val said.

* In her study of Mormon polygamous families, which was based on interviews of family members conducted in the 1930s, 1970s, and 1980s, Jessie L. Embry found that 25 percent of the plural marriages involved sisters, which is known as sororal polygyny. See *Mormon Polygamous Families: Life in the Principle* (Salt Lake City: University of Utah Press, 1987), 141.

"What? I wasn't doing that at all. Not at all!" I told her.

Alina, who joined us at that moment, chimed in. "No, Val; Vicki wouldn't do that," she said.

I knew how terribly Val had been hurt in her first marriage, but I underestimated what it would take for her to believe that our desire for her happiness was sincere. I had naively figured that all Val needed to be happy was two super sister wives and a terrific husband! But, as it turned out, we had much more work to do.

CHAPTER SIX

Time to Speak Out

But little children are alive in Christ,
even from the foundation of the world.

—MORONI 8:12

Alina

WITH VAL JOINING OUR family at the same time I gave birth to my fifth child, it felt like a fresh start for our family. We were on the right path, we felt, and God was truly blessing us. But after the birth, we were faced with a challenge we could never have anticipated.

It had been a special pregnancy for me. Before I even conceived this baby, I knew she was coming. I had dreamed about this child, my second daughter, and I already had a name picked out for her: I would call her Kyra.

The pregnancy started out much like the other four had: I had a little bit of morning sickness, a little fatigue. I craved prime rib and Caesar salad. I would go to the grocery store, get a bag of salad mix, pour on that good dressing, and eat the whole thing in one sitting. I'd developed diabetes after my second pregnancy, so I diligently went for checkups and monitored my blood sugar, but wasn't having any problems. I felt great and the months passed quickly.

By October 6, Kyra's due date, I was down to one outfit: a pink and black striped shirt and black stretch pants. I refused to buy any new clothing; this was going to be my uniform until she came. Each morning, as the days ticked by and Kyra stayed tucked inside me, I stared at the tired shirt and well-worn pants and grudgingly put them on one more time. At last, on October 12, the labor pains began. They progressed so fast that I was ready to deliver by the time the midwife and her assistant arrived at our home!

"Stop pushing, Alina," the midwife told me after checking things out. She didn't want me to tear. "Stop pushing," she repeated.

"I *can't*," I said, pushing some more.

She smacked my nose. "Stop it."

Kyra slipped into the world moments later. She was pudgy, pink, and perfect. She weighed nearly ten pounds and had beautiful brown eyes and a smattering of dark hair. The midwife ran through the basic checks and found nothing amiss. Kyra took to nursing easily, sweetly inspecting the new faces around her. I was blissful.

Two days later, I felt good enough to participate in the marriage ceremony as we accepted Val into the family. My life was so full of joy, so complete, matching the hope I'd always held before me.

Kyra was a content little baby at first, but within a few months she grew fussy with what seemed like colic. That winter, there was an outbreak of respiratory syncytial virus (RSV) in Utah, and sick babies overwhelmed local hospitals. Two of my sisters had babies with RSV; one had taken her infant to the emergency room, but she'd been told her baby wasn't sick enough to stay and was sent back home with instructions to watch him. When Kyra developed congestion and a cough, I figured she had RSV, too.

We had fifteen children at the time, and combating winter colds and bouts of flu was just part of our routine. We didn't run to the family doctor for every little sniffle, and I thought I could get Kyra through whatever was ailing her.

But as my sisters' babies slowly got over their sicknesses, Kyra's lingered. One day, it would seem she was turning the corner, and the next she was getting worse again. Kyra just couldn't pull out of it, and I began to worry she had pneumonia. On March 16, I called our family doctor. No one answered at his office, so I left a message that Kyra was sick and needed to be seen. I still hadn't heard back by the end of the day and planned to try again in the morning.

That evening, Joe, Vicki, Val, and I went out to dinner. I took Kyra along, and she slept through most of the outing. Back home, as I got Kyra ready for bed, I made a mental note that she hadn't had a bowel movement that day and added it to the list of things I planned to tell the doctor. It was Joe's night with me, and he climbed into bed shortly before midnight, but Kyra was fussy so I put *Gone with the Wind* in the VCR and settled into a rocking chair to nurse her. She eventually dozed off, and I followed not long after.

Some hours later, I woke up and drowsily looked down at Kyra, who was still nestled in my arms. It took only seconds for me to realize she wasn't breathing.

I leaped out of the chair and cried out, "Joe, come quick! She's not breathing!" I put my ear to her mouth. "*Is* she breathing?" I asked, unwilling to give up hope.

Those first minutes were a blur: Joe put his shoes on, grabbed his cell phone, and took Kyra in his arms to begin mouth-to-mouth resuscitation as we ran to the car. He handed Kyra back to me as he got behind the wheel, and I took over breathing into her tiny lips. Joe punched 911 into his cell phone and pushed SEND as he slammed the car into drive, hitting one of our other vehicles as we lurched forward. The call didn't go through. Joe tried to dial it again, and then again and again as he raced through the empty streets toward the nearest hospital. Cell phone service was spotty in our neighborhood back then, and between that and his state of shock, Joe couldn't get his phone to work.

I looked over once at the dashboard, and the needle on the speedometer was edging to the right faster than I'd ever seen it move. Joe ran every red light. I rocked Kyra as I gave her little puffs of air, holding her upright because I thought it might help her breathe better. Once or twice I was sure I saw her chest move. And then I wondered if I'd imagined it. I vacillated between hope and despair.

"I can't get her to breathe," I told Joe, my voice tinged with desperation.

"Keep doing it," he urged.

Joe pulled into the emergency center at the hospital and we hurried out of the car. He grabbed Kyra from my arms and ran through the lobby straight to a doctor. Joe frantically thrust Kyra at him and said, "Save my baby! She's not breathing."

"Help us," I pleaded.

The doctor glanced at me but didn't reply. I didn't want to acknowledge what I saw in his eyes.

The doctor then placed Kyra on a bed in a small room, where a knot of staff quickly formed around her. I watched as they cut away Kyra's clothes and began to work on her. They tried to shock her heart into action. Once, maybe twice they tried—and then they stopped and looked at each other. A nurse came out of the room, walked over to me, and put her arm around my shoulders.

"I'm so sorry," she said.

I collapsed against Joe, who caught me. He was bawling.

The nurse led us to a little room so that we could have some privacy. I sat, stone still and sobbing, while Joe, his tears subdued for now, called Vicki and Val.

"Get to the hospital," he said. "Kyra's gone."

"What do you mean *gone?*" Vicki's voice was so loud and panicky that I could hear it, too. Joe couldn't bring himself to say more; he simply hung up.

A nurse then called Joe out of the room. I didn't move, trying to quiet my anguished thoughts: *How can I go on? How am I going to go home without my baby, without Kyra? I can't just* leave *her here.* I turned my head slightly in the darkened room and there, next to me, I saw a vision of Joe's father, who had died six years earlier. He was holding Kyra on his hip, and she was looking at me and waving good-bye. *Oh Kyra, I can't believe you're leaving me like this!* I thought. For a brief moment, as I took in that image, peace filled me. I knew in my heart that Kyra was okay, that her spirit lived, and that she, an innocent little baby, was on her way to heaven.

A nurse, her eyes wet with tears, brought Kyra to me, wrapped in a baby blanket, and told me I could hold her as long as I wanted.

I rocked the little bundle back and forth, instinctively seeking to comfort her as I so often had, until Vicki and Val arrived. They wept as they took turns holding Kyra before handing her back to me. After a while, the nurse came back. "Are you ready yet?" she asked.

No. I was *not* ready. I would *never* be ready. I held Kyra tighter.

Joe joined us then. He put an arm around me and said, "We need to let her go." But I couldn't, despite the earlier, fleeting moment of acceptance. *Who would watch her? Who would hold her? Where would she be once I left? Would she be all alone?*

Finally, Joe said, "Let me take her." And then I had to give her up.

Walking out of those hospital doors with empty arms was one of the hardest things I've ever done.

Vicki and Val drove me home, while Joe stayed behind to answer questions and fill out paperwork. I carried Kyra's car seat, spotted with her spit-up, into our house. A day earlier, I'd had a baby daughter to hold and to love. Now, nothing. An empty car seat. Clothes she'd never wear again. A baby blanket still infused with her scent.

I curled into a ball on the couch, clutching Kyra's blanket to my nose, trying to grasp the horrible reality that my baby was gone. Vicki and Val sat on either side, grieving with me. I was wracked with guilt. *Why had I allowed myself to fall asleep? How could this have happened? Why Kyra? What did I miss? She was sick, but how could she have died?*

When Joe got home, I wanted to know only one thing: *Why* did she die? He didn't have an answer. Moments later, a Salt Lake

County sheriff's deputy arrived at our house to question us about what had happened. In a daze, we answered his questions, giving our ages, Kyra's date of birth, the names of our midwife and family doctor. The deputy wanted to know if Kyra was allergic to anything and whether I had eaten any seafood before nursing her to sleep. He wanted to see the blanket I had swaddled Kyra in as I cradled her in the rocking chair. I let him examine it and then quickly grabbed it back. The deputy was kind, his questions routine, but I noticed his eyes sweeping the house, taking in all the people. Vicki, Val, and I were temporarily living separately in two trailers and an apartment on our property while we waited to move into a larger home that was being remodeled. But everyone had gathered at my home that morning.

There was an autopsy, as required in cases of unexpected death. We learned the results just before Kyra's funeral. Kyra had been born with defects of a sort that sometimes don't show up for months. She had a heart abnormality and her intestines were contorted—the ultimate cause of death. Had the defects been detected while she was still living, she would have needed surgery, though even that might not have been enough to save her. I tried to take some comfort in knowing she'd died peacefully, in my arms, without having to endure any of that trauma.

Hundreds of people turned out to support us as we buried Kyra. Joe's uncle made her a tiny casket, and his aunt lined it with pink satin imprinted with roses. Vicki's mom made Kyra's gown, which was white and, by coincidence, had the same rose pattern as the casket's lining, and three pink rosebuds across the bodice. One of Joe's sisters sang Billy Joel's sweet song "Lullaby (Good

Night My Angel).” Our hearts almost unbearably heavy, we laid Kyra to rest next to her Grandpa Darger.

We were numb in the days that followed, stuck in a newly hollowed space in our lives. I would sit with Vicki's eighteen-month-old son for hours, rocking and rocking, taking solace in holding his warm, little body close to mine.

Not long after the funeral, the deputy we'd met the day of Kyra's death called again; he had a few more questions and wanted to come by the house. Joe tried to assure me it was all routine, no big deal, but I felt a growing sense of alarm. During this visit, the deputy asked detailed questions about how long Kyra had been sick, the nature of any home or natural remedies we might have used to treat her, and why we hadn't called an ambulance that night.

“Was there any particular reason you didn't take her to the doctor sooner?” he asked. “Finances? Fear?”

Then, the deputy dropped a bomb.

“Some members of the committee reviewing Kyra's case are concerned you might be affiliated with the Darger polygamist family,” he said. The state's Child Fatality Review Committee, which investigates the death of every child up to age nineteen, wanted to know whether money or a reluctance to ask the state for help had been an obstacle in seeking medical care for her, he added.

“They want you to know services are available,” the deputy said.

For a moment, I could hardly breathe. I kept my eyes on Joe, who calmly told the deputy that we had health insurance, and that while his family had been involved in polygamy, it wasn't an issue for us.

How else could Joe respond, given our uncertainty about what the state might do if he told the truth? In my grief, I wasn't sure I'd understood what the deputy was trying to tell us. At the time, I had no idea who was on the committee or what role it played in investigations into deaths like Kyra's. What I knew was the thing I had feared most of my life—the state's power to use my lifestyle to break up my family—was now before me.

At the end of the visit, Joe asked the deputy what we should expect to happen next.

The deputy said, "As far as I'm concerned, this investigation is closed, but there's no telling what the state will do."

I stared at him, confused. What did that mean? He *was* the state. His comment heightened my concern that there might be trouble ahead.

A grief nurse contacted me next to see how I was doing. I told her I had a lot of support and thought I was handling things pretty well, but she insisted on bringing some pamphlets to our house. I remember her first comment: "Boy, I had a hard time finding your place!" She asked again how I was feeling and how our children were adjusting. As she left, she told me, "You seem okay. You've got a good support structure. Call if you need anything. I like to stay out of people's business as much as I can, but you know the government!" There it was again: a hint that there was more to come.

The next day, we were just leaving our home to go to a funeral for a friend's child, a boy who had died of cancer, when a vehicle pulled into our driveway. A woman got out and introduced herself as a state Child Protective Services investigator. She told us that a medical neglect investigation into Kyra's death was under way, and as part of that she wanted to interview our children. Joe told her she'd have to come back later. That's when I realized the grief counselor had come mostly to scope us out.

Despite my increasing trepidation, I was shocked. I sat through the funeral for our friend's child in a daze. I believed with all my soul that Kyra had gone straight to heaven, but that didn't automatically take away the ache in my heart. Now I feared that the state might be after the children I still had with me.

That night we learned that the investigator, unaware we were educating our children at home, had gone to the nearby elementary school and questioned all the children with the last name Darger. None of their parents had given permission for their children to be interviewed. The investigator had asked each child who his or her parents were, which is probably how she realized none of our children attended the school. Nevertheless, she continued with the interviews, asking the children if they knew our family, how many mothers there were, what kind of mother I was, what our children were like, and how we disciplined them.

A recurring nightmare began to fill my nights: fierce storms raged around our house and, as thunder and lightning cracked the sky, the door blew open to reveal an officer who swept in, grabbed all my children, and vanished into thin air.

My days weren't much better. I was grieving for Kyra, but I had to be strong for my other children and do everything in my power to make sure they weren't taken from me. I was terrified.

When we first met the investigator in our driveway, Joe had let her know that she would not be allowed to speak to our children alone. We had no idea what our rights were, but we knew we needed to figure them out fast and be proactive in defending our family. The state legislature had recently created the post of "investigator of crimes within closed societies." That investigator, newly hired, had been dubbed the "polygamy czar" by the media, and he'd participated in investigations of other Fundamentalist Mormon families we knew. I worried we might be next on his list.

I was a wreck as I worked feverishly to keep my house spotless and my children freshly scrubbed and immaculately dressed, with every hair perfectly combed in place. I worried the state might show up at my door unannounced, wanting to look things over. I felt so desperate I even thought about hiding my children. Instead, I stayed put and began searching for an attorney to represent us in what increasingly looked like the battle of our lives.

The original Child Protective Services investigator called to arrange a meeting at our house with our children, and Joe again said she would not be allowed to speak to them alone. We were afraid she would try to influence and twist whatever the children said to build a case against us. Joe asked the investigator to bring a deputy or some other third party along. Instead, the investigator agreed to let Joe stand outside the room, and out of the children's view, where he could listen to her questions and their responses. That worked for us.

The investigator came out to the house and we set her up in a bedroom with our three oldest children. Our two-year-old, Ashton, was too young to understand the seriousness of what was happening, and raced in and out of the room and up and down the hallway. The investigator tried to put the children at ease with questions about what kinds of things they liked to do and where they liked to play. She then got more focused: Have your parents ever taken you to the doctor? Did you know Kyra was sick? What did your parents do when they found out Kyra was sick? How do your parents discipline you? Does anyone ever make you feel afraid? What happens when you fight?

Our oldest child, Joseph, who was ten, gave a detailed answer to that last question. "Lots of times, my mom just makes us sit by each other until we work it out," he said. The investigator laughed.

Joseph told her about his trip to the emergency room to get stitches after falling and cutting his brow, and about the time-outs I'd given him when he misbehaved. Shad, who was nearly five, gave what was apparently a hilarious answer to one question, based on how much laughter it drew from his siblings.

When it was over, the investigator had one more question for Joe and me: she asked for the name of our midwife. "I'll be in touch," she said, her face a mask that revealed nothing.

The next day, I got another call from the investigator. She asked a few questions about our family doctor and then dropped the zinger: "Is he a polygamist also?" I knew he was a Fundamentalist Mormon, but I had no idea if he had more than one wife. "I don't know," I told the investigator.

But I was freaked out by her question. What did the doctor's family structure have to do with Kyra's death? My worries about my own family redoubled, because there could be no doubt now that polygamy was an issue. I was sobbing when I called Joe to describe the conversation.

As we spoke, my phone kept beeping to indicate incoming calls. I could see that it was the investigator again, but I ignored her calls. Every aspect of our life was being scrutinized, from our decision to educate our children at home to our lifestyle and our religious beliefs, which the investigator insinuated included an aversion to medical care.

Later that day, the investigator called Joe at his office. He managed to keep calm as she asked more questions, some phrased multiple ways to see if he'd slip up. Then it was his turn to ask a question: "We're a grieving family. You have nothing on us. I want to know how long this inquiry is going to take."

The investigator told Joe she had a few things to wrap up, including an interview with our midwife. She also said she needed to speak to me one more time before she was finished. Joe lost it then: "No more! It's too hard on my wife," he shouted.

But I *did* speak to the investigator one last time, and it was a spiritual experience for me. I had been praying fervently, asking God to help me find the words to express what kind of parents we were and how much we loved our children, how much I had longed for and loved Kyra. An incredible confidence finally came over me, and I was ready when the investigator called again.

I took the phone into a bathroom and locked the door so I wouldn't be interrupted. The investigator began probing me about my midwife and family doctor, asking about the care they had given Kyra. "Are you mad at them?" she asked.

"I know what you're trying to do," I answered, "and if you're going to place blame on anyone, it's got to be me. You are not going to drag my doctors, who did everything they were supposed to, into this."

The investigator told me that she would be turning her report over to a screening panel that would make the ultimate decision about the case. She said it was too close a call for her to make the decision on her own.

"Why?" I asked her. "They've never met me, never seen my family. How can they be impartial?"

"The panel will rely heavily on my opinion," she said. That wasn't exactly comforting since I didn't have a clue what she thought about us.

"They don't know what a caring mother I am," I said. "They haven't been in my home. *You* have. *You* know!"

Then she asked a surprising question. "Are you planning on getting pregnant again soon?"

Less than three months had passed since Kyra's death. Pregnancy was the last thing on my mind, and I told her so.

"Well, if you do, I would suggest you deliver at a hospital," she said, adding that she'd be in touch after the panel made its decision.

In June, Joe and I went to Boston for a long weekend. Some friends had collected donations to send us on a much-needed vacation. We were sitting in a restaurant when my cell phone rang. It was the investigator. The screening panel had concluded there was no neglect on our part, and the state was closing the case. Then she added a "but."

"But the case will remain on file, and if anything else comes up it may be reopened. I strongly advise you to have your future babies born in a hospital," she told me again.

Joe was angry, but I just melted. It was over at last. Kyra was in heaven, and my other children were safe. But my sense of relief proved to be elusive.

Shortly after we received that news, the deputy who'd first questioned us after Kyra's death called. He'd retired, after twenty-four years of service, while the case was ongoing, and he was now selling life insurance—his reason for calling. But he also wanted to know how the investigation had ended. He had been kind to us, so we agreed to meet with him, and we ended up learning more than we'd expected.

The deputy told us about the discussion our last name had triggered among the Fatality Review Committee members. He said he'd objected to any further inquiry into Kyra's death, asking, "How can you base something like this on a person's last name?" He reminded the committee of his reputation as an officer whose integrity was highly trustworthy. He then let the committee members in on a secret: "Well, let me tell you something. My father was a polygamist."

The deputy had told the committee he would review the case again and, if he found anything amiss, would make sure justice was served. But there was no basis for a medical neglect investigation, he said he'd told the committee, a conclusion he repeated after meeting with us again.

But that hadn't stopped the child welfare investigation, which moved on its own, separate track. The former deputy's account confirmed what I had suspected all along: a full-scale investigation into our daughter's death had been launched because we were polygamists.

As I listened to the man's story, I realized I would never again be the person I was before Kyra's death. There was no going back to that naive state of being. The concern I had always felt about how my lifestyle might be used against me had proved to be well grounded. In the months after my baby died, I asked myself the same set of questions over and over: *What can I do to prevent another mother from experiencing what I did? Is there any way to take my sorrow, my terror, and turn it into a tribute to Kyra?* With these thoughts in mind, I began to speak out in hopes of educating people about my lifestyle.

CHAPTER SEVEN

Sister Wives

The faults and weaknesses which are born in us are the enemies
we are to grapple with, and those who have the greatest,
and can put them under their feet, are the greatest conquerors
and will wear the brightest crowns.

—HELEN MAR WHITNEY, PLURAL WIFE OF JOSEPH SMITH,
IN *Why We Practice Plural Marriage*

Plural marriage isn't easy. We're the first to admit that. It's a lifestyle that requires of each woman a constant gentle empathy for her sister wives and a respect for boundaries and fairness. We face the same struggles that monogamous wives do, but those trying times are often magnified because there are multiple partners whose perspectives and feelings have to be considered. This way of life must be freely chosen to work. And once a plural marriage has been undertaken, healthy relationships are critical; there is no room for abuse or force or mistreatment. It starts with the husband and his character, but what really makes success possible? It's that woman who's agreed to take the journey with you, your sister wife.

Alina

KYRA'S DEATH BROUGHT ME closer than ever to my sister wives. They shared my grief and comforted me in a way that no one else could. Vicki and I had already experienced a great many highs and lows after living together for a decade, but my relationship with Val was fresh and fragile, and Kyra's death compressed the time it took for us to bond as a family. Val was tender and thoughtful during those dark days, knowing without being asked when I needed comfort and a shoulder to cry on. Now, after our shared grieving, we had a history together, and staying power for the future. But we still had a long way to go to be the family I'd always envisioned. I realized just *how* far several months after the investigation into Kyra's death ended.

I'd been out running errands and rushed into the kitchen with my arms full of groceries. "Where's Joe?" I asked Val, who was seated at the table. It was an innocent, reflexive question, just my way of checking in to see what was going on with the rest of the family.

Val stared at me. "Why do you always have to know where he is every minute?" she asked with an edge to her voice. I was flabbergasted.

In Val's first plural marriage, every relationship, whether between Donald and a wife or between one wife and another, was compartmentalized. We were the complete opposite of that. Vicki, Joe, and I talked about and shared nearly everything, and that openness created problems for Val and me at first. In my earnest efforts to accept and include her, I was too much for Val: too open, too inquisitive, and too involved. I didn't realize at first how controlling I was coming across to Val, and her mistrust that day in the kitchen was like a slap in the face.

I had opened my life to Val, willingly agreed to share my husband with her, and now it felt as if she didn't even *like* me. At first I was defensive, trying to explain myself to her. But then I began to examine my own behavior. After all, the whole point of living this way was to see how closely we could model Christ's teachings about love, acceptance, care, and compassion. And she was right. I tried harder to give her more space after that, and when I found it hard to cope with Val's mistrust, I would say a prayer, flip open the Bible or the Book of Mormon, and read whatever I found on the page to give me strength and comfort. Even so, it took time for us to understand and trust each other completely. We'd make it past one barrier only to bump up against another one. It's the same growth process that creates the foundation of any long-lasting relationship; there are layers that rest on the good times, and layers that develop by getting beyond the bad times.

About four years after Val married Joe, she miscarried early in a pregnancy. Joe was at a football coaching conference and couldn't be reached. Val and I were having a lot of friction at the time, but I decided to do everything I could to help her, without worrying about being rejected or misunderstood. I went to Val's bathroom, where she was bent over on the toilet, in great pain. She'd never miscarried before. Having experienced a miscarriage myself, I understood what she was going through. I sat beside her, my arm around her back, and talked her through it. The intimate hours I spent with Val in that crisis brought a new dimension to our relationship. No words were spoken about it, but from that point on, Val and I seemed to be able to give our all to each other with no reservations.

Does that mean everything was now perfect? No. When people say I "practice" polygamy, they've got it right: my efforts to live this lifestyle are constant and ongoing. There are many religions that have practices aimed at deepening spiritual insights and expressing faith, such as fasting, saying the rosary, and making a pilgrimage. That's what plural marriage is for me: a daily practice that focuses my attention on the highest ideals of my religion. The benefits to me, in terms of spiritual and personal growth, joy, and completeness, far outweigh the hard work and sacrifice it takes.

My relationship with Vicki and Val is a hybrid found nowhere but in plural marriage. We have the closeness of sisters and the camaraderie of friends. I love it when I head for the kitchen late at night for a taste of chocolate and find Vicki or Val there, spoon in hand and ready for conversation. I find joy in knowing that the bond between sister wives often lasts beyond marriage. Val is still close to some sister wives from her first marriage; my older sister continued to live with her sister wife after their husband died, just as Joe's grandmothers did after their husband's death.

As sister wives, we also have a unique respect for each other—a respect that is found among women in our culture who know they love the same man. It is that connection that prevents our relationship from being identical to that of sisters or friends. There are some things we just do not share with each other, mostly involving our private, intimate relationships with Joe. Absolute privacy on that issue is one of the unwritten rules of our plural marriage, though I've seen that respect violated by sister wives, inevitably creating pain and damaging relationships.

Not long after Val joined the family, we were having a girls' night out with a bunch of women; some were plural wives and some married women from outside the culture. The laughs and conversation flowed freely, from raising children to the appropriate age to teach them about sex. Then the talk took a turn to marriage and wedding night experiences. A friend of mine shared some rather intimate details of her wedding night. "Did anyone feel the same as me?" she asked, looking around the room. "Come on, now. I shared. It's your turn!"

There was an awkward silence. I looked at Val across the circle of women, and her one raised eyebrow said it all. No way would we ever discuss our sex lives in front of each other—or with anyone else, for that matter. Our intimate relationships are sacred. And what if something was said that got back to another wife? There was too great a possibility that such talk might cause hurt feelings or feelings of inadequacy, or lead a wife to start making comparisons, which are a deadly trap in a plural marriage.

A few women shared stories of their first experiences with sex, but the plural wives kept silent. On the way home, I said to Val, "She sure didn't get it, did she? I can't believe that!"

"Nope," Val said, laughing. "That was clueless."

When I entered plural marriage, I knew full well Joe would be intimate with other women, and I soon learned that would require me to respect certain boundaries in our distinctive relationships. I'm sure some of that understanding came from watching how my mothers interacted, but mostly it came to me the hard-knocks way. Early in our courtship, Vicki and I agreed we would rotate sitting in the front seat next to Joe whenever we went somewhere in his car. Sometimes Joe would reach over and take the hand of whoever was up front with him, a gesture that I always enjoyed. But one day, as I sat next to Joe, *I* reached over for *his* hand.

Vicki was really upset I had done that, and later confronted me. "Why did you do that?" she asked. "I always wait for him to reach for my hand first."

"I'm sorry," I said. "When I'm not the one in the front seat, I don't pay attention to who instigates the hand-holding. I just notice, now and then, that you're holding hands."

Vicki had one expectation about what was appropriate and courteous when it came to public displays of affection, and I had another, as that example shows. We had to do a lot of talking to figure out our boundaries. And when Val came into the family, we had to mark the boundaries all over again, because she had her own ideas and expectations.

As a plural wife, I need intimacy with Joe that is mine alone, and I need my sister wives to respect that space. We share a great deal, but not everything. This unspoken policy extends to many aspects of our individual relationships with Joe. For example, when Joe and I go on a date, we don't necessarily share our plans with Vicki and Val, and vice versa. And afterward, I don't gush about what a great date we had or complain to them if something went wrong.

But the reality is, we are all affected by what goes on in each relationship, from the good to the bad. When one relationship is going well, it can have a spillover effect—generally positive—on the other relationships. Conversely, if Joe and one of my sister wives are having a spat, and he and I have a date that night, his mood will be affected. We don't interfere in each other's couple disagreements, though we sometimes confide in one another about our individual problems. The fact is, each of us considers our relationship with Joe to be monogamous, which means that our family, at one level, consists of three separate marriages. One marriage may be flourishing at the same time another marriage is fragile, which can affect the overall dynamic of the family. Sometimes I am closer to Vicki and sometimes closer to Val; our relationships shift depending on what's going on in each of our lives.

As a family, we had a very difficult time when Vicki experienced severe postpartum depression after her seventh child. I sometimes felt she directed her resentment at me and turned to Val for comfort. She seemed so irritated with everything I did, but how was I supposed to change who I was? One night, as the three of us were talking, all my emotions bubbled to the surface and I broke down crying. Once I'd composed myself enough to form words, I poured out my heart. Vicki and Val both came over to me and hugged me for a long time. Having put down my defenses, I could see how alone Vicki was feeling. We were able to forgive, let go of the bad feelings, and move forward again with more empathy for one another.

During this time, I gave up some of my nights with Joe because Vicki's relationship with him needed attention. I am married to both Joe and my sister wives; when their marriages succeed, mine is better, too. It's the "weakest link in a chain" philosophy: the stronger each relationship becomes, the more strength we have as a family.

Vicki, Val, and I also sometimes trade nights to accommodate *happy* occasions—a birthday or anniversary, or a special event involving one of the children. I bought tickets to see Kenny Chesney in concert months in advance, for example. The concert happened to be on a Friday night, and when it turned out my night with Joe was Saturday, Vicki willingly swapped nights with me.

I love my time with Joe, but I also love my time without him. That's when I stay up late reading, take a class on interior design, go to a movie with my girlfriends or children, or just get a good night's sleep. I know myself, and if it were just the two of us—Joe and me—we would probably be taking each other for granted after twenty-one years of marriage!

As Joe's legal wife, I often attend public functions with him. But having that status has created its own set of complications. There are times when I feel I cannot truly be myself with people who don't know the whole story of our lives. For example, if I am with Joe at a business function and someone asks how many children we have, what's the correct answer? Seven? Twenty-four? In the early years of our marriage, I really didn't know how to deal with such questions. I had to adopt a facade when I went with Joe on business trips, hiding a big part of my life.

One year, I accompanied Joe to a meeting in San Diego. We were the youngest couple there, and the wife of Joe's boss took a special interest in me, inviting me everywhere with her. By the next trip, Joe's boss had learned we were polygamists and his wife openly expressed her disdain for me. I was pregnant, and at the first luncheon with the other wives, she ridiculed me for having so many kids. I spent the rest of the trip by myself. As a plural wife, I often experience an emotional tug-of-war between having pride in my family and fearing I'll be ostracized if people find out how I live.

I have never wanted Vicki or Val to feel bad or left out because I'm the legal wife. In the early years, when Vicki and Joe and I were first married, Joe tried to balance things out by taking Vicki on a separate trip following a business trip with me. There were often times I would gladly have swapped the work trip for a pleasurable vacation on which I didn't have to worry about keeping secrets. When Joe changed careers and began dealing with a new group of associates, we decided Vicki would be the public wife. Eventually, we resolved it this way: I went on all the East Coast trips, while Vicki went with him to meetings on the West Coast.

We use similar strategies within our own community to mask our relationships with Joe, but despite those efforts there have been times when I've been on a date with Joe and bumped into someone who'd previously met Vicki or Val in the role of wife. That requires some explanation! I am constantly thinking through what someone already knows about us before I say anything. It is such a relief when I'm in settings where I don't have to hold back and can truly be myself. As I've gotten older, though, I find I don't care as much what others think about my family.

I've evolved, too, when it comes to conflicts. In the beginning, it was more about jealousy: Did Joe look at Vicki a little differently compared to the way he looked at me? Did he reach first for Val's hand? Sit closer to her? Talk to Vicki more? The little things I used to take so personally don't bother me anymore. Now the conflicts are more about the annoyances inherent in any long-standing relationship and the logistics it takes to keep a family that consists of more than two dozen people running smoothly.

At this point, I hope we're beyond any chance of failure, but I am often asked what would happen if one of us left the marriage. We believe that our commitments are sacred and that we should do everything possible to avoid divorce. But we all share the view that if one wife left, the rest of us would have an obligation to support her and her children.

A friend once told me Joe was lucky to have three wives who like each other so much and get along so easily. There's no question it was helpful that Vicki, Joe, and I were able to create a family culture from the inception of our marriage, and that Val adapted to it so readily when she joined us. The fact that we are all roughly the same age also aided our compatibility. Having twins as sister wives isn't a big deal to me. There are things Vicki and Val understand better about each other than I do, and they have a family history that will never include me. Yet there's a side of each of their personalities that is a perfect match with mine—for Val it's fashion sense and for Vicki it's organization skills!

But luck has nothing to do with the success of our marriage. Our relationship is the result of commitment and hard work. It's the result of good communication and not letting resentments build up, of being willing to consider someone else's point of view and respecting boundaries. I'm human, I make mistakes, but I'm really trying to be the best I can be. I have found that love has a boundless capacity to grow, and when I love, it comes back to me in even greater amounts. I made this choice; I want these challenges. I love Vicki and Val. They are the family I always hoped for, the family I worked so hard to achieve. If one of them were missing from my life, I would feel incomplete.

Vicki

I LIKE TO COMPARE my decision to live the Principle to climbing Mt. Everest: from the minute I decided to do it, I knew it would be a challenge, but I was excited to see what I could conquer. I drew courage from the examples of those who'd succeeded; I could see that the experience changed them forever. I knew others who'd tried and given up, and even some who'd lost their faith in the attempt. At times, I've been afraid, unsure if I would make it, but I am still forging ahead. When I reach the summit, I may be tired and full of aches and pains, but I will have a great sense of accomplishment.

Plural marriage, for me, is about overcoming weaknesses and selfishness, about having compassion for others, and about relying on the Lord in daily life. It is sometimes a pain to have to consider what everyone else in my family wants, from where to hang a mirror in the house to how we interact with Joe in public. It's easy on the good days, and nearly impossible on the bad ones. But that's the life I've chosen. I try to stay focused on what will benefit me eternally, and that's not likely to be an extra ten minutes with Joe now, or getting upset because he loves someone else just as much as he loves me.

In the first year of our marriage, I felt awkward any time Joe showed affection to Alina in front of me. If I walked into a room and they were huddled together, close in conversation or hugging, I wasn't sure what I was supposed to do. Some plural wives make it clear that they never want to see affection between their husband and another wife. But I realized that if I tried to quash these displays, I might miss an opportunity to know a whole different side of Joe—the *real* Joe. I had to let go; I had to trust; I had to accept. To me, that doesn't mean settling for less.

Alina, Val, and I each believe we are Joe's eternal soul mate. But we consider each other to be soul mates, too. It's that belief in our female connection that drives our commitment to each other and gets us through tough times. Our friendship and love have grown over the years, to the point where the little jealousies are far outweighed by the knowledge that my sister wives always have my back.

But jealousy is an unfathomable emotion, one that can surface for no apparent reason and stage an attack when you least expect it. It can be the result of a misunderstanding, or rooted in the realities of plural marriage. A great personality can set it off; so can physical characteristics. I've had jealousy triggered by pretty ordinary-seeming aspects of living the Principle: a look Joe gave someone else, an occasion when he slept late into the morning with another wife, and times when he seemed to go on more dates or to have a better connection going with one of my sister wives. Anyone who is human knows that jealousy is not always rational!

I was a guest on a New York City–based morning television program in 2007; Keith Ablow, a psychiatrist, author, and talk show host, was also on the program. Ablow, who the previous year had invited others in my family to be on his own show, commented that the jealousy inherent in plural marriage *could be* good if it served as motivation to take better care of yourself and work at your relationship. In other words, if you put it to good use! While it helps to know that Joe loves us equally, it is my strong faith that brings me back from the destructive edge of jealousy.

It is a constant, inner-directed labor to live this lifestyle, one that regularly pushes me out of my comfort zone. Because of the extra work it takes, I think my relationship with Joe is better than the relationship many of my monogamous friends have with their husbands. In fact, friends have told me they're envious of the depth and richness of our relationship! I cherish that and certainly don't take it for granted.

Many people's reaction to plural marriage could be summed up in one word: yuck. They assume the men are perverted or have a huge ego or are overly sexual. Quite the contrary: if a man *has* any of those characteristics, his plural relationships are not likely to last. I certainly wouldn't stay with Joe if he had any of those traits. I'm not here to be a toy for a man, nor are my sister wives. Most men don't enter this lifestyle so they can have more sex; rather, they have a sincere sense of a higher purpose. I heard a comedian once say, "Any man who isn't married thinks, 'Oh yeah, I'll take three wives. Polygamy sounds good!' And any man who has a wife thinks, 'Why would anyone in his right mind want more than one?'" I find that funny—but true, too, which adds to my respect for Joe and other men who live this way. I'd rather share Joe than have a hundred men of lesser quality to myself. I consider

Joe to be a monogamist. He is faithful to me, and faithful to the people I expect him to be faithful to.

I've learned during my darkest times just what a gift this lifestyle can be. What I wanted most in life was to be a mother, yet motherhood has turned out to be the very thing that has tested me most as a woman and, from the very beginning, as a sister wife. We had been married only a month when Alina sat me down in the kitchen to give me the news. "Guess what?" she said. "I'm expecting!"

I feigned a smile. "That's great! Exciting!"

In reality, though, I was devastated. Alina wanted children as much as I did, and we'd hoped to have our first children as close together as possible. I was caught off-guard that she was pregnant and I wasn't, and I was shocked by the range of emotions I felt at her announcement. As Alina's belly began to swell, I had to face her intimate relationship with Joe in a way I hadn't before. I tried not to let images of them together seep into my thoughts, but it was hard. It was one thing to consider their intimacy in the abstract, and an altogether different thing to experience it concretely. As each month passed and I still hadn't conceived, I felt like a failure. After all, there clearly was nothing wrong with Joe.

I tried to share my feelings with him, but he was just as thrilled as Alina about the baby that was on its way. "And you should be, too," Joe said encouragingly.

The only thing that got me through my disappointment was a strong belief in what we were trying to do. I held fast to the thought that the family we'd long desired was now becoming a reality, and this would be a child I would love, too. Alina invited me along to her prenatal appointments and, unexpectedly, I found it just as exciting as she did to hear how the baby was progressing. We began planning for the birth together, shopping for baby clothes, toys, and educational games, and sharing ideas for a nursery. At yard sales, we bought children's books by the armload. With each passing month, I continued to worry I might never get pregnant, but I was such a part of Alina's pregnancy that I no longer resented the fact that she'd conceived so easily.

About a month before Alina's due date, a sign came that my prayers had been answered. It was Thanksgiving, and we were supposed to take mashed potatoes to the family dinner. I felt so nauseated that even preparing that mild dish was too much for me, so Alina took over the cooking duties. When we arrived at Joe's parents' home, the smell of roasting turkey made me so queasy that I had to go outside for fresh air. "Vicki, do you think you might be pregnant?" Joe's mom asked me once I returned to the kitchen. I suddenly realized I might be experiencing morning sickness, and I couldn't wait until the next day, when the stores would reopen and I could get a home test that would confirm I was pregnant. Sure enough, I tested positive, and we were all thrilled!

When Alina's baby was born, I thought I loved her son, Joseph, just as much as she did; when I had my son, Caleb, seven months later, I realized that the connection between a mother and her own child was unlike anything else. As the years passed and our family grew, my ability to love my sister wives' children just like my own increased. And so did my love for Alina. We did *everything* together. If I went to see my mom, Alina and her kids came along, too. If someone invited me on a picnic, it was understood we all would go together. We were inseparable, and it was thrilling to watch our family expand. By the time Val joined us, I had six beautiful children and was well on my way to having the ten children I'd always dreamed I would have with Joe.

But suddenly, it seemed I might never come close to realizing that hope. Motherhood, which had until then given me such joy, presented me with my greatest challenge—one that rocked my marriage to its core and tested my relationships with my sister wives in unexpected ways.

After a five-year break between pregnancies, I had trouble conceiving my seventh child, and then had a miscarriage. I feared my childbearing days were over, but I finally got pregnant again. I was extremely excited at the prospect of once more being a mother to a newborn. My relationship with Joe was at an all-time high, and my interactions with Alina and Val flowed easily. My life seemed perfect.

But something felt off right from the start of this pregnancy. My morning sickness, severe from the outset, never let up. I also was plagued by constant headaches and exhaustion. A sweltering heat wave that summer made me feel miserable. I couldn't sleep at night because I was too hot; as a result, I was too tired to get up early enough to exercise, which always made me feel better during my pregnancies. The final link in that chain of consequences was that I gained weight. And it was *all* Joe's fault! Joe couldn't win no matter how hard he tried to meet my emotional or physical needs.

As my due date approached, I was a mess, crying in private and standoffish in public. I wasn't sure I was capable of getting through the labor I knew lay ahead of me, or whether I would ever get over this attitude, this *thing* that seemed to have taken hold of me. I couldn't stand myself, but that didn't keep me from lashing out at Joe, which added to our strained interactions. Our nights together were filled with tension, and instead of taking time to talk and connect, we would tumble into bed exhausted.

It didn't help that as my relationship with Joe withered, his relationship with Alina blossomed. For the first time in my life, I wondered if I had the strength and staying power necessary for plural marriage.

At the time, none of us understood pregnancy-related depression. Val had had a bout of postpartum blues, so she was best able to relate to what I was experiencing. I didn't recognize my symptoms as the same thing, however—nor did she; I was, after all, still pregnant.

I was a grueling ten days overdue when labor began, and it was the roughest delivery I'd ever experienced. That rigor of delivery led to a much slower recovery than I was used to. With my previous pregnancies I'd stayed in or near bed for around ten days to let my body rest, even though I felt good almost immediately. This time, I needed every minute of that and more. I felt helpless and incapable of rejoining my busy life. But Alina and Val were both working, and there were eight little children at home who needed care around the house or help getting off to school. I kept telling everyone I couldn't handle it, that I was overwhelmed, but no one seemed to grasp my desperation. With no other options, I tried my best to step up. That's when my emotional spiral really began.

I was on a crazy-train I couldn't get off. I'd go to my closet to get dressed while the baby slept and end up on the floor crying for long periods of time. Every thought and emotion I had conflicted with another. I didn't want Joe anywhere near me; I was upset when he stayed away. I knew something was wrong with me, but I was unable to accept any help or advice from my well-meaning mother, sisters, and sister wives. I wanted to get out of the house; I wanted to stay shut in so no one would see how much weight I'd gained. I wanted God's help, but I had a hard time praying.

I wallowed in self-pity, insecurity, confusion, and indecision. I crafted long, emotional letters to Joe but, thankfully, never gave him the worst ones, which were full of mean and nasty barbs. I thought seriously about moving with my children into the trailer on our property; if the mobile home hadn't needed so much fixing up, I might have gone for that informal separation.

I'd lie in bed at night, my thoughts roiling. I'd get up to tend the baby and then be unable to get back to sleep. I stared into the darkness one night, thinking about how Val had seemed emotional and distant for weeks after having her last baby. Yes, I had judged her at the time as ungrateful and self-absorbed: *Why didn't she just get over the negative feelings and enjoy her good life?* I'd wondered then. Now I was ashamed of myself, finally recognizing that she'd gone through something similar to what I was experiencing.

I got out of bed and made my way to Val's room, knocked softly at her door, and went in. I shook her awake. "Val, I have to talk to you," I said. "I'm so sorry I didn't understand what you were going through after your last birth, that I didn't try to understand. I had no idea."

"It's okay, Vicki," Val said. She sat up and I crawled onto the bed next to her and poured out my feelings.

"I don't know if I can do this," I said. "It's burying me. All my thoughts and feelings are irrational, but I don't know what to do to make them right. How did *you* do it? How did *you* get through it?"

Val listened, holding my hand as I cried quietly. "I wish I could give you a simple answer, a formula. I can't—but Vicki, you *will* get through it. I did," she said. "It's hard and it hurts. I know it feels crazy. I felt that way, too. I wanted to curl up in my closet and hide from the world for a while."

Over the next few months I sought Val's comfort often when my swirling thoughts—which were mostly about Joe, who I didn't think was taking my condition seriously enough—kept me awake at night. Val gave me encouragement and kept reminding me things had gotten better for her, and that gave me hope I'd make it.

Somehow, though, I just couldn't connect with Alina during those difficult months. I went to St. George one weekend, and while I was gone she sent me text messages of encouragement and support, which only fueled my irrational anger. I didn't think she understood what I was going through at all. Joe would tell me how worried Alina was and how much she cared, and my unspoken reaction was *Okay, so she's now a saint in your eyes and I'm a devil. Great!*

The situation finally got so bleak that Joe confronted me, leading me to my bedroom one afternoon and shutting the door. As we sat down, he took my hands in his. "Vicki, I'm really concerned about you," he said. "I'm worried you might try to hurt yourself, and I'm concerned about our baby. Have you had any thoughts of wanting to hurt our son?"

I couldn't believe that he would even suggest such a thing. "Joe, I'd just as soon throw *you* out the window right now—what a thing to ask me!—but my baby is my only joy, the only thing getting me through every day," I said. "So, no—the answer is no. Boston is safe, but I'm not sure about us."

I needed help, and I finally got it when I hit bottom and took my family's advice to seek outside assistance. I began getting vitamin B shots weekly, started exercising again, and joined a support group for women from the polygamous culture. The therapist (who was not a fundamentalist) helped me understand more fully how crippling pregnancy-related depression can be. She also helped me understand that my anger was sometimes justified, though perhaps blown out of proportion. But most important, she reminded me there were physical explanations—a difficult labor, a prior miscarriage—for the hormonal imbalance that was driving my depression and emotional upheaval. I wasn't crazy!

As I emerged from under the black cloud, I realized how much hurt I had caused my family. I was humiliated by my behavior and spent a lot of time praying for forgiveness and the courage to apologize to Joe and Alina, who'd taken the brunt of my anger.

In the end, what got me through this rough time was the steadfast devotion of my husband and my sister wives. They never gave up on me. They saw me at my worst and still loved me. When I was unable to give my children all the attention they needed, Alina and Val were there to make sure they were cared for and loved. Joe never stopped listening or walked away, even when my criticisms stung. I came out of that experience more grateful than ever for my family and for the resilience of my relationships.

Living in a couples' world, as I call it, makes our lives harder than if we were part of a community that accepts plural marriage, such as Centennial Park in Arizona or Pinesdale in Montana. But even in those communities, there are many different approaches to relationships, just as there are in monogamy. Some women have completely separate lives from their sister wives, with very little interaction. Some live near each other, but not together. And some live just as we do, all in one house. At the personal level, there are some women who have domineering personalities that affect their relationships with their spouse and sister wives, but alpha females who dominate relationships aren't exclusively found in polygamy. In our family, we don't have any sort of hierarchy among the wives. When Val came into our family, she instantly became a full and equal partner. We've created a marriage that is a true collaboration, which ensures that our opinions are valued, our needs met, and our lives tightly linked together.

Living the way we do, all in one house, can be stressful, no doubt about it. Did sharing a house with Alina and Val add to my struggles when I was deeply depressed? Maybe. But I also couldn't have survived that time without Val's support and understanding, or without Alina's unyielding patience, her help with my children, and her faith in me. It works for some people to live together, for some to be married, and for some to love another person of the same sex. None of those relationships is immune from the challenges we've faced in our family. But this is the lifestyle that works for me, the one I've chosen, the family structure that gives me the love and support I need.

Val

AFTER I MARRIED JOE, I had to learn how Alina and Vicki interacted with each other and with him, and how I could fit in without stifling who I am. I discovered that the new arrangement was quite different from my first plural marriage, where there wasn't equality between the wives.

When we lived in Mapleton, one of Donald's wives had a nicer, bigger bedroom and he kept all of his personal belongings there. That meant he showered and got ready for the day in her room. That same wife also had a job as his secretary, and they drove to work together every day. It seemed she had everything: all his time, all his attention, and a greater influence on him. I was envious, because I felt my relationship mattered less to him.

Compounding that problem was the fact that there was generally a free-for-all in other areas, such as when we went somewhere together; there was little effort at balance among and toward the sister wives. Usually, the last person to the car slipped into the front seat beside Donald—to grab that seat first would have been perceived as flagrantly selfish—which meant some wives were always trying to be the last out of the house. There was no equality among our various relationships, which contributed to the erosion of my bond with Donald and made it hard to trust that he had everyone's best interests at heart. I brought that attitude of mistrust along when I joined Joe's family.

At first it was really awkward for me when the four of us would go out together. I didn't know the new protocol, so I simply followed the routine I was used to. When all of us wives were along, I would usually just get in the backseat, for example, even if it was my night with Joe. That's what I did one evening when we went to dinner, but it didn't feel right. I stressed about it throughout the meal, and on the ride home (backseat again!) Joe must have sensed my frustration. When we got home, he asked us all to sit down in the living room.

"Obviously, Val is feeling uncomfortable and unsure about how to fit in and about who sits where and when," he said. "We need to figure something out."

"I'm just trying to sort out how you do things," I said defensively. "You clearly have some unwritten rules that I don't know about."

"We've just always rotated and that seemed to work out, but I see your point," Alina said.

Vicki admitted she hadn't really thought about how to work a third person into this aspect of daily life. By the end of the night we had a new plan: when it was one wife's night with Joe, she would sit by him in the car, at a restaurant, or wherever we happened to go that day. It may seem strange to have to discuss these details, but we've learned that it helps us avoid a lot of confusion and insecurity.

We also try to deal with our feelings head on. A couple years after I married Joe, we were still adjusting as a family and had the added stress that comes with having five children become teenagers at once! We also were feeling financially pinched. Joe was changing careers again, Alina and Vicki were both working, and I was staying home with the children. Joe would come home after a long day of job hunting and head straight for the kitchen to chop vegetables, a task that he found cathartic. Later, as we ate the stir-fry he'd made for the four of us, we'd talk about our teenagers, our jobs, Joe's search for work, and how our newly blended family was coming together. We joked that it was our own little therapy group. And there was something to that: those frequent discussions helped us understand and draw closer to each other.

When I see how hard Joe works at each of his relationships, and how hard Vicki and Alina work at their individual relationships with him, I don't see any malicious intent to take something away from me. I don't feel like I'm getting only one-third of a man. Joe is there when I really need him, every time. I don't feel I have to have him every minute of every day. But my time with him is precious. I try to clear everything else out of my schedule when it's my night so we can spend quality time together reuniting, reconnecting. I know my sister wives need the same quality time in their relationships with Joe, and I respect that need.

Women who've never lived this way often focus on jealousy: "Aren't you jealous of your sister wives?" they'll ask. Of course I get jealous! I'm human. But I'm seeking an expanded heart and mind so that I am able to want my sister wives to have as much happiness as I have. It's something I have to work at all the time.

I married into this family knowing that there were two other wives and—though Joe has spent countless hours talking each of us through our emotional upsets—when I feel jealous or insecure, it's a problem I have to take responsibility to resolve.

One night, I really wanted Joe to help me sort through the insecurities I was feeling, but he had a date with Alina. I watched from the window as they drove off together, feeling very sorry for myself. Then I collapsed on my bed in tears. The next day, I treated Joe with indifference. I didn't want to see him or talk to him or even kiss him good morning. It hurt him, and I knew it. I was acting immature—I knew that if I needed him, all I had to do was say so—but I couldn't help it!

I finally realized that the only person who could help me overcome these bad feelings was myself. Joe could love me, listen to me, and be supportive and understanding, but he couldn't stop me from having negative thoughts. I had to pick myself up and learn a better way of processing my feelings. What I have developed in my marriage to Joe is a sense of empowerment: I can speak my mind, express my needs, and make my own decisions, including saying no, without worry of any repercussions.

I learned a lot about self-reliance from Joe's grandmother, Maurine Owen Barlow. She had two sister wives and moved constantly as her husband did his best to provide for his families. Grandmother Barlow had thirteen children, one of whom died days after birth. During the early years of her marriage, she had to work incredibly hard to provide for herself and her children. Despite that, she felt she had everything she needed and was wary of expecting too much from her husband. "I feel that that's one sacrifice a woman in this law must make," she said, referring to the Principle. "She should take care of herself and children as much as possible." That's something a lot of people miss when they look at this lifestyle: it requires a willingness to take personal responsibility and be accountable for yourself.

I loved growing up in a plural family, but those fond memories alone are not enough to carry me through the trials inherent in plural marriage. That's where my faith comes in. I wouldn't have chosen this lifestyle if I had not received a spiritual confirmation that it was right for me. I have to constantly examine my behaviors and my motives to see if I am really working for the betterment of us all, which is how this lifestyle becomes a spiritual practice.

CHAPTER EIGHT

Love Times Three

It is a pure and holy principle; and, therefore, persons,
either male or female, who have not the desire in their hearts
to become pure and righteous, have no business to practice it,
for it cannot be practiced acceptably before God on any other
principle than that of purity and righteousness.

—JOSEPH F. SMITH, SIXTH PRESIDENT OF THE LDS CHURCH, 1878

Joe

VICKI AND I WENT to a friend's home to watch the debut episode of HBO's *Big Love*. Val and Alina were at a birthday party and planned to meet up with us afterward. They arrived just as we were getting ready to head for home. As we stood in our friend's driveway, we had our own "big love" moment. We'd had a lot of scheduling changes during the week and couldn't remember whose night it was, which would determine who was going to ride home with me.

"I don't remember. What did we trade?" Alina asked.

We all looked at each other. "I can't remember, either," I said.

"I thought it was my turn," Vicki said tentatively, "but I'm not sure."

"Well, this is awkward," I said. "We've got to make a choice here. Talk about 'big love'!"

We all laughed. Alina called home to see if one of the kids could check the calendar (this was in our pre-BlackBerry days), but no one answered so we made an on-the-spot decision knowing we could sort things out later. We made it Vicki's night.

So . . . let's get right to it. What you really want to know is how I manage "sleeping" arrangements with my three wives, right? Yep, there is a schedule. At the beginning of our marriage, we based the order on age and rotated nightly. That's still the way we do it: Alina, Vicki, and then Val, in one big circle. We now put the schedule in our BlackBerrys and stick to it as much as we can. I know some plural families who live and die by the schedule, with no flexibility for life's unplanned events. We try to be reasonable. When Val recently had surgery, Alina and Vicki gave up nights knowing Val needed extra attention from me. Other times, we swap because of a business trip or special event. The problem, though, is that once one wife's night is skipped it can take a while to catch up and get her back into the rotation.

For example, say it's Vicki's night on Saturday but I take Val on a weekend getaway, leaving on Saturday and returning on Monday. Vicki trades her Saturday night for Val's Wednesday night. Val thus gets Saturday and her regular Sunday. Monday is Alina's night, as scheduled. Vicki then has Tuesday and Wednesday nights. Then it's Alina's night, Vicki's night again, and finally, a week later, Val's turn. See why we get confused sometimes?

I've really been surprised by the prying questions I routinely get about our sex lives, from whether we sleep together, all four of us, to how I would feel if one of my wives wanted to sleep with another man. Do monogamists get asked that last question? Of *course* I wouldn't like it!

I have three separate sexual relationships with my wives. There is absolutely no kinkiness. When Alina, Vicki, and I were first married, we heard that there were rumors we were having a ménage à trois. I didn't even know what the phrase meant! It's a prurient idea that many people can't shake, though it couldn't be further from the truth.

In 2006, author and psychiatrist Keith Ablow invited me, my wife Val, and daughters Laura and Amanda on his talk show. They were identified only by first name. For legal reasons, I participated without being shown or identified. I thought I was prepared for just about any question, so it caught me off-guard when Ablow asked me what I would do if one of my wives brought home another woman and wanted to have a sexual relationship with her. I told him my wives are free to make that choice, but it's just not in keeping with our religious values. And that goes both ways. The behavior of Bill Henrickson on *Big Love*—his unscrupulous courting of a fourth wife, the way he had sex with one wife in another wife's bedroom—was terribly offensive to me. That was Hollywood, not our life.

I consider my intimate relationships sacred and don't talk about them with anyone, which has left me feeling quite alone at times. When a problem surfaces, it's not as though I can go talk to another wife about it. That's really taboo for us. Besides making sure each intimate relationship is 100 percent private between the two of us, I have learned not to make my time with each wife all about the sexual experience. Otherwise, they assume that's my focus when I'm with the *other* wives, which only causes jealousy and competitiveness. If my wives thought my interest in them was only sexual, it would be difficult for them to trust each other and respect me. Having multiple relationships has reinforced for me that the intimacy a woman really craves involves being cherished and cared for, understood and valued.

Each of my wives brings a uniqueness and richness to my life. I appreciate the time I have with each wife, as well as our time apart. When it's one wife's night again, I genuinely find that I've missed her and am really looking forward to having time to connect physically and emotionally—connections that are as important in a plural marriage as they are in a monogamous relationship. But as any couple knows, there is more to a good relationship than what goes on in the bedroom. The essence of plural marriage is *not* sex. There are much easier and cheaper ways for a man to get sex than promising to love, support, and care for multiple women in a spiritually based, committed marriage. The essence of plural marriage is self-actualization and, especially for men, learning to overcome a carnal nature. From the beginning, I knew our relationships would require more than romantic love to sustain them. I want my wives to have my unconditional love—what the Greeks called *agape,* a higher and purer form of love. When I am in touch with pure love, there is no desire to possess, no desire to hold on to or control.

Living this lifestyle requires me to focus on fundamental gospel principles and work to overcome the slothful, selfish, jealous, lustful, and prideful aspects of my character. I can't be controlling or manipulative, behaviors that have doomed many plural marriages. And I've learned the hard way that I have to keep my temper in check.

In the early years of married life, I found myself becoming my father at times. Once, Vicki's car broke down and I had to tow it behind my truck to the repair shop. Vicki was steering her car. We came to an intersection where we had to make a left-hand turn. I started to make the turn but Vicki braked, slowing us down as oncoming traffic approached. We narrowly avoided getting hit. After we cleared the intersection, I pulled over to the side of the road and was shouting at Vicki before I even climbed out of my truck.

"What the hell were you doing? I *told* you what to do!" I yelled. She burst into tears, which made me stop short. She hadn't done anything wrong, and I was taking my frustration out on her, just as my father used to do to me. To this day, Vicki won't help me tow a car.

I sometimes snapped in other stressful situations, too. Alina would just argue back and tell me I was being a jerk when that happened, but it would crush Vicki. Her father had never been harsh or aggressive, and she expected me to be as gentle as he was. I would tell Vicki not to take my actions personally, and she'd say, "How can I not?" She was right, of course—and learning to control my temper was a big issue for me.

A lot of men are like the trainer I met at a local gym. He didn't believe me at first when I introduced Alina, Vicki, and Val as my wives; then, grinning, he said, "I'm so jealous! I'd like to try that. I wish I had five wives."

"Yeah, right," I said. "Everyone says that, but they haven't thought through what it means."

This lifestyle has required me to give up many worldly things in order to provide for my family. I rarely indulge in hobbies or activities I used to enjoy, such as skiing and golfing. I've given up certain career opportunities because of my family obligations, including a great job offer that would have required me to travel frequently out of state. I would have been a much wealthier businessman if I had opted for a different kind of family.

But those sacrifices are nothing compared to the pressure on me to sustain three healthy monogamous, but interwoven, marriages. I have to provide what each of my wives needs in her unique relationship with me while simultaneously making sure the relationships are harmonious with each other. My wives' personalities are different, and so is the "love language" that works best for each of them—distinctions they expect me to recognize and appreciate!

Vicki's personality is analytical, determined, and deliberate; she is a peacemaker. She also is adventurous and athletic, likes creative dates, and needs plenty of quality one-on-one time with me. One year for her birthday, I staged a treasure hunt that took her throughout the Salt Lake Valley, from a floral shop to a chocolate store to a shopping mall—where I met her and helped her pick out a new dress—and, finally, to the Anniversary Inn, where we spent a romantic evening together in the Romeo and Juliet room. That's her idea of a good time!

Alina comes from a boisterous family, and she's strong-willed, assertive, opinionated, and decisive—a real take-charge person.

She enjoys trying new restaurants, attending cultural events, and spending a day being pampered at a spa. For Alina, nothing expresses love more than acts of service, such as having me take over her Sunday breakfast duties when she isn't feeling well or replacing a broken fan in her room without being asked.

Val is affectionate, loyal, loving, and a great listener. Like me, Val is a bookworm, so a perfect date with her is a trip to a bookstore, where we get a treat and browse the shelves, or a quiet night at home, with just the two of us snuggling on the couch to watch a romantic movie I've picked out just for her. Val wants affirmation of my love through physical touch—holding hands, hugs, and kisses.

My wives know that I really open up and feel connected when I hold hands or have them close to me. This was a problem at first for Alina and me. She would never kiss me in public and wouldn't even hold my hand or hug me when we were at her parents' home. I thought at first that she wasn't attracted to me. Vicki was the complete opposite, and I soaked up her affection, which then made Alina feel rejected.

When we'd been married five years, I took Alina to Seattle for her birthday. We had a wonderful, romantic time and she was more affectionate to me than she'd ever been. "I like this a lot," I told her. "I wish you were more like this all the time, instead of being like a stove that goes from cold to hot with no warm setting in between."

I am not, however, usually affectionate in public when I am with all three of my wives. There are a number of reasons for that. If I hold hands with Alina and Vicki, how is Val going to feel? If I put my arms around two wives at once, will strangers be uncomfortable? I am respectful of other people's views and try to be discreet. At a movie, for example, I may have a wife on either side of me and I will take turns holding their hands. Sometimes, observant people will notice and wonder what's going on. We are sometimes watched closely even by family members and other fundamentalists, who are looking at us as an example or to see if I have a favorite. I feel a lot of pressure to make sure my behavior is not misinterpreted, including by my wives. I got so gun-shy about this when we were first married that I avoided the whole problem by not being affectionate to either Vicki or Alina when we were all together. They didn't like that solution, either. Now I just try to be more aware and balance the attention I give each of them, though my wives' different personalities make that challenging.

Alina is more outgoing, naturally drawing more interaction from me and from others as well. Vicki was used to that after their shared time at my parents' house, but after Val came into the family, she was jealous because she thought I paid more attention and gave more respect to Alina. We were at a restaurant one night when I noticed Val shut down all of a sudden. When we got home, she stalked to her bedroom and slammed the door. I knocked and went in after her.

"What's wrong?" I asked.

"You were looking at Alina during our entire conversation tonight," she said.

"No, I wasn't."

"Yes, you were. It was obvious."

It's no fun to be worried about which way you turn your head in a conversation. I told Val I couldn't live my life worrying about every move I made, from whose hand I grabbed first to where my eyes rested in a conversation. But I also realized I needed to be more aware of how my behavior might affect her.

Sometimes, though, I can't win for losing. Trying to meet one wife's needs gets me in trouble with another. After I married Val, she needed so much attention from me that I soon felt smothered. After ten years of marriage, Alina and Vicki were fine with simple dates—a trip to visit relatives or an afternoon in the park. But Val was a newlywed and wanted romantic interludes and fancy dates— and expected me to plan them. I couldn't handle it and began acting with indifference toward her. A typical conversation went like this:

VAL: *It's our date night on Friday. Where are we going?*

ME: *I don't know; I don't have anything planned. I'm fine if we just stay home.*

VAL *(with sarcasm): Oh, great!*

ME: *Well, why don't you plan something then? Tell me what you want to do.*

But Val just shut down. One time, I was looking for something in her nightstand. Her journal was open, and I happened to see that the page was peppered with four-letter words. *That* certainly let me know how she felt! The pressure got to be too much, and I purposely began to not plan anything fun on our nights together.

Val finally went to Vicki and asked her for advice. Not long after their conversation, Val took the initiative and planned a day trip to Park City. She asked Alina to watch her children and arranged several fun activities for us, including a concert.

Afterward, we walked to a gazebo and I held Val close, my jacket draped around her. I opened up about the stress I'd been feeling in our relationship. Val told me she'd taken to heart Vicki's advice, which was to be a giver, not a taker, and was working to change her expectations of me. We were able to talk through our feelings so productively that time got away from us. When we noticed how late it was, we decided to stay overnight. I thought Val had called home, and she thought I did. People think there's no such thing as a doghouse for polygamous men, but there is, and by the next morning, I was in it.

As we pulled into the driveway, I could tell that Alina was furious before I even parked the car. She was in the front yard, and I'd never seen her pulling weeds so fast. I heard her call to the children, who were playing nearby, and tell them to go to the backyard. I got out of the car and said hello, but I'd hardly gotten the word out before Alina shouted that she needed to talk to us. We went inside and sat in the living room.

"I had no idea you planned to stay the night," she said accusingly. "Why didn't someone call me? I felt grossly disrespected by both of you. That was so unfair!"

"Alina, you're just being jealous," I said placatingly. "Val and I really needed this time to connect." (Picture foot in mouth after I made this really dumb comment.)

"Well, I'm so glad you had a breakthrough moment with Val, but you could have taken one minute to call me!"

I started to respond, but Alina cut me off as she stood up. "Go to hell!" she said, stomping off. She slammed her bedroom door so hard a shoe-holder fell off it and broke.

(By the way, we don't normally have big, loud fights, but I do get the message when a door is slammed.)

Alina was right. I should have taken the responsibility to let her know what we were doing. I had been thinking only of Val, not Alina or Vicki, and that wasn't fair. That experience refocused me on the importance of thinking through every move I make. It took weeks to work through the hard feelings.

But I'm a man, and I sometimes repeat my mistakes before the lesson really sinks in. It wasn't too many years after this episode that I took Alina on an overnight date for Mother's Day. I fully intended to do the same for Vicki and Val, but in the meantime, I picked up a potted plant to give each of them when we got home. Wow, did that ever bomb! For one thing, Val hates potted plants.

Other special occasions can be really tough, too. Alina and Vicki share an anniversary. Vicki and Val share a birthday. And what about Valentine's Day? Now *that's* a complicated holiday for polygamists. One year—this was pre-Val—I ordered roses for Alina and Vicki. The florist looked at me like, "Yeah, you're a player!" I had arranged for the roses to be delivered separately but mistakenly put Alina's name on both bouquets.

One of the hardest things for me to do is to take one wife on a trip or a special date, leaving the other two at home. But the prejudice against our lifestyle also makes it hard for us to publicly acknowledge our connections to one another. (Even among other Fundamentalist Mormons, it is bad form to ask someone to identify a spouse or spouses or to ask how many wives or sister wives someone has. When one close friend took a third wife, I didn't learn about it until nine months later.) I had all three wives with me during a recent business trip to San Francisco, where I met with a new client. "And these are . . . ?" he asked as his eyes circled our little group. What was I supposed to say? During that same trip, I faced a dilemma while checking into our hotel. I had two rooms, and the clerk asked me who would be in each room during our three-night stay. I paused before remembering it was Vicki's night. I wrote her first name next to mine on one slip, and then Alina's and Val's first names on the second slip. The clerk pressed for last names. Vicki and Val use my surname informally, so now it got awkward: Alina, the one who legally shares my last name, wasn't sleeping in my room.

I despise shopping, but with three wives who all like to shop, I've done my share of it. I developed a shopping strategy, though, after an experience at Christmas one year. One night, I went to a mall with Alina while she chose a special outfit. A few nights later, I ended up in the same store in the same mall with Vicki, who picked out the identical outfit. The same clerk was on duty and remembered me. I got the dirtiest looks I'd ever received. Now I have certain malls and stores reserved for each wife, which spares me embarrassment on many levels.

My motto is *Fair, but not equal.* There are three ways I evaluate gifts for my wives: cost, number, and quality. I don't strive for equality in all three criteria individually, but for fairness across the board. Circumstances often affect what I do. Say it's Alina's birthday, and I take her on a nice romantic trip. Months later, when it's Vicki and Val's birthday, I'm crazy busy at work and can't get away, plus money is tight. I simply can't do the same thing I did for Alina. Over time, I try to even it out. But I sometimes get tripped up.

One year I spent the same amount of money on Christmas gifts—mostly clothes—for Alina and Vicki, but Vicki had a few more boxes to open. That upset Alina. Only later did I figure out what was really going on: Alina happened to be feeling insecure about her weight that year and thought Vicki looked far better in her new Christmas clothes. In her mind, that's why Vicki had more packages to open: she got more gifts of clothing because clothing looked better on her.

There are times when I connect more with one wife than another, and there are times when all three relationships are working smoothly. Unfortunately, there are also times when all three are *not* working and it seems I can do nothing right, especially when all three women's hormonal cycles align. I've found that when that occurs, it's best to stay low, keep my mouth shut, ignore my male tendency to want to fix things, and just listen. I've sometimes wondered what I'm in for when the empty-nest and menopause years arrive!

Vicki and I went through a rough period of marriage after the birth of our seventh child in 2007, when she experienced severe pregnancy-related depression. My wives had had baby blues previously, but nothing like this. Vicki and I had been very close as we planned for this baby, but after Boston's birth, she descended into a deep despair. I was blindsided by the fact that things Vicki had taken in stride before, such as sharing a husband and the demands of motherhood, were now causing her deep hurt and insecurity. I couldn't seem to do anything to make her happy or help her understand how much I loved and valued her. I remember wondering who had kidnapped my wife. Vicki blamed me for many things and constantly made comparisons among the three relationships, which put pressure on all of us. I felt extremely rejected by her attacks and mistrust. It was as though everything I had done, sacrificed, and given to her over the years meant nothing. I wasn't sure what to do, and for the first time in my life I had no idea how to fix my marriage.

My relationship with Alina happened to be at a pinnacle at the same time, causing even more distress for Vicki and strain between her and Alina. In the best of times, watching me go off in the arms of another wife requires a tremendous amount of mutual trust and respect. In bad times, a modicum of trust and respect has to remain; those qualities are the only things that make our lifestyle possible. It crushed me that my closeness with my other wives was a hardship for Vicki. Interestingly, Vicki grew closer to Val, who had been on the same emotional roller-coaster after a pregnancy. Val also gave me insights, reminding me how important it had been to her that I never gave up and kept working at our relationship during that tough time. It helped that both Alina and Val were very generous in giving Vicki and me the time and space to work through our difficulties. We had to almost start over in our relationship, rekindling the excitement, appreciation, and trust of our earlier years.

I am often asked what the hardest thing is about living this way. I would say it's feeling overwhelmed, or that I'm not enough of a man to meet all the needs of my wives. This experience with Vicki accentuated that difficulty for me. Whatever I did seemed inadequate. Ultimately, the love and support Val and Alina gave me, though painful to Vicki, supplied me with the strength and confidence I needed to keep pressing forward. Vicki, to her credit, recognized that she needed help and began to see a therapist. She learned to verbalize her feelings. I had some changes to make, too: I learned that I was not triggering, and thus could not fix, what Vicki was experiencing.

Relationships have cycles, and the highs and the lows both pass. No matter where Alina, Vicki, Val, and I are on that wave, I still have to give the same quality of attention and love to each wife—and that's true even when the love, passion, and intimacy are at an ebb. It would be grossly unfair if I gravitated to whichever woman was treating me sweeter or looked more attractive on any given day. I have to go beyond the superficial and connect on a deeper spiritual and emotional level with each of my wives, every day.

That said, there is an aspect of personal responsibility that is even more critical in plural marriage than in a monogamous relationship. Even if I wanted to, I couldn't carry three women's luggage through the airport. I can't carry three women's emotional baggage, either. If I tried to fix and take care of every need, whether it was physical or emotional, there would be no end to the work and I would be little more than a packhorse. The best thing I can do if, for example, Alina and Val are having a disagreement is to listen to each of them and let them work it out. The minute I take on their emotional baggage, I enter a no-win situation that leads only to dependency. In our unique family structure, we have to maintain a healthy degree of independence and responsibility for meeting our own material and emotional needs.

But someone has to lead the family, which may be one of the most misunderstood aspects of polygamy. That yoke falls on me.

As the head of the family, I'm like a CEO of a business. My wives are my vice presidents. We are all part of the family's administration, nearly equal in office. We make decisions together when it comes to big things, such as moving, going on a vacation, or making a major purchase. If we can't make the decision unanimously, we don't do it. (That was another shortcoming of *Big Love*. The husband rarely tapped into the resources of the powerful women around him.) We had a lot of competing ideas, for example, when we remodeled our backyard, from whether to include a volleyball pit to how big to make the sandbox and where to place the water feature. In the end, the design we adopted was the result of collaboration and compromise. If no one has a strong opinion about something, I will usually make the decision. And in a family the size of ours, someone has to be the ultimate decision-maker on many small, day-to-day issues, such as what time we're going to leave the house to go visit the grandmothers. That's my job.

Early on, I often tried to assert my status as the husband to get my wives to do what I wanted, but playing the patriarchy card wasn't working for me. Alina and Vicki weren't having anything to do with it. That, and scripture, set me straight. I realized I was trying to *drive* them, not *lead* them. Unrighteous dominion, the concept of trying to impose one's will on another, is an abuse of my priesthood authority—that is, the God-given power and responsibility to lead my family and perform certain religious ordinances for them. If I can't lead my wives through gentle persuasion to go in a certain direction, then I need to reexamine my reasons for wanting a particular outcome.

I have had varying challenges in each of my relationships, and I am keenly aware that any one of my wives could choose to leave me at any time. I have an uncle who was in a plural marriage; his second wife left him, and he was very hurt by it. "She's been my friend and shared so much of life with me," he said to me one day. "I feel like I've lost a part of myself." My uncle also was in turmoil about the pain and disruption his children were experiencing. He asked me this question: "If Vicki, say, were to choose to leave you tomorrow, what would you do?"

I thought for a moment before responding. "I have to let go of that fear, and focus instead on giving all I can so that I'm not the catalyst for such a decision and have no regrets about my contribution to our relationships," I told him.

Divorce is a very serious matter in my view, and is permissible only for the most egregious problems. The need to get along and work through problems, to treat each other with respect and unconditional love, is critical, because when one relationship is in trouble the discord ripples throughout the family. We have learned that problems have to be dealt with quickly or they have the potential to destroy the family—something also true in monogamy, where it takes personal growth and sacrifice to love and give fully to a partner so that the relationship succeeds.

The decision to pursue plural marriage was, for me, similar to the choice people make when they decide whether or not to have children: I felt it promised a richer, fuller life, one with challenges and sacrifices but also more varied experiences and enjoyment. I am head-over-heels in love with each of my wives and awake each morning thrilled to spend another day with them.

When everything is in sync and working, my plural relationships are a little bit of heaven on earth. Seeing the sacrifices my wives make for our plural marriage and receiving their unconditional love is humbling and makes me want to be a better man—one who is not ruled by his passions, but gives all that he can.

So here's the other big question I get all the time: What about a fourth? While not opposed to the idea of another relationship, we are not actively pursuing another wife. There would have to be a fit, everyone would have to want that change, and it would need to be a spiritually guided process. To be honest, the prospects of expanding my family seem to fade as I get older. There are so many demands on my time and resources that it is not something I dwell on. Still, I felt this way before I married Val, and accepting her into our family turned out to be one of the most fulfilling experiences of my life.

CHAPTER NINE

Children by the Dozen

*Lo, children are an heritage of the Lord and the fruit of the
womb is his reward. As arrows are in the hand of a mighty man;
so are children of the youth. Happy is the man that hath his
quiver full of them: they shall not be ashamed, but they
shall speak with the enemies in the gate.*

—PSALM 127:3–5

Vicki

ON JUNE 7, 2010, I gave birth to Victoria Berlynn Darger—Tori—
at home with the help of a doula and a midwife. Joe was there, as
he had been for the births of all our children. So were Alina and
Val, along with our three oldest daughters, who were witnessing
a birth for the first time. Having all my family close by during this
miracle is one of the things I enjoy most about giving birth at home.
The rest of our children were lined up outside the door, waiting
to hold their new sister. Later on, in keeping with a family tradition, they all voted on her middle name.

Tori is my eighth child, and the nineteenth for Joe, who also is the stepfather of Val's five children from her first marriage. We have thirteen girls, eleven boys. If there were a movie about our family it would be called *Cheaper by the Two Dozen*! Being the middle child in a large family, I was surrounded by siblings as a kid, so it feels natural to me to have my own big family. When Alina, Joe, and I were first married and still childless, we would often invite our youngest siblings to stay overnight with us because we enjoyed them so much; it didn't feel like a home without the pattering of little feet. I love everything about the experience of creating a family: the pregnancy, sacredness, and joy of giving birth, and then watching each personality unfold.

Our lives are centered on family, for reasons that go beyond the enjoyment of parenthood. We believe in the Mormon doctrine that teaches that we were God's spirit-children and dwelt with him in heaven before coming to earth. During this preexistence, each of us agreed to be born and receive a physical body so we could be tested here in the second stage of our spiritual development. Many spirits are awaiting the opportunity to come to earth, through parents chosen in heaven. By living righteously, which includes raising our children properly, we hope to qualify to live together again in God's presence.

It is definitely a sacrifice to have so many children. There are many things we've each given up to make our children a priority. For me, it was guitar lessons, traveling, developing my computer skills, and interacting with clients when I worked in an office. But mothering is what brings me the most joy in my life. The decision to have another child is something Joe, Alina, Val, and I have always prayed about and discussed together, because it affects all of us. Alina, for instance, has diabetes and thus a pregnancy puts her health at risk, which concerns us all. She needs careful monitoring and has many doctor appointments when pregnant, which makes it hard for her to work every day. As you might imagine, Joe, Alina, and Val greeted with trepidation my announcement, two years after the deep depression I experienced with my seventh pregnancy, that I was ready to have another baby. We discussed it among ourselves for several months, weighing the pros and cons. Ultimately, though, having another child has always been a carefully considered decision made individually by each wife with Joe.

When Joe, Alina, and I were first married, we read stacks of parenting books and then came up with a plan for raising our children and developing a strong family culture. We wanted our children to grow up together, so one of our first decisions was to share a home. That makes it easier for Joe to see all his children every day, and helps the children bond as siblings. Kyley, one of Val's daughters, was nine when she wrote her mom a letter complaining that all the "kids were being mean, except Jed [my son]. He is nice no matter what and he always loves me." It would be much more difficult to foster these kinds of bonds if we lived in separate homes.

I interact most closely with my own children, but Val, Alina, and I are available to and love all the children equally, regardless of who their biological mother is. It doesn't always come as naturally to love another child as much as you love your own, something a lot of today's blended families can relate to! There are times I have to work at it. Joe more fully understood that challenge when

Val came into the family; as a stepfather, he had to love and treat her children just as he did his own offspring.

I don't think any of us anticipated how difficult it would be to blend our families when Joe married Val. We had different family cultures that sometimes clashed, especially regarding childrearing. Some of our mothering practices were better, and some of hers made more sense. For instance, Val relied on her oldest children to help with the younger ones far more than we did. Bedtime was a problem because, while her children were used to getting into bed and going right to sleep, ours were night owls who took hours to settle down. Now, with new siblings sharing their rooms, they thought it was one big slumber party every night! We exchanged a lot of parenting ideas as we discussed such issues, and we adapted our style to benefit all the children and get them into the same routines.

All three of us would prefer to be full-time mothers if it were financially possible. It's not, but we decided it was a priority to have at least one stay-home mom. We take turns working and being at home, depending on which of us currently has an infant. The working moms take great comfort in being able to leave their children with a woman who truly loves them. After Tori's birth, I became the stay-home mom, with four other children to watch over at that time: my two-year-old son; Val's daughters, who were nine months old and four; and Alina's four-year-old daughter. I try to fill the role of mother as completely for the other children as I do for my own. One day, Alina's daughter Allie was sad because her mom was at work. I scooped Allie onto my lap as I sat in a rocking chair, but she resisted me when I tried to comfort her. "I'll be your mom when your mom is gone," I said. "And when your mom gets home, *she'll* be your mom!" Allie had been worried that accepting comfort from me was being disloyal to her mom. When I worded it that new way, though, she was fine, and so was I!

Our goal in raising our children is one shared by most parents: we want them to grow up to be good, decent people who are able to make the most of their God-given talents. There are aspects of this lifestyle that help us accomplish that mission. In a big family like ours, children learn to be unselfish, to be helpful, and to understand, from a very early age, a wide range of personality types. They also learn to respect each other and, when possible, take responsibility for themselves. One example: by age five, our children serve themselves at meals, while the older children serve food to the youngest children. They learn to eat up whatever they dish onto their plates, with no wasting allowed—in theory, that is!

Sometimes, our children become *too* responsible. One day, Alina went into the kitchen to make my baby a bottle and found her four-year-old daughter Vanessa already there, carefully measuring formula into a bottle. When Alina asked how many scoops of formula she'd used, Vanessa answered, "Three, just like Maddie showed me." I finally had to hide the formula because we were going through it so fast! Vanessa, in an excess of preparedness, would get five or six bottles ready at a time and leave them lined up on the kitchen counter waiting for a baby to get hungry. Some inevitably sat out so long that their contents had to be poured out.

Another time, Alina and I told all the children to get into the car so we could visit one of the grandmothers. Her son Joseph was five at the time, and she told him to put on his seatbelt.

"You can't make me," he said. "I have my freedency [free agency]." Alina had to explain that free choice comes with consequences, and the choice not to buckle up meant he might get hurt if we got in a car accident.

"You *do* have a choice," she said. "Buckle up or stay home." He buckled up.

We limit our children's "screen time"—television, video games, and computers. There is plenty of fun to be had in our big backyard, which is equipped with a volleyball pit, an in-ground trampoline, and a bicycle and skateboard track that circles our property. Our children all have a playmate close to their age within the family, so they can keep each other entertained for hours on end. The neighbors' children often want to come to our house because there's always something going on. A few summers ago, five of our boys decided to build a fort in the backyard (no girls allowed, of course). They worked on it from sunup to sundown, day after day, and any friends who came over were quickly enlisted to help. They gathered scrap wood, discarded carpet, and every spare nail or screw they could find. They happily took an old couch off a neighbor's hands and begged for furnishings they thought we might part with. By the end of the summer they had a fully decorated, carpeted hut!

Our children know from the time they are toddlers that they can't be unruly. There just isn't a place in our crowded house for such behavior. Our sons Tavish and Ashton were about four and five years old when a friend of mine came to visit, bringing along her two boys to play. The young visitors immediately ran through the house, bouncing from one thing to another and leaving a path of destruction in their wake: a broken figurine, a ripped book, a decapitated Barbie. When the boys finally left, Tavish came to me and said, "Mom, that wasn't very fun. They just don't play right."

In many plural families, each mother, along with the father, disciplines her own children. In our family, because we have a unified parenting style, we discipline each other's children when they are young, but each mother takes responsibility for her own children as they get older and the problems get more complex. If I catch an older child lying, for instance, I let the other mother deal with it. Sometimes, Dad has to lay down the law. Joe didn't like how long one son's hair was getting and gave him a choice: get your hair cut, or I'll do it for you. It was an easy decision!

Val got her daughter Maddie a new bicycle for her eighth birthday and wanted to keep it a big surprise. The day Val brought the bike home, she asked one of her sons to conceal it in a blanket and carry it into the house. My son Jed, who was thirteen, happened to be walking by the front door just as the bicycle was being carried in. He went straight to Maddie and said, "Maddie, you're getting a bike for your birthday." The party was hours away but the surprise was ruined. Val was furious, but instead of talking to Jed about it, she let Joe and me handle the situation.

Another time, I found a chair leaning up against the house, just below a certain child's bedroom window, and figured someone was sneaking out at night. But it was Val's child, so I told her what I'd seen and let her deal with it.

We have to work hard at being fair referees in our children's disputes to avoid favoring our own kids and appearing one-sided. It can be pretty tough for a child not to be automatically backed by his or her mother, but if we didn't have that philosophy our family would break down into warring tribes! Of course, the children try to play us against each other. If one mother says no, they've been known to go ask another in hopes of getting a different answer.

Kyley, Val's nine-year-old daughter, is a very free spirit who loves to make up stories, dance, and dream the day away. It's not easy to get her to focus on chores. She always has something much more interesting to do! Alina was trying to get Kyley to pick up toys in the playroom one afternoon. Kyley would pick up a few and then get distracted and start playing with her younger sisters or wander off to her bedroom to work on a story she was writing. Alina finally sent the younger girls out of the room and told Kyley she had to stay until her pile was picked up and sorted in the toy bins. Three hours later, after Alina had had to search for Kyley and take her back to the playroom several times, the task was finally finished.

That evening, Kyley went to Val and said, "Mom, there are some things I've been wanting to talk to you about." Val could tell by her tone that this was something important, so she led the way to a private spot and invited Kyley to explain.

Kyley was very serious as she went on. "I have this thought that comes in my head over and over. I don't *try* to make it come in; it just does. The thought is that I want Aunt Alina out of my life. I try to make it go away, but it just keeps coming."

Val had to help Kyley understand that she might not always like what Alina wanted her to do, but she still had to do it.

We use time-outs, loss of privileges, and grounding to discipline our children. Rather than bribing or yelling at them, we try to validate their feelings, to listen and talk to them. Our goal is to teach them to express and take responsibility for their feelings and behavior, right from the start. But have you ever tried to send four little girls to time-out together? One day, our four youngest girls went into a bathroom and dumped all the shampoo and bubble bath into the tub. When they turned the water on, there were bubbles everywhere! I had them come out of the bathroom and made them fold their arms and sit at different spots in the hallway while I cleaned up the mess. Soon I heard giggling. They were squished up against each other laughing. I made them move apart and went back to the bathroom. Soon there was snickering. They had scooted close enough together to touch toes.

Our children refer to us collectively as "the moms." We each have our own parenting personality, which together makes us a great team. Alina is protective, but also fun and really good at relating to teenagers. Val is easygoing and a good mentor, but less strict because she doesn't like conflict. I'm strict, but also like to let the children experiment. It's nice to have another mom to lean on for help when I need to give special attention to one child, or when I'm not sure which approach to take in a difficult situation.

Once, I was going the rounds with a daughter who had just turned thirteen. She was constantly on the phone with her friends, and had pulled away from the family. Her grades had slipped as her social life took center stage. I grounded her until she caught up in school. When she finished some missing assignments, I relented to show my love and appreciation for her efforts, and gave her permission to go to a friend's house for a few hours. She was due home in thirty minutes when I got a call from the friend's father. He asked me to let his daughter know he was on his way to pick her up. You can imagine my reaction! I told him I'd thought the girls were at *his* house. It turned out they'd lied to both of us in order to hang out with some boys. I was worried and hurt, and I felt manipulated. When we tracked down my daughter, I was so angry I wanted to yell and scream. But Val and Alina talked me down, helping me separate my emotions from the situation and settle on an appropriate consequence for my daughter's behavior.

We obviously don't hide our lifestyle from our children. We allow them to decide for themselves, though, how much to disclose to their friends. If they forget to fill in the blanks, some interesting moments can result. Once, one of my daughters brought a friend home who knew I was her mom and Joe was her dad. The friend saw Joe kiss Alina as they worked together in the kitchen.

"Who's that?" the friend asked a niece who was at our house.

"Oh, that's Alina," my niece answered.

"But that's not her mom," the friend said.

"Oh, yeah—well, they're polygamists," the niece said.

Another time, a classmate asked one of our daughters, a first grader, why she always brought a sack lunch instead of eating the school lunch.

"Because I'm a polygamy!" she answered cheerfully. She knew we were different and thought *that* was why she got the cheaper brown-bag lunches. She hadn't yet grasped the concept of frugality!

Polygamy wasn't a persistent topic of public discussion when we were growing up, but times have changed: our children are often confronted with it in negative ways, directly and indirectly.

One of Val's sons was appropriately suspended from school after he called a classmate a "fag." But there was no similar repercussion when a classmate derogatorily called Val's son a "plig."

One year, Joe's little brother and his niece attended the same middle school as our children, and they were in some of the same classes. One of the teachers required her students to bring current-event topics for the class to discuss. Someone brought in a newspaper clipping about a marriage that FLDS leader Warren Jeffs had conducted between a young girl and a man referred to as her first cousin.

"What's a first cousin?" one student asked the teacher.

The teacher, who knew about their family background, pointed at Joe's niece, whose last name was also Darger, and then at Joe's brother. "That would be like those two marrying," she said. Having been singled out because of their well-known fundamentalist surname, they were humiliated.

When Joe heard the story, he went straight to the principal to explain how insensitive and hurtful her behavior had been to children from our culture, and how such comments emboldened other children to be rude. This wasn't the first instance of school staff saying insulting things about children from fundamentalist families. Joe asked the principal to put on a sensitivity training program for his staff; to his credit, the principal agreed and did it.

If one of our children is struggling in school academically or socially, we sit down together and discuss it, making use of our very own family think tank. We each have an investment in every child's well-being and success. Everyone makes suggestions and then we agree on a solution. The same thing happens when a child is acting out in some way. Often, one of the other mothers in the family is able to provide a perspective or intervene in a way that helps resolve the problem.

Alina was having a tough time once with one of her sons, who was going through an adolescent phase of being loud and obnoxious. He was constantly playing jokes on people—jokes that he thought were hilarious but that his victims did not find funny. Alina didn't have the patience for his antics. One day, we were having our weekly family meeting and he burst into the room. "Hey, why did the chicken cross the road?" he yelled out, and then squawked. I began laughing. When he left, Alina brought up how irritated she was with him. I reminded her it was just a reflection of his preteen insecurity and would pass. Alina later said my comment helped her remember how much unconditional love her son needed during this awkward period.

In a typical plural family, the first wife often has at least several children before the second wife comes along, so there is a spread in the children's ages. In our family, the children are close in age, so we really got slammed when we suddenly had a bunch of teenagers. We've gotten to be really good at raising small children, but we're still getting a crash course in parenting adolescents!

Compared to their friends, our teenagers have more responsibility at home, and more rules: we have a curfew, limit their Internet use, and require them to pay some of their own expenses. We discourage our children from dating exclusively, something we think they should postpone until they have a serious interest in someone that could lead to marriage. Since we don't belong to an organized religious group, it can be hard for our children to find friends who share their background and values. With that in mind, we encourage them to participate in activities hosted by a wide variety of religious denominations, including the LDS Church, the AUB, and several evangelical churches in our area.

I am often asked whether I expect my children to follow this lifestyle. I *hope* my children choose to live this way, because I value it so much as a true principle and a good way to raise a family. But they know it's absolutely their choice. If they don't, I hope I've raised them to be autonomous, responsible adults who have integrity, follow a strong work ethic, and take family and parenting seriously. And if I'm blessed, they'll think I was a pretty good mom, too!

Joe

THERE'S A SPAN OF nearly twenty years between the birth of my first child and that of my youngest, but the thrill of birth has never diminished for me. Neither has the joy of being a dad. There's nothing quite like coming home from work and being greeted by a dozen small children, all of whom want to give me a big hug. Or being out of town on business and receiving a singing message from three daughters, who've adapted the Faith Hill lyrics "Where are you, Christmas? Why can't I find you?" to "Where are you, Daddy? Why can't I find you?" That melted my heart.

When Alina, Vicki, and I were courting, we talked about how many children we wanted. It was a few more than we have so far. There are Vicki's eight, Alina's seven, and Val's nine children (five from her first marriage). Having a large family is an important aspect of our faith—every child we have is a spirit-child that has gained a chance at embodied life—and we see it as the purpose of our marriage. Because of the tremendous responsibility involved, my view is that the size of a family should be a choice based on the parents' ability to provide financially and emotionally for each child. I want to connect with, relate to, and support *all* of my children. It also is important to consider my wives' health, both physically and emotionally. I'm not just trying to have as many children as I can; quality of relationships matters more than quantity of offspring.

Since my marriage in 1990, nearly every year of my adult life has been marked by a birth in our family. People often ask me if I know all my children's names. I turn the question around and ask if they know the names of more than two dozen people. Of *course* I know each child's name, as well as all the nuances of his or her distinct personality and personal details such as birthday.

Some people find two or three children to be as much as they can handle. That's fine. But in this lifestyle, it is natural to have *many* children. I genuinely love children, enjoy the culture a big family creates, and appreciate the responsibility it requires from me, from my wives, and from each of our children.

My children are fortunate to have three incredible mothers. That's no accident, though: we planned it this way. We each grew up with lots of siblings, which provided a good understanding of the dynamics of big families. We also actively prepared for parenthood. Alina, Vicki, and I knew we were going to have lots of children and wanted to be the best parents we possibly could be.

We prepared by reading parenting books—*Parent Effectiveness Training: The Tested New Way to Raise Responsible Children* by Thomas Gordon was an early favorite. Before the birth of our first child, we also attended a conference at the Institutes for the Achievement of Human Potential in Pennsylvania. We learned about brain development, teaching techniques, and the best ways to discipline children, all of which have served as our parenting blueprint over the years.

We get a lot of questions about how our big family works. I like to describe it as being similar to a football team, which functions best when there's discipline, there's structure, and everyone acts in concert. Sometimes, I have six little children, all close in age, with me when I am running errands or going on an outing. People invariably assume I am with a school or church group until they hear the children all calling me, "Dad, Dad, Dad!" Strangers typically are amazed by my children's good behavior. Self-discipline is something we teach our children from a very young age. When I see a four-year-old throwing a tantrum in public, I'm amazed! With as many little children as we have, it would be chaos if we allowed that sort of meltdown to occur.

When you treat children with the respect that's due to capable human beings, they live up to and model that respect. That's our method, but I had it reinforced for me the hard way when I had five stepchildren enter my life at once—one of the times I felt most maxed out as a parent. My oldest children felt displaced by Val and her children, not understanding the process we had gone through before accepting them into our family. One day, my oldest son, who was nine at the time, came along when I went to get a haircut and got upset when I engaged in friendly banter with the hairdresser. He figured I was trying to get another wife. When he talked to me about that concern, I knew I had some educating to do.

Because Val kept her marital problems hidden from her children, they didn't understand what was happening when their parents separated. Val's son, who was ten at the time, really resented me. He and Amanda made their feelings toward me known by being rude, inconsiderate, or noncommittal. Even an offer to go to a movie or to get ice cream was met with a sullen, "I don't know."

Val is a good mother and her children are well behaved. At that time, though, her children were also fearful and wounded, and they often misinterpreted my efforts to correct their behavior. I am not a physical disciplinarian, but my children know that when they get out of line I'm not going to tolerate it. Much as I didn't want to model myself after my dad in this respect, I was a much harsher parent at the time Val joined our family than I am now. I had a short fuse and used anger to intimidate my children. I'd grab my older sons by the collar, yelling as I marched them down the hall to have a time-out. Val's children weren't used to such discipline, and they were shocked. They'd never seen someone act that way. Their reaction was a learning experience for me; it caused me to reexamine my parenting behavior and adopt better ways of dealing with all our children, especially the older ones.

Teenagers are hard, all right—but imagine having three or four all at once! That can really test a parent's character. An uncle of mine who has more than thirty children likes to say, "Having teenagers isn't for the kids. It's for the parents. Adolescence teaches the adults a lot, and the kids don't even remember it."

In our most trying parenting moments, we have found the different perspectives within our plural family to be a real benefit. When my oldest son was about sixteen, he became very hostile about our lifestyle. He blamed polygamy for everything he thought was bad in his life, from having a curfew to being expected to pay his own cell phone expenses. When he didn't pay his phone bill one month, I turned his cell phone service off. That was when I realized we had a generation gap. When I was a teenager, the worst thing that could ever happen to me was to lose my driving privileges. But losing access to his cell phone, which cut off his social network, was the ultimate punishment for my son!

None of my son's friends were required to pay their own cell phone bills, and my son figured that the reason *he* had to was that there were so many children in our family. It goes deeper than that, though. I see requiring my older children to contribute to their expenses as a great way to teach them accountability, not reduce our bills. But my son, perceiving this as unfair, blew up one day and ran away to a friend's home. He wouldn't talk to me or to Alina, his mother. But Vicki was able to reach out and get my son to vent his frustrations to her, which led to his returning home ten days later. Having our own family safety net and being able to rely on each other's strengths is one of the best things about living this way.

It is a priority in my life to have strong relationships with my children and make sure they get time with me that matters. That doesn't mean I'm there for every event in their lives; it's just not possible. For example, I don't go to a parent-teacher conference unless a child is having major problems in school. Instead, the mothers go; I meet with each mother and child later to hear the report, a time when I get to both offer congratulations on a job well done and help set goals for improvement. But I have coached each of my sons' football teams, which has given us quality time together and provided a great forum for me to teach them life lessons. I put together daddy-daughter dates with my girls for the same reason.

One of my daughters began to show signs of anorexia as she entered adolescence, and her grades dropped in school. Nothing we tried was getting through to her; nothing revealed the real problems underlying her behavior. I asked her to go for a drive with me one Friday afternoon—a pretext for a weekend away where we could spend time together. She was in crisis, and I knew she needed my full attention to feel safe enough to disclose whatever was going on. As a result of that time together, I was able to get my daughter the professional help she needed. But it was our relationship, built over the years through my strong presence in her life, that allowed me to recognize the signs of trouble and made it possible for my daughter to trust my efforts to help.

While my faith is the center of my life, I know it is not something I can force on my children. All of my children have to determine for themselves what they believe, and not rely on the faith of their parents. As my children get older, I encourage them to attend different churches to learn what others believe and how they worship. For a time, LDS Church missionaries visited our family; they were amazed how much my children knew about the scriptures. Many of my children also have attended LDS Church religious education classes that are offered as an elective option in Utah's public secondary school system.

I worry that some of my children will blame our lifestyle for every mishap and hardship in their lives. Statistics and family history tell me that not all of my children will choose to follow this religion or to enter plural marriage. That's okay; that's their choice. I will love them regardless. Our decision to enter this lifestyle wasn't about perpetuating polygamy; it was about creating a family and following what we believe to be true.

Whether or not living the Principle is in their path is between each of my children and his or her Father in heaven. I am raising my children to be capable of living this lifestyle if they choose it—to have the faith, wisdom, and emotional intelligence to be successful at it. Even if their path leads elsewhere, that grounding means they will be well prepared for life. My ultimate hope is that my children will view our decision to live this way with respect and pride, rather than shame.

CHAPTER TEN

A Day in the Life of a Polygamous Family

*Our children should not be neglected; they should receive
a proper education in both spiritual and temporal things. That is
the best legacy any parents can leave to their children.*

—WILFORD WOODRUFF, FOURTH LDS CHURCH PRESIDENT,
Journal of Discourses

Alina

IT IS DARK OUTSIDE as our children stumble, one by one, into our
downstairs family room. At six thirty in the morning, a few of the
oldest kids are already dressed and ready for school, but most of
our children are still in their pajamas. Joe asks Ashton to give the
prayer this morning. We bow our heads and fold our arms as
Ashton speaks softly, asking God to give us a good day, to keep
the family safe, and to help Grandma T. get over the flu. He fin-
ishes, and then it's Joe's turn.

"Don't forget we have Jed and Caleb's concert tonight at eight. Who still needs a ticket?" he says. A few hands go up. "Okay, and we will be celebrating Maddie's birthday on Sunday evening at six thirty. Plan for it."

Now it's time for one of my favorite parts of the morning: we rise and exchange hugs and good-mornings! I'm on breakfast duty, so I head upstairs to set cereal, milk, and some fruit on the table, and soon I am surrounded by a half dozen hungry little children. Welcome to our home!

There isn't just one way to structure a plural family. As the others have noted, some families live in one home and some are in separate homes side by side or near each other; there are also families that live in different cities, and even families living in different states. At the beginning of our marriage, we decided we wanted to live as a single family, with all the challenges and benefits that come from sharing one home. I love seeing all of my family each morning—definitely one of the pluses of living together.

We live in a suburb of the Salt Lake Valley. When Joe's family bought the property more than two decades ago, the area was lightly populated and offered space for our family to grow. It's changed a lot since then but still has a bit of a country feel to it. We're friendly with some neighbors and, over the years, have been involved in city and school organizations, but this is an area where people tend to be private.

Our first home was a trailer that Joe moved onto the property and fixed up before Vicki and I married him. It was small but cozy: two bedrooms, a bathroom, a living room, a kitchen, and a dining room. We converted the dining room into Vicki's bedroom; it was larger and at the opposite end of the trailer from the master bedroom, which gave us more privacy. The little bedroom became the nursery when our first child arrived. We quickly became cramped with that arrangement. We had five children between us within five years, and trying to make a place for all our belongings and keep things tidy was tough! Joe and various members of his family finished a large home on our property just before I had our sixth child in 1996. It became our second home and seemed wonderfully spacious when we first moved in, but we eventually outgrew it, too.

Today, we live in a 5,500-square-foot two-level, brick home that Joe helped build on the same property, and we need every bit of that space. All but three of our children still live at home. From oldest to youngest, we have: Joseph, twenty; Laura, eighteen; Jed, eighteen; Grayson, sixteen; Liesl, sixteen; Shad, fifteen; Louis, fourteen; Logan, thirteen; Ashton, thirteen; Madison, twelve; Tavish, eleven; Kyley, nine; Sabrina, eight; Kadence, eight; Allie, seven; Vanessa, five; Angelina, five; Boston, three; Krista, two; and Victoria, fifteen months. Caleb, twenty, is close by, so we see him often; and Amanda, nineteen and in her second year of college, rejoins the family on weekends and breaks. Val's oldest son, Sam, twenty, lives a couple hours away and visits frequently, too. That's three twenty-year-olds, nine teenagers, eight children between the ages of five and twelve, one preschooler, and two toddlers!

We had a craft room, an office, and an exercise room in our home, but over time those have been converted to bedrooms. Maybe we'll get to reclaim them after we send more kids to college

THE DARGERS, BY THE NUMBERS

I husband
3 wives

24 children (23 living)
II boys
13 girls

5 stepchildren, Joe
7 children, Alina
8 children, Vicki
9 children, Val
19 (18 living) biological children, Joe

3 twenty-somethings
9 teenagers
8 children between ages five and twelve
I preschooler
2 toddlers

$500–$700 weekly grocery bill
36 rolls of toilet paper used weekly
10 family cars
10 laundry loads a day
10 cell phones
6 laptop computers
5 desktop computers
3–5 loaves homemade bread consumed daily
5 kids in diapers at one time
5 bathrooms
4 TVs
2 gallons of milk consumed daily

or as they launch their own lives! We currently have eleven bed-rooms and five bathrooms. Each wife has her own master bed-room, which she shares with Joe. He keeps clothes in each of our closets. There are eight bedrooms for the children. We initially sat down with a map of the house and grouped two or three children into each bedroom based on gender and age, but personality has turned out to be a bigger consideration in matching up children in rooms!

Sharing a single home requires a lot of give-and-take. One issue that became contentious when we were remodeling the kitchen a few years ago was how high to make the counters. Small detail, but it was a big issue! Because I'm tall, I wanted counter heights that matched my size. Val, who loves to cook, is much shorter, and she wanted counters that fit *her*. One day, Val came across a split counter design that was a perfect compromise, one that accommodated everyone's wishes. We made decorating deci-sions together for the common areas of our home, such as the formal living room, the family room, and the sunroom adjacent to the kitchen, which can accommodate a table long enough to seat the entire family. The common rooms are modestly furnished, in a traditional style and neutral colors. We let our designer talents shine in the bedrooms. Mine is traditional, with a robin's-egg blue and chocolate color scheme. Vicki's room has a Victorian look, while Val's bedroom has a beach cottage theme that uses shades of pink, green, and dusty blue.

We have two refrigerators, two freezers, and two laundry rooms. We often joke that we would rather share a kitchen than a laundry room any day. With up to ten loads of wash to do each day, the laundry room can be a battle zone at times! I'll put in a load and plan to follow it with another batch. Meanwhile, Val, who has no way of knowing it's a two-load day for me, moves my clothes to the dryer and starts her own load—and my agenda is shot. More than one person can work in a kitchen at a time, but the laundry is a solo affair.

Joe, who has his own business, is the primary wage earner for the family. At least two wives are usually working, while the third is the stay-home mom. Right now, Val and I work in our family-owned residential and commercial cleaning service and also do seasonal decorating. Vicki is at home with the youngest children and also works from home as a bookkeeper. We've all had other jobs in the past. Val was a baker, for example, and I worked for a mortgage company. We've never received welfare or relied on food stamps. One thing that has been tricky is health insurance. At times, Joe has been able to carry all our children on his health plan. Vicki and Val can't legally be included on Joe's family plan, however, and thus have to provide their own insurance (and sometimes coverage for their children). We've also had periods where we've had no health coverage.

We pool all our earnings to cover major and ongoing expenses, and then split what's left so we each (including the stay-home mom) have our own spending money. We budget for everything, from major purchases to vacations and groceries, but have found it works best if we each have our own bank account and make our own spending decisions. One time, Vicki was saving to buy a piano. Val and I knew how much Vicki wanted it, so we agreed to use our discretionary money to help pay for it.

Vicki, Val, and I share other duties, such as cooking for the family. Each mom is in charge of meals two days a week; on Sunday, we each take one meal. We divide up the rest of the home labor, with each of us taking responsibility for certain tasks. Vicki handles the mail and bills. Val keeps us supplied with homemade bread. I do the weekly grocery shopping. We are extremely frugal and have a reputation for being amazing shoppers. We appreciate hand-me-downs, aren't above frequenting yard sales, and recycle like crazy. We rarely pay full price for anything and shop sales, discounts, and clearances. There is a network of plural wives that gets activated whenever there's a really good deal going on, whether it's a sock sale at Macy's or a three-dollars-a-pair pants clearance sale at J. C. Penney. At the end of each season, we buy marked-down clothing that we store in big Tupperware bins, labeled by size and gender, so the children have something to grow into. We don't usually buy brand names, which is tough on our teenagers. One of our children really wanted a pair of True Religion jeans. Joe told him, "You want true religion? Come to Sunday school. Otherwise, buy your own jeans!"

We buy flour and sugar in twenty-five-pound bags and purchase as many items as we can in bulk. We go through two gallons of milk and three to five loaves of homemade bread every day. Toilet paper? Thirty-six rolls every seven days! Our grocery bill runs $500 to $700 a week. Our children take sack lunches to school, which they put together each morning assembly-line style—though whichever mom is on that day has to make sure there's a sandwich and a piece of fruit, and not just cookies, in the bag! To save money, we've learned to cut hair. We have Haircut Friday once a month, when all the boys and some of the girls get a trim at home. Sometimes there's a pile of hair a foot deep on the kitchen floor.

We set a budget, based on age, for birthdays and Christmas. Each mom shops for her own children, but if I see something I know is on Vicki's shopping list, I'll call to ask if she wants me to pick it up. We try to make sure the piles around the tree are similar in size. One year, though, my two oldest children wanted iPods, and that took their whole share of the Christmas budget. We have several Christmas Eve traditions that keep the focus on fun, rather than funds. We gather the children in one big circle and give each child a wrapped present. Joe reads "'Twas the Night Before Christmas," and every time he says the word "the," a present has to be passed to the next person in the circle. That word occurs thirty-four times (though Joe has been known to throw in a few extras), which means the anticipation really builds until that final "the," when the children get to open whichever present they're holding. The surprise can be anything from a candy bar to a five-dollar bill.

Unless they have a job outside the home, we expect our children to do weekly, rotating chores. The youngest children may be tasked with wiping down doorknobs, light switches, and kitchen stools, or folding towels. At age seven or eight, our children start dusting and vacuuming the family room, cleaning bathrooms, and helping with the dishes. Given the size of our family, dishwashing is the worst job, followed by bathroom duty! At age ten, each child becomes responsible for his or her own laundry. By age thirteen or fourteen, the children make bread, prepare simple meals, and clean out the fridge. Our children learn that if they don't get a job done, it affects the entire family. We hold them to it, too. There is no playtime or other privilege until their chores are finished. We expect the teenagers who work to cover their own expenses as much as possible for such things as gas, clothes, and cell phone. And as long as they live at home, they help in the kitchen and yard, with car maintenance, and, once they can drive, with carpooling.

I don't wait for Joe to do many things monogamous women expect of their husbands. There are three of us, and if he tried to play princess to us all the time, he'd never get anything done. If there is a broken light on the Christmas tree, I fix it myself. Once, Vicki and I decided to remodel a bathroom. I used a mini-jackhammer to remove the old tile and then, with her help, replaced it with new tile. Conversely, there was a period early on when Joe was between jobs, Vicki was working part-time, and I had a full-time job, so he made dinner every night.

When we were first dating, Vicki, Joe, and I wrote a mission statement listing the things that were important to us as potential parents. We wanted to provide our future children with a united family, teach them to be responsible and productive citizens, and give them a strong spiritual foundation. Education also was high on our list, and initially we chose to homeschool our children.

Once we were blessed with young ones, we set up a preschool with some friends and relatives. Neither Vicki nor I were working; we would spend the morning teaching our children letters and sounds, colors, shapes, and numbers, and then take them to the park or the county pool in the afternoon. Typically, our children were reading by the time they were four years old (still true today). From there, we kept adding grades. We knew we could give our children more attention than the public schools could, and we could focus on their areas of interest more fully. There was a strong homeschool movement in Utah at the time, and we attended the association's annual convention and its parent training classes and support groups. We designed a detailed curriculum and adhered to the typical hours of a school day, covering all the required subjects. We also amassed an extensive library of children's books, which we supplemented with educational aids and learning games.

We encouraged our children to pursue specialized interests, such as music, and took them on field trips to concerts and plays and even to an ice-making factory. We joined other homeschool groups for activities like science and history fairs. Many of our children also participated in Little League sports, which gave them an opportunity to interact with other children from the neighborhood.

To check their progress, we periodically gave our children an achievement test supplied by a national agency, which scored the results. Most of our children tested up to two grades ahead of their age group.

I love the experience of watching a child read her first word or understand a new concept. I consider it my duty, but also my privilege, to be my children's first teacher. But, as much as I loved teaching our children at home, I always knew a time would come when their educational needs would surpass our ability to meet them. That moment came in 2002. Joe had changed careers and Vicki and Val started working to help support the family. My oldest son was eleven and he really wanted to go to school with his friends, and the other kids were also interested in trying that approach. For all those reasons, we enrolled our children in public school. Much to the surprise of their teachers, our children tested ahead of their peers. I still kept involved in my children's schooling by volunteering in their classrooms, helping with class parties, and grading papers.

We now have a hybrid approach to education, using whatever system works best for each child. At one time, we had children in nine different schools in order to provide the best educational environment for each one. It was crazy! At present, we are using several different settings to meet our children's educational needs, including charter schools and public schools. We have three children attending two different colleges, too. During the school year, our days are much like those of parents everywhere: hectic! Generally, each mom takes care of getting her children wherever they need to be, but if we have three or four children going to the same school or activity, such as football or soccer practice or music lessons, one mom handles it.

Our annual family vacation is always an adventure. One year, we went to San Diego. We drove in three cars, but everyone still had to pack light. Vicki was in charge of booking three condos, Val was in charge of planning meals, and I oversaw the packing— a division of labor that is one of the great benefits of plural marriage! All but the youngest children were responsible for their own suitcases. I then checked them over. I had to pull roller skates from one suitcase and put in underwear and socks. When we travel out of state, most people we encounter are less familiar with polygamy and mistake our large family for a church or school group. During this particular trip, we were at the beach and a woman came over and asked if she could borrow some sunscreen. "I saw you were a day care and figured you would have some," she said.

Given the size of our family, it's easier (and cheaper!) to create fun at home. For years, we set aside Monday evening as Family Night, a time when we'd gather to read or recreate together. That has become more difficult with teenagers and with Joe's current work schedule. But we find plenty of opportunities to join together as a family. A typical summer weekend involves a lot of backyard games, from volleyball to dodgeball, and a family barbecue. From our large deck, we can watch the children as they ride bicycles and scooters around the path that circles our yard. When the sun goes down, we build a bonfire in the backyard pit and gather to roast marshmallows and sing songs, accompanied by our own little band of guitar, mandolin, banjo, and harmonica players.

In the winter, we gather everyone up to go sledding or ice-skating; at night, we hunker down in the family room for pizza and a movie—favorites are *Star Wars* and *Willy Wonka and the Chocolate Factory* and *Napoleon Dynamite*. It's on nights like that, as I snuggle on the couch next to Joe, with Vicki and Val close by and children piled around us, that I feel like I'm sitting in the middle of the dream I first had twenty-one years ago.

Val

IF THERE IS ONE day of the week in our lives that looks different from what goes on in many families, it is Sunday. Sunday is sacred to us, a day of worship, family, and reprieve from the hectic pace of daily life, just as it is for many other people of faith. But instead of traveling to a church or meetinghouse, we head downstairs to the family room for our weekly service.

It still takes teamwork to feed everyone a small breakfast and then get them dressed in their Sunday clothes; for one thing, there are eight little girls whose hair has to be done! But we are usually gathered by 9:30 A.M., ready to worship together. Joe will ask someone to give an opening prayer and then one of the mothers will take the children who are younger than eight to another room for their own class. The moms take turns giving the little children lessons on basic principles of our religion and ideals like kindness, serving God, and having love for others.

For the younger children, we use teaching manuals published by the LDS Church. These "primary" manuals, designed for different ages, include lessons, songs, poems, art activities, and things to memorize. A lesson might discuss the Heavenly Father's plan for us, present a simplified version of the Articles of Faith (thirteen statements that describe basic Mormon beliefs), or explain the origin of the Book of Mormon.

Meanwhile, Joe leads a discussion for the rest of the family. As a priesthood holder and father, Joe is responsible for making sure our family understands the principles of the gospel, which is the focus of our Sunday school. This is when we talk about, read, and study our faith, usually spending one to two hours together. Joe's lessons draw from what we call "the standard works"—the Holy Bible, the Book of Mormon, Doctrine and Covenants, and the Pearl of Great Price, as well as other less-well-known Mormon writings. These include *Gospel Doctrine, Priesthood Government,*

Teachings of the Prophet Joseph Smith, and the *Journal of Discourses,* a multivolume compilation of early LDS Church leaders' sermons.

Joe also draws from other ethically oriented materials that complement gospel principles and offer ideas about living a good life, from *Mere Christianity* by C. S. Lewis to Viktor E. Frankl's *Man's Search for Meaning.* For a lesson on virtue, Joe talked about the Internet and online safety and used written material and a video presentation from the National Center for Missing and Exploited Children. Other lesson topics have ranged from repentance to finding grace and the atonement of the Savior. He applies the messages in these works to our daily lives and shows how they can help us improve ourselves.

Joe often calls on the children to speak on a topic of their choosing, and the truth is, not all of them like this task! On some Sundays we also have a sacrament service, when we renew our commitment to follow Jesus Christ and his teachings.

Some Independents gather together for services, while many others hold family meetings as we do. This is one of the ways we differ from the organized Fundamentalist Mormon groups, who have meetinghouses where they gather. With the exception of the plural families seated in the audience, those church services do not look or sound much different from those taking place in LDS Church meetinghouses on Sundays. The organized Fundamentalist groups sing the same Mormon hymns, give similar testimonial speeches, and hold a sacrament service in which consecrated bread and water are distributed to the congregation.

Once our Sunday service is over, the moms get busy in the kitchen making a traditional brunch, a feast worth the weeklong wait! It is the only day we make sure we are all together for meals. We also often invite friends and extended family to join us for brunch, which makes it an even bigger affair. It is common for us to go through five dozen eggs, sixty to seventy waffles, bags of potatoes, and several gallons of milk and juice. You can imagine how the children dread landing dishwashing duty on Sundays! But there are many helping hands. We always have a special, more formal Sunday dinner, too.

After brunch, the children go off to play or engage in quiet activities in their rooms. Joe often gets wangled by the children into a game of touch football or an outing to the park. Joe also likes to meet individually with the children on Sundays. With the little ones, Joe might spend a quiet moment reading a story. With the older children, it's an opportunity to talk one-on-one about goals, concerns, work and school, successes, and areas for improvement. Some Sundays, we load everyone into three or four cars and go visit relatives. We also set Sundays aside for birthday celebrations. There are just two months—January and May—when there are no birthdays; in April and December we celebrate a birthday every week, which makes for a busy month.

At some point in late afternoon or early evening, we parents gather around the kitchen table to plan the coming week. Our BlackBerrys are crammed with comings and goings, appointments and logistics, as we figure out who will be where and what activities the children have coming up. We often have six or eight kids in sports and music activities at a time, so figuring out how to get it all covered takes high-level strategizing. And it seems like every other day one or another of our ten cars is broken down or has a flat tire, which makes scheduling even more complicated. A typical discussion goes like this:

> VICKI: *I have a dentist appointment on Monday at four o'clock for Sabrina, Tavish, and Boston, which means someone else will have to get Ashton and Logan to football and I'll need help with Tori. Oh, and Louis has soccer practice at five.*
>
> ALINA: *Well, I was going to pick up Maddie at Safety Patrol, so I can get the boys to football. I'll take the Nissan and you can have the minivan. But Laura's car isn't running and she has a job interview Monday at three. Is there another car she can use? Plus, Joe, you need to help her tow it to the shop when you get home from work. And I have my sister's birthday party at six.*
>
> VAL: *I can make the soccer run and I'll watch Tori.*
>
> JOE: *Laura can use the truck.*
>
> VAL: *Great! We're covered.*

But that's just Monday!

We also take time during the Sunday planning session to deal with any conflicts or problems in the family, which can range from a child who is having homework trouble to a teenager who is staying out too late. Quite often, we have different ideas about what to do, and we find it really helpful, as parents, to hear those other perspectives. When one of our teens started breaking curfew repeatedly, I suggested taking away her cell phone. Joe wanted to give her one more chance to see how she responded. Vicki proposed grounding her for a week. In the end, we settled on a warning talk and a second chance.

During our planning session, we also go over the triple Honey-Do list. Joe's typical reaction: "Holy cow!" Despite the fact that Alina, Vicki, and I aren't shy about taking on household repairs ourselves, there can be dozens of fix-it projects and other tasks on the list, from major projects like building a shed to smaller ones like repairing a closet door. Here is one Sunday's list: Fix dryer vent; fix leaky toilet; finish shelving in garage; put doorknobs on shed doors; fertilize lawn; get oil changed in truck; buy and put on new tires for Nissan; install wood trim in Vicki's bedroom; pick up gravel for driveway; fix lighting in mudroom; hang new light fixture in Alina's room; fix broken chair in dining room; install ceiling fan in Val's room; patch leak in dining room ceiling. There is always plenty to do. This also is when we discuss any changes needed in the spousal sleeping schedule, depending on trips or events that are coming up.

Our religion, though, is not just what we do on Sunday or the family structure we've established; it is how we try to live our lives, using the gospel of Jesus Christ as a template. We strive to make our faith present every moment as we interact with each other and with people outside the family.

Throughout the week, our days end just as they begin: with a family prayer. In the evening, before we put the little kids to bed, we gather once again in the family room and Joe asks someone to offer the prayer. It's a time to think about our relationship with our Creator and how we lived that day. We follow the tradition of the Lord's Prayer, expressing gratitude, examining shortcomings and trespasses, and seeking forgiveness. We regularly pray for our country, expressing appreciation for the Constitution, with its freedoms and liberties, and our hope for wise leaders. We pray for people we know who are experiencing financial hardship, medical problems, or some other challenge. It is important to us that we teach our children to remember in their prayers those who are suffering, so that they develop compassion. And we always end with appreciation for the love we have for each other and the family we have created. There's one last round of hugs before we tuck the children into bed.

On most evenings, the house is usually quiet for only a few minutes before a chorus of children's voices breaks the silence: I'm scared! I can't sleep. I'm hungry. I need a drink. I have to go to the bathroom. She won't be quiet. I forgot to brush my teeth. Mom, will you sing me a song? We've even heard this one: Hey, Mom, I never got breakfast today!

That's when we look at one another and just have to laugh.

CHAPTER ELEVEN

My Three Moms

Our lives begin to end the day we become silent
about things that matter.

—MARTIN LUTHER KING, JR.

Laura, age eighteen: Alina's oldest daughter

WHEN I WAS LITTLE I thought there were two types of families: some had one mom and some, like mine, had two. Neither kind of family seemed weird or wrong to me. I knew that Alina was my real mom, but I could go to Mom Vick, too, if I needed anything. My mom was good at some things, and Mom Vick was good at others; she was the one who taught me to read even before I was old enough for school.

Our home was on a large property where several other families within the Darger clan lived. I was as close to their children as I was to my siblings. We didn't play video games or watch much television when I was young. Instead, we were full of imagination. We had a closet full of toys, and loved playing with the little plastic cowboys and Indians, ponies, Lincoln Logs, and Legos. Mostly, we were outside, playing together. We could turn a pile of rocks into a five-star hotel.

When I was seven, my dad married Aunt Val, bringing her and her five children into our family of eleven. Val had always been my fun, cool aunt, and thinking of her as a mom felt weird at first. I had a hard time getting used to them being part of our family. Val's daughter Amanda is eight months older than I am, and, despite our totally opposite personalities, we had been best friends. Now, I had to accept her as a sister. We began competing with each other, especially for my dad's attention. Amanda needed a lot of love, support, and guidance, and I sometimes felt overlooked.

I was homeschooled until third grade, and one of my first lessons in public school was that my family was different. I took the school bus, as did several children from another polygamous family, whom I'll call the Smiths. They were Fundamentalist Mormons like us, but were much more conservative. The boys wore dark pants and long-sleeved shirts to school, while the girls wore long dresses that covered their bodies. The children spoke with a southern Utah drawl, which made them stand out further. One day, as the bus stopped to pick up the Smith kids, a boy leaned out the window and yelled, "Polygamists!" All the kids on the crowded bus laughed. As the Smiths took their seats, some kids began teasing them. For the first time, I felt a twinge of embarrassment. *Is a family like mine a bad thing?* I wondered. No one knew that, like the Smiths, I came from a polygamous family. The teasing was relentless for the rest of the year. But I never spoke up to defend the Smiths, even when other kids joked about starting a movement they called Polygamous Pants Anonymous to get them modern clothing.

I changed schools almost every year between fifth grade and my last year in high school—mostly because I was in the gifted and talented student program and it was available only at certain schools, which were not in my neighborhood. One good thing about that: I was able to avoid being shadowed by my polygamous background since my siblings and cousins went to different schools.

I found out the hard way that some people's attitudes changed once they knew about my family. I had a big circle of friends, and I invited one girl over to my house without telling her anything about my parents. I didn't explain anything at the house, either, but she saw all my moms. The next time I went to her house, her mom drilled me: Who's your dad? Do all your moms live together? Not long after that, the other girls ostracized me. I never invited a friend from that group to my home again. I learned to change the subject whenever I was asked personal questions. Mom Vick became "my aunt." Whenever we talked about these kinds of situations as a family, my dad would say, "If someone asks if you're a polygamist, ask if they're a bigot!" I appreciated his support, but it was not particularly helpful advice for a fifth grader! Still, I learned at a young age about the misunderstandings and prejudices people have about fundamentalist culture.

I learned to divide school and home into different worlds. Life at home was pretty good. I never saw my parents in a disagreement. Any issues my parents had were worked out in private, rarely affecting family time or their relationships with us. My parents taught me to work out my own disputes, as they did, whenever I had a fight with a sibling or a friend. I was aware of how much respect and love my parents had for each other and for every child in the family. My mom and I have a great relationship, but I'm emotionally closer to my dad and turned to him a lot as a child. I can talk to my dad about anything and always count on him to be there for me. The moms are all good at different things, so growing up it was like having a supermom at home. If I needed help with cooking or sewing, I would ask Aunt Val. If I wanted to talk about personal problems, I would seek out Mom Vick.

I was a really good student and excelled at my studies. In eighth grade, my parents placed me in a charter school they thought would offer a better educational challenge for me. That year, a girl named Margaret was in my class, and everyone suspected she came from a polygamous family. She wore long skirts over pants, socks, and sneakers, and kept her long hair twisted into a French braid. She got teased mercilessly. One day at lunch, a friend wondered aloud whether Margaret wore the skirt-pants combo because she was a polygamist or a hermaphrodite. For the second time in my life, I didn't say anything when someone else was taunted for a way of life I shared. But my thoughts were in turmoil. *How is that fair to her?* I thought. *What if I were on the opposite end of that comment? Someone has to stand up for the Margarets of the world.* I thought back to my bus rides and how I'd kept silent when the Smith children were teased, and I was ashamed of myself.

That summer, I finally had a chance to speak up on behalf of all the Margarets and Smiths and other kids I knew who were treated unfairly because they came from polygamous families. I participated in a youth rally in Salt Lake City, which was organized to give kids a chance to speak about their experiences growing up in plural families. There were a couple hundred people there, and dozens of kids spoke. I talked about our constitutional right to practice freedom of religion, and how preservation of that right is so important. I really enjoyed seeing so many teenagers whose families and values were similar to mine. For once, I could be openly proud of my polygamous heritage—despite the people driving by the rally who shouted insults at us.

In September, I went with Aunt Val and Amanda to New York to appear on *The Dr. Keith Ablow* show. I thought Keith Ablow was friendly and respectful, allowing us to respond to his questions with our own opinions. It was really interesting to watch the audience during the show. There was a lot of tension in the air at first, and I could tell people weren't sure if they could take us seriously. After a while, though, I could feel the audience lighten up as they realized we aren't so different after all.

But as I entered high school, my rebellious side began to emerge. I resented my parents for the teasing, scrutiny, and rude comments I had to go through because of our family. I felt alone and unsure of who I was and what I believed. I was proud and stubborn; I wouldn't ask for help when I needed it, and the lessons I learned about dealing with prejudice and standing up for myself were learned the hard way. I became a real smartass at school. It was so bad my science teacher had me moved to a different class.

All I cared about was how I looked, my friends, and hanging out with the cool crowd, especially boys. I began sneaking out of the house at night.

I wanted nothing to do with the polygamous culture, and at home all I did was fight with my parents. They never reacted with anger, no matter how difficult I was. My moms simply gave me the same loving support they had always offered. My dad would tell me, "Teen rebellion is a choice," and I'd respond, "Oh, I'm choosing it all right!"

I was still in this rebellious phase as I started tenth grade. Every kid raised in a polygamous family reaches a point where she (or he) has to come to terms with the lifestyle and decide what role she wants the fundamentalist faith to play in her own life. I was sixteen when I reached that moment.

My older brother Joseph was a senior that year, and he was very popular. Everybody called me Little Darger. For once, it felt okay to be identified with my siblings. Telling people about my family wasn't such a big deal anymore. I didn't care what they thought, and I was encouraged that our lifestyle was even accepted in some ways, due to Joseph's paving the way. There were rude comments here and there, but overall the misunderstandings and misperceptions only served to make me a stronger person. It was a turning point for me in accepting my family and wanting to live according to the gospel principles of love, virtue, and honesty.

I graduated a year early from high school and took a year off before going to college. I lived at home and helped supervise the homeschooling for some of my younger siblings. In my free time, I took up painting and taught myself to play the guitar.

I love spending time with my family. We always have fun, whether we are celebrating someone's birthday, spending the day in a park, going to visit our grandparents, or taking a drive through the mountains to see the leaves changing color. My parents took us on a lot of three-car road trips to places like Disneyland, Lake Tahoe, and Mexico. Everywhere we went, people stared, but we didn't care.

There are a lot of different character traits in my family, which makes living together interesting and lively. I have funny siblings, shy ones, and logical, athletic, and outspoken ones. As one of the oldest children, I often look after my younger siblings. I love kids and I've never minded babysitting at all; because I look forward to having my own family, I'm glad to experience what works and what doesn't work in raising children. Every one of my brothers and sisters contributes to my life, like different colors in one vast painting. It is difficult for me to imagine a family without so many people in it. Today, some of my closest friends are the cousins I grew up with. And, with enough love and support, Amanda and I were able to work out most of our differences and develop into two different but equally beautiful people. She's one of my best friends.

However, living in such a big family can be a challenge. All of my siblings have different ideas, preferences, beliefs, talents, and ambitions. It can be difficult to reconcile so many points of view, which is often a detriment to family harmony. My parents do an incredible job of keeping the peace and keeping our family running smoothly, managing, with our help, what would normally be three separate families—from three meals a day, laundry for over twenty people, housecleaning, gardening, and yard care. My parents are great examples of hardworking, selfless givers. I really admire them for that. Everything they earn goes to the family; my parents think of themselves only after their children are taken care of. Greed has no place in a family like ours.

My parents gave me a foundation of strong values: responsibility, respect, communication, honesty, self-control, selflessness, and, most important, accountability and repentance. Looking back at my childhood, I realize that the teasing and questions made me face my fears and insecurities and develop a strong character at a much younger age than most people do.

My parents encouraged me to explore other religions while I was growing up, but nothing I saw in organized religion drew me in. I've embraced my fundamentalist faith. Some of my other siblings don't share the same belief in it. People often ask me whether I expect to live plural marriage. I can't answer that question. I'm still changing and developing. I know it's a hard lifestyle, one that requires a lot of sacrifices. It's not for the faint of heart! I am nowhere close to making that kind of decision right now, but I deserve to have the choice open to me.

Caleb, age twenty: Vicki's oldest son

I was the second-born in our family, arriving on the scene seven months after my brother Joe. My parents had me in violin lessons by the time I was four, and within a couple years I was performing in a family band called the Silver Strings. We played at fairs, banquets, and company parties and were quite a hit. When I was seven, I was photographed performing with the band and landed on the front page of *The Salt Lake Tribune,* Utah's biggest newspaper. Everyone was really excited for me, but I was nervous and almost paranoid. From a young age, I knew my family was different from most other families, and I was afraid the state would use that photograph to come find me and take me away from my parents.

My parents taught us at home at first, but when I was ten homeschool became too much for my parents to handle. Midway through the year, they enrolled my siblings and me in public school. My dad sat us down the night before our first day, prepared to answer our many questions. Some of us were already involved in community sports, so we weren't completely backward socially. But some siblings had questions: "Will they be rude to us?" "Do they know about us?"

Joe, Aunt Alina's son, was in the same grade at school, but we were put in different classes. We've always been close, growing up like twins. But now we avoided each other so we didn't get the inevitable questions, such as, "How are you related?" Saying we were brothers would bring on a slew of new questions: "How does that work? You don't look anything alike." We tried telling people we were cousins, but that didn't work, either. "How come you live in the same house?" "Why do you get picked up in a different car every day?" Eventually, we decided to call ourselves stepbrothers, but that still didn't stop the questions. Kids are relentless, and we were easy targets. Luckily, I was good at making friends.

One day, I was hanging out with a friend I'd known for a while when my mom called me home. My friend, who lived about a mile from my house, insisted on going with me. He wouldn't take no for an answer. I spent the whole walk trying to figure out a way to tell him about my family. As we neared my driveway, I finally said, "My dad's a polygamist."

"I know," he said. That was it. I'm sure he figured he would have all his questions answered in about thirty seconds. My siblings were certainly surprised to see someone not related to them in our house. It was the first time any of us had brought a school friend over.

Some people had a lot more questions once they caught on to our lifestyle, but they didn't know how to ask them. I loved the questions because I loved changing people's misconceptions about my family. There were some questions, though, that didn't deserve an answer. One time, a friend's mom asked if all my siblings slept in the same bed. I laughed in her face; she'd watched too many cartoons in her life. I had nineteen siblings by the time I was fourteen, but take away the numbers and we were like any other family.

A lot of times my family would get wrongly associated with people like Warren Jeffs, the FLDS prophet. I didn't like it when that happened. I didn't know anything more about him or his group than the average person does. And the things I heard about him didn't sound anything like what my experience had been.

Music has always been a huge part of my life. When I was in eighth grade, I saved up a hundred dollars and my dad put in another hundred so I could buy myself an electric guitar. This new guitar was black and white and gorgeous, my most prized possession. I would race home from school every day to play it. After a few months, I had written several songs. That Christmas, one of my friends got a bass guitar and another got a drum set. We decided to start a band. I would walk a mile every day to practice. Our early influences were bands like Blink 182, but as I got older, I gravitated toward darker music—bands like Senses Fail and Atreyu. My band collected a small following, and I was getting a good amount of attention at school, especially from girls.

I started secretly dating one girl in particular. I was in love, but she was like the devil on my shoulder. I began sneaking out in the middle of the night, sometimes just with her, sometimes with other kids. One night, my parents found my bed empty. I didn't have a cell phone, so my dad called a friend who happened to be with me.

"Anyone recognize this number?" my friend asked, since the number came up without a name. I looked at the screen, which showed my parents' number. I figured I was already in trouble so I didn't bother responding. Then a text came in: "If you're not home in five minutes, we're calling the cops." I ran the whole way home. My iPod, skateboard, and guitar had all been confiscated in my absence, and I was grounded.

Shortly after that episode, I came to my senses and dumped my girlfriend, but I was still making stupid decisions. My friend had an older brother who was about one color short of a rainbow. One night, we talked him into driving us to meet up with some girls. One girl's mom bought us two six-packs of Bacardi coolers. *Wow, what a cool mom,* I thought. *I can't imagine my mom doing this.* I drank a couple and got a little buzz.

It got late and we headed home. We had made sure my friend's brother didn't drink anything, but he was spacey enough by nature that he forgot to turn on the car's headlights. We got pulled over by a cop, who immediately smelled alcohol and called for backup. Three more cop cars pulled up. One officer called my parents and my dad drove up within minutes, screeching to a halt and then storming across the street toward us. He approached the officer who was writing out a ticket for me. The cop took one look at my dad and dropped his pen. "I think he is going to be worse off in your hands," he said, putting away his pad.

After I got in my dad's car, he drove upward of a hundred miles an hour along the deserted streets leading to our house. Finally, he pulled over to the side of the road. He seemed so mad I almost expected him to hit me, but I sneaked a peek at his face and realized he looked like someone had died.

"Of all my children, I never thought it would be you," he said. "You are old enough to make your own decisions, but do you really want this on your conscience?"

He went on for a bit in that vein. I didn't say a word. I expected to be grounded at the least, but there was no punishment named. My dad didn't talk to me for a week, though—he was that upset. I guess that was all I needed. It was a major turning point for me. I realized that being honest and upfront was so much easier than trying to keep track of all my lies. From then on, I had a really good relationship with all of my parents.

By the time I got to high school, I didn't really fit in anywhere. I didn't relate to the jocks and I didn't do drugs or drink, but I didn't feel accepted by most of the Mormons, either. I found a place with the Straight Edge kids—a subculture of the punk music scene that called for a clean and sober lifestyle, abstaining from tobacco, alcohol, and drugs. Some Straight Edgers were militant about their views, which is why my parents didn't like where I was headed. They told me I would be judged because of my clothes, music, and friends, but I didn't see it. They were worried, particularly since a couple years earlier, a cousin of mine was with his Straight Edge friends when they got in a fight and ended up killing someone. I was never very rigid about it, but putting a label like that on myself made it almost impossible to avoid violence. Still, doing so helped me stay away from a lot of other negative behaviors.

Music became my outlet. I started another band and we began to play wherever we could. Our drummer got into a lot of hot water by becoming involved with other people's girlfriends, and he dragged us into his drama. Normally, I would never hang out with someone like him, but that was one of the sacrifices I made to play music. Eventually, it started becoming unsafe to play or be seen in certain areas because of his antics and other developments in the local Straight Edge scene.

One night, we played a show in the garage of a friend's house. We were just packing up when a group of Straight Edge kids appeared out of the night. They were wearing bandannas and hoods, and carrying weapons—quick sticks, baseball bats, brass knuckles. A huge fight broke out. We fought them off for a while, and then they retreated down the road. My friend and I decided to get out while we could. We had parked at a church down the road. It turned out that's where the attackers had gathered to plan their next move. They saw us across the parking lot and started running toward us. Just as we got in and locked the doors, they swarmed my car. It was like an awful scene in a movie. I could hear them crawling over my roof and punching at my car windows. I was fully aware of the situation, but completely calm. It was as though something or someone was controlling me. I started the car and backed up. Then someone bashed my window in. I snapped out of my trance and sped off.

I quit my band and began to rethink the direction my life was heading. I had felt good about the Straight Edge movement until that point. But after that night, I lost whatever passion I had left for it. We were supposed to be standing up for the same things, and yet here we were all fighting with each other. It wasn't what I'd signed up for.

By my last year in high school, I'd started listening to different artists and styles of music. One that I particularly connected with was Bob Dylan. I immersed myself in his songs, dissecting each and every word. I started writing folk songs of my own under the name the Mighty Sequoyah. I began to love everything about folk music. It's so timeless, gives me a lot of creativity as an artist, and allows me to reflect my cultural roots. After going through lots of different lineups, my brother Jed and I now have a full band.

I was seventeen when I graduated from high school. I've since moved out and am going to college. I have no reservations about my family. I'm very close with all my mothers, though I'd be lying if I said there wasn't a special connection between my biological mom and me. People often ask me how my dad does it with three wives and twenty-plus children. The answer is pretty simple: my dad has incredible time management skills. He doesn't come home and turn on the television; when he's home he catches up with his kids and works to stay involved in all of our lives. I love my family, and my background hasn't been nearly as much of an obstacle for me as for some of my siblings. I was always pretty open about it. Even though some people had misconceptions and prejudices, I always felt that after meeting my family their negative opinions would go away. For me, my parents are a great example of people living the best way they know how and making it work.

I have a strong testimony of Jesus Christ, but I struggle with faith all the time. Right now, I don't see myself following in my parents' footsteps; it's hard enough to find *one* woman who's a good match. But I can't say definitely yes or definitely no, because there's no telling what the future holds.

Amanda, age nineteen: Valerie's oldest daughter

MY EARLIEST CHILDHOOD MEMORIES are from Pleasant Valley, where I grew up surrounded by lots of sisters who were my age. Aunt S., Aunt C., and Aunt C. C., my other moms, cared for me just like any of their own kids. We went freely from one house to another to eat and play, but unless there was a sleepover, we always went home at night. We had a great time playing with the cows, lambs, and chickens our family kept. But the best times we had were in a huge junkyard at the edge of the property—an area full of old cars. We'd climb in one and pretend we were going some- where. There was a giant truck that had a steering wheel so big you could slip your legs through its openings and rock back and forth. We'd fight at times as siblings do, but after a twenty-second rebound, we'd be back at it.

As far as I could tell, our lives were perfect. But when I was seven, my mom moved us to Montana. We stayed at a grandmother's house on the way, where my mom sat us down in a spare bedroom to tell us what was happening. When she said she and my dad were divorcing, I started bawling. My older brother, Sam, looked at me and then said to my mom, "She's so stupid! She always cries." Then *he* started crying, and soon all of the younger kids were crying, too—not because they understood what was happening, but just because *we* were crying. My mom tried to make us feel better about the change, but it was hard. I missed my family that was still in Pleasant Valley, though I figured we would be going back there eventually. That's the idea my dad planted in my thoughts the few times he called: one day, all his wives would come back to him, he said.

Sam, who was nine, stepped in as the father figure in our family. My brother was awesome at taking care of me, no matter what. One day, a bunch of kids got into a huge snowball fight. One of my brother's friends threw a snowball that hit me in the stomach hard enough that I started crying. My brother tackled his friend and said, "Don't you ever hit my sister again!" Sam made sure I always had someone to walk with to school and never let anyone pick on me. My parents' divorce was harder on him than anyone else. Sam was more scared about the situation, which is why he thought he had to be so strong.

We hadn't been in Montana too long when we moved again, this time to a trailer next to my cousins' house in Utah. I had a hunch what was going on, but I didn't want to believe it. A few days after our move, my mom told me she was going to marry Uncle Joe, my cousins' dad. I didn't want my mom to marry someone else because that meant she wasn't going back to my dad. My older brother had a hard time with it, too. But I knew it was really happening after I saw Uncle Joe give my mom a quick kiss one day. After their marriage, we continued to live in the trailer for a couple years. My brother would talk to us at night as we fell asleep, telling us it was all going to be all right.

I had always been close to my Aunt Alina's daughter Laura, since we're the same age, but we developed an instant rivalry when my mom married Uncle Joe. When I was ten, we moved into the main house with the other families. Our parents put Laura and me in the same bedroom. We had fun together at times, making up songs and planning a future band, but mostly we fought. It got so bad, our parents moved me into a bedroom with my younger sister. My new bedroom was next to Aunt Alina's room, so we became really close. She was the mom I could joke with and always have a good time with; she also was the mom I talked to when I was too scared to go to my own mom. For a time, my relationship with Aunt Vick was more strained. I'm stubborn, and Aunt Vick is blunt. She didn't hold back in telling me when I fell short, which often hurt my feelings. It made me a better, stronger person in the end, and I love her very much now.

As for my new dad, he was "Uncle Joe" and I was determined to keep it that way. I was angry when I saw how easily my three younger siblings—who were twenty months, three years, and six years old—accepted Uncle Joe as their father. Like my older brother, I resisted Uncle Joe's efforts to build a relationship.

Sam had such a hard time adjusting to our new family that when he was fourteen, he went to live with my dad. I really missed him; I felt I had lost my big brother and my protector. And it was devastating for my mom, who felt helpless and didn't know how to reach out to him. Since then, Sam has drawn closer to my mom again.

My mom and Uncle Joe often talked to me about how important it was to be open and communicate, to work at a good relationship. I didn't want that to happen, but despite the wall I put up, I began to see how much Uncle Joe really cared about us and how hard he was trying to make everything work. I slowly began to accept him, but I continued to call him Uncle Joe even though I knew it would mean a lot to him to be referred to as my dad. Finally, when I was fifteen, I wrote Uncle Joe a letter on his birthday about what he meant to me. As I handed it to him, I gave him a hug and said, "Happy birthday, Dad!" Almost crying as he finished reading my note, he told me it was the best birthday present ever.

With so many people living together in one house, we all had to learn to share belongings and space. There was competition, followed by compromise, when it came to nearly everything: a seat on the couch, what television program we watched, space to work at the kitchen table, use of the bathroom. With a houseful of little kids and their little bladders, I heard a lot of, "Get out of the bathroom—you're taking too long!" I learned to show up on time at meals and eat fast if I wanted seconds.

As one of the older children in the family, I did my share of babysitting, but the moms mostly helped each other out with that. My mom would generally ask me to watch only her kids, so it never seemed like I was being given too much responsibility or being burdened. If all the parents went somewhere, there were usually several of us older kids watching over our own younger siblings.

It took me a few years to catch on that not everyone accepted my family. I probably didn't get as much attention about it because my last name is different from that of Aunt Alina's and Aunt Vick's kids. In seventh grade, my history teacher was giving a lesson on how the Mormon pioneers came to Utah, and he brought up polygamy. "Personally," he said, "I think all polygamist men are slut dogs." That night, I told my parents what the teacher had said. They contacted the principal to complain about the teacher's comment.

My parents always told us to be careful whom we talked to about our family—not because they feared being arrested, but because they knew that some people would make fun of us. I wasn't afraid to tell people; I just didn't know how to bring it up, so most of the time I didn't. Sometimes, my friends learned about it through their siblings who knew my older brothers. I mostly went to my friends' homes, inviting only friends I really trusted to my house. I was more afraid to tell people how big my family was than to tell them I had three mothers. If I was asked how many kids there were in my family, I would usually answer very carefully: "My mom has . . ." and fill in however many she had at the time. Sometimes, I would say my aunts and their children also lived with us.

By high school, my family background didn't seem like a big deal. Most of the kids I knew were open-minded and made up their own opinions about my family and me. Their parents were more likely to be judgmental. I played club soccer for years and was on my high school's team. I had never said anything to my teammates about my family. But in 2007, after my mom went on *Oprah* to talk about polygamy, one teammate's dad started acting really standoffish. If I said anything to him, he would just stare without acknowledging me, though he was friendly and talkative with my teammates. He kept it up for weeks. One day, that dad came to our house to give me a ride to a game. I was still getting ready so my friend had to come knock on our door to get me. When I got in their car, my friend's dad turned to me and said sharply, "Don't you ever make me have to send my daughter to your door again!" Shortly after that, I quit catching rides with them. It was too uncomfortable.

I sneaked around behind my parents' backs with boys during high school and even kissed some of them. I really liked one boy who was a Mormon and a super-good kid. He would get so scared when he came to our house that he would literally shake when he saw my dad, who was buff and bald and intimidating. The boy felt guilty because he knew we were engaging in inappropriate behavior. I learned a lot about guys and about myself and wouldn't take it back, but I soon realized I didn't want casual relationships like the one I had with that boy. I set higher moral standards for myself about how to dress, whom I associated with, and the kind of behavior I wanted to engage in before marriage.

My parents were consistent and sincere, but not forceful, in teaching us about their faith and what they believe. We learned good principles during our family Sunday school but also during family activities. On some family nights, we'd read together from such books as *To Kill a Mockingbird,* a family favorite, and *The*

Work and the Glory, a nine-part series about a fictional Mormon family. My dad has always said that he hopes we all will get a testimony about the religion—in other words, that we will feel our hearts touched personally by the Holy Spirit in a way that reinforces the truth of our religion—but that we each have to make that decision for ourselves. He encouraged me to attend different churches, from Baptist to other fundamentalist churches, while I was growing up, so I'd understand what others believe. My mom is the same way. We've talked about her decision to live plural marriage, but she's never told me I have to live it myself.

I recently had a testimony about my faith and now know I want to live plural marriage someday. I came to that decision by watching my parents' example and through my own prayers. I know it will be hard, but I know it's the right thing for me. But that's in the future. Right now, I am attending college in southern Utah and plan to become a dental hygienist.

My real dad has never been a big part of my life. By my choice, I see him only about three times a year. I am really close, though, to some of my sisters and their mothers from my first family. Our family ties remain strong and I love and care about them very much.

People think plural marriage is all about what's going on underneath the covers. That's not it. In 2006, I went on a television talk show with my mom and my sister Laura. The host asked if I thought my dad loved my mom more than the other moms. I was shocked by the question and responded with a loud, "No!" The audience cracked up laughing, which was embarrassing. I thought it was an absurd question. My dad loves all my moms equally.

We're pretty much like any other family, and aren't better or worse people because of our choice to have this particular kind of family. I don't think I should be treated differently or judged unfavorably just because I have a lot of brothers and sisters and more than two parents who love me.

CHAPTER TWELVE

Going Public

*In spite of the problems they face, some of these new forms of close
relationships—including plural families among contemporary Mormon
fundamentalists—are here to stay in American and Western society.
They are not likely to "go away"; they are not fads or fancies; they are
not aberrations. They will be part of the family life scene
well into the future. We must therefore learn about them, learn
from them, and even help people live the lifestyle of their choice.*

—IRWIN ALTMAN AND JOSEPH GINAT, RESEARCHERS AND AUTHORS
OF *Polygamous Families in Contemporary Society*

Val

IN 2006, POLYGAMY WAS a hot news topic as FLDS leader Warren
Jeffs made the FBI's Most Wanted list of fugitives. He was arrested
that August during a traffic stop in Nevada, triggering a massive
amount of media coverage, but there was little effort to clarify that
the FLDS do not represent all Fundamentalist Mormons. It
seemed all the educational efforts we'd undertaken in recent years

had achieved nothing, which was hard to take because it hadn't been easy to be more public about our lives. In fact, when we were first asked to be on the cover of *Mormon Focus*, we were filled with terror about the possible consequences. Posing for that 2003 cover was a bittersweet experience. Vicki and I held our youngest daughters, but Alina's arms were empty. Kyra was on each of our minds that day.

In the years that followed publication of the magazine, we'd done a handful of media interviews. Despite our familiarity with the process, the avalanche of interest in polygamy after Warren Jeffs's arrest was intense. National media, from CNN to NBC's *Nightly News,* reached out through Principle Voices with the same request: Can you get us a family to interview? Back then, the FLDS were notoriously averse to media, as were most plural families. Once again, we decided to step forward, even though every request brought a new round of anxiety and soul-searching about whether to further expose ourselves publicly. We accepted interview requests from reporters and college students around the world, who wanted to know more about our lifestyle and why we choose to live this way. We also gave numerous presentations to college classes and at conferences for social workers, child abuse experts, attorneys, and law enforcement officers. For the most part, Joe stayed in the shadows, while Alina, Vicki, and I took turns sharing our view of the plural life. Typically, we were identified only by our first names. Nonetheless, the criminal status of our lifestyle—in Utah, polygamy falls under the bigamy statute and is a third-degree felony—made us cautious in our answers to certain questions.

Before the second season of *Big Love,* the show reached out to the polygamous culture, and Vicki and I were among a handful of plural wives interviewed for a promotional documentary that launched the new season. My interview captured the hesitancy most polygamists feel when asked for personal information. A producer asked me what Joe does for a living.

"He . . . manages," I stuttered.

"So he's a professional?" the producer asked.

"Uh-huh," I said.

"So you're being discreet with me."

"I am. I don't want him to lose his job," I said.

I wasn't exaggerating. Joe's boss, who knew about our family, had explicitly told him to avoid being public. One major client had stopped doing business with Joe after a competitor e-mailed him a link to an interview Joe gave on CNN in 2006, even though Joe was shown in silhouette and not identified by name. That had chilled Joe's participation, even in a limited way, in interviews, but we carried on. One of my favorite experiences came in 2007, when Oprah said she had an "Aha!" moment when I appeared on her show to talk about my family.

"I heard your point, I really heard that when you said we live in a country with so many alternative lifestyles, and you're saying I want the right to be able to not be considered a criminal if I choose to live this way," Oprah said on air.

Then, as we said good-bye, Oprah added: "You have shed a different light on it. Just looking at you has been an eye-opening experience for me."

To hear Oprah—Oprah!—say that was really rewarding, because changing perspectives is what we're all about, why we put our family at risk for persecution when we go public in this way.

I was on the TV show *Larry King Live* the next year, in April 2008, and the CNN talk show host asked me if polygamy is better than monogamy.

"You could have monogamy because you're very attractive. I'm sure you could have been with many men and had children. Why is it more attractive to you?" King asked.

"That's exactly the point," I said. "I'm a thirty-eight-year-old woman who *chooses* to live this way, and I should be able to if I want to. . . . This lifestyle has been going on for centuries.* It didn't just start up recently with the Mormon church. And there are challenges. I think there are challenges in and struggles in any marriage relationship."

"But you prefer it, right?" King prodded.

"I certainly prefer it," I told him.

But it was Troy Roberts of the TV show *48 Hours* who asked me the question that stumps many people I've met: "How does sharing your husband with other women enhance your spiritual lives?" Roberts asked.

"We learn a lot of things about ourselves; we learn about our emotions," I said.

"Can you see living your life any other way?" he asked.

"I can hardly imagine it," I told him.

---

* Stephanie Coontz, author of *Marriage, a History* (New York: Viking, 2005), is among researchers who note that plural marriage is found in "more places and at more times than any other" marital form in the world (p. 10). According to the 1998 *Ethnographic Atlas Codebook*, of 1,231 documented societies, 186 were monogamous, 453 had occasional polygyny (a man with multiple wives), 588 had frequent polygyny, and 4 were polyandrous (a woman with multiple husbands). See J. Patrick Gray, "A Corrected Ethnographic Atlas," *World Cultures* 10, no. 1 (1999): 24–85.

The point is, I don't feel I have any less love or joy in my life because Joe has relationships with Alina and Vicki. In fact, I have more. And, as I told Oprah, in this day and age of alternative lifestyles, I should be able to make this choice—just as other adults, such as homosexuals and polyamorists, are able to structure their personal relationships however they choose.

Altogether, Joe, Alina, Vicki, and I have nearly a hundred siblings. Some of them knew they would pursue plural marriage from childhood; others sought it out later in life. We have siblings who believe in plural marriage but have never had the opportunity to live it, and some who entered plural marriages that, for one reason or another, didn't work out. We also have siblings who, as adults, never followed the fundamentalist faith.

Joe, for example, is the only one of his father's seventeen children who is in a plural marriage. This is a typical pattern among the fundamentalists we know: not every person raised this way decides to adopt the lifestyle. Our family is typical in another way, too. Mega-families in which a man, such as Winston Blackmore of Canada or FLDS leader Warren Jeffs, has dozens of wives are an anomaly. Most plural families we know consist of a husband and two or three wives.*

Plural marriage is only one aspect of our faith, and it is not the only acceptable form of marriage in our culture. It is not *essential* to get into heaven, as many critics of the lifestyle falsely assert. Mormon theology holds that there are three different degrees of

---

* Historian Jessie L. Embry, in her earlier-cited book, found that 60 percent of men who practiced polygamy in the nineteenth century had just two wives, while 20 percent had three and 10 percent had four (p. 34).

glory (or levels of heaven) that a person can attain in the afterlife, with the highest being the celestial degree. Fundamentalist Mormons believe that to reach that level, it is necessary to live celestial marriage.

My capacity to love has changed as a result of living the Principle, and so has that of my children. I see that every day, in many ways. Not long ago, our sons Caleb and Jed, who have a folk band, put on a concert for family and friends to raise money to produce a music CD. The event became a family affair. Their little sisters helped prepare snacks and cookies for a bake sale. Their brothers built a stage and set up lights and chairs in our big garage. As the concert got under way, we found that the boys had a surprise for us: the warm-up act was our sons Louis, Grayson, Tavish, and Logan, who accompanied Jed on a number. The older boys had taught the younger ones a song, taking time to practice it with them so it was show-worthy. Caleb and Jed also arranged for their sisters Amanda and Liesl to perform during the concert. As I stood watching our children come together like this, I felt wonderfully gratified to know we'd helped them form bonds that will last beyond a lifetime. My tears really flowed when Caleb performed a song he'd written for us moms about growing up in a plural family where there was always "love, love, love." This is the kind of family moment many people don't connect with our lifestyle, and yet it is at the heart of it all.

And just like Larry King and Oprah, a lot of people are surprised by my appearance—very mainstream!—and think I'm an anomaly. Trust me, I'm not. I know and associate with many people in our culture who look and dress and act just like anyone else in society. Sometimes when I meet people, I can tell by the look on their faces that I don't fit their preconceived notion of plural wives as oppressed women who are forced into this lifestyle. It is an inaccurate stereotype that is hard to shake.

When Joe and I were on our honeymoon in Hawaii, we met a guy who asked us where we were from.

"Salt Lake City," Joe told him.

"Oh, so you're one of those polygamists!" the man said.

"Yes, I'm the third wife and this is our honeymoon," I replied.

Laughing uproariously, he walked away never suspecting that we had told him the honest truth. The point is, a lot of times people don't know when they are looking a polygamist in the face. That said, I respect the choice of some Fundamentalist Mormons, such as the FLDS, to wear clothing that distinguishes them and reflects a group identity and religiously based modesty. In that regard, they are not unlike the Amish, who also use clothing to reflect their spiritual principles.

Over the years, I've sometimes faced hostile audiences and interviewers who have spoken as though all polygamous experiences were the same, or have claimed that polygamy is inherently abusive and that no women in this lifestyle are happy. It's just not true, and I don't appreciate blanket assumptions of that sort being made about me or about my family. Sometimes, attempts to belittle the way we live are outlandish. In January 2011, Alina testified about her experience as a plural wife in historic court proceedings before the Supreme Court of British Columbia, which was deciding whether Canada's law against polygamy is constitutional under the country's Charter of Rights and Freedoms. Alina described the free choice she exercised in entering plural marriage, how it is a spiritual practice for her, and how much love there is in our family. She was asked whether she had the freedom to choose to live with multiple husbands. Alina answered the way any of us would, telling the court she has the freedom to make that choice, but it isn't in keeping with her personal values.

As a family, we have come a long way since our first tentative steps into the public spotlight with *Mormon Focus*. The questions we get now run along familiar tracks: Do you get jealous? Are you treated badly? Do you have arranged marriages? What is the doctrine behind it? Do you encourage your children to live this way? Given that polygamy is against the law, why do you still choose to live it? Are you afraid of prosecution? Persecution? You now know the answer to many of those questions.

My goal is for people to see how human I am, to realize I could be their neighbor, and to understand that I deserve as many rights and as much respect as they do. My message is simple: I live this way *by choice,* and I am content with and fulfilled by my life.

We've had mixed reactions from some Fundamentalist Mormons about our decision to go public. The old-school folks say it won't do any good and we are putting our family in jeopardy. The younger people say it's awesome that we are willing to stand up for what we believe and our right to structure our families as we choose. We get that mixed reaction from our relatives and children, too. We allow our older children to make their own decisions about whether to participate in media interviews. We let our children, even the younger ones, know when one of us is likely to be in the news, and try to insulate them as much as possible from the repercussions of our public appearances. But at times a backlash is inescapable, such as Amanda experienced with her soccer teammate's dad (described in the previous chapter). Our children have had a particularly hard time on those occasions when we've agreed to do an interview and then had our comments subsequently misused, twisted, or dismissed. The online comments posted with some stories have been hurtful and even scary. We've had friends and business clients shun us. Once, a stranger showed up on our doorstep wanting to get to know our family after one of us appeared on a talk show. These experiences have drawn us together as a family to talk about the value of civil rights, free speech, and correct principles.

We consider our marriage sacred, and very traditional in all respects. Its foundation rests on five of the six marriage dimensions identified by the Coalition for Marriage, the Institute for American Values, and other marriage proponents. There is a financial partnership, a sacred promise, a sexual union, a personal bond, and a family-making bond. The dimension it lacks is legal recognition.

I am not asking for and don't expect plural marriage to receive official state approval, but I believe unique bigamy laws that make polygamy a felony are unfair. Utah's bigamy statute reads: "A person is guilty of bigamy when, knowing he has a husband or wife or knowing the other person has a husband or wife, the person purports to marry another person or cohabits with another person." Several states have similar statutes. Massachusetts and New Mexico, for example, explicitly refer to polygamy as a crime. Prosecutors turn a blind eye to other bigamous relationships— when a spouse is separated or not yet divorced and lives with a new partner, for instance—but threaten, and sometimes use the law to go after men who want to acknowledge, honor, and support their multiple partners through a religious bond.

Decriminalizing polygamy would go a long way toward bringing the practice out of the shadows so families like ours can live openly and honestly. It would also make it more likely that when problems do occur, people who need help can seek it without fear that their lifestyle will take the focus off real issues. Decriminalization would end my fear about how much I can tell people about myself and about my family, and what my children can say about their parents, their brothers, and their sisters. Ultimately, I want my children's generation to grow up with pride in their cultural and religious heritage, and—if they choose this lifestyle— without worry that the state might raid their homes and remove their children simply because of the way they've put together their families.

Joe

AFTER KYRA'S DEATH, I was angry about what my family had been through, angrier still that our lifestyle had driven the state's suspicion, and downright furious that the state now wanted to dictate how I lived. I had a choice: stand up for my faith or cower behind my fear. I picked the first option. I vowed to get to know the people who were using negative assumptions about my lifestyle to bring the power of the state against me. I decided I would put meaning and purpose to Kyra's death by trying to correct misguided notions and stereotypes about our culture. When a relative invited me to give a presentation about my experience to a nonprofit advocacy group called Utah Children, I readily accepted. It was my first time speaking publicly about my lifestyle.

That led to an invitation to serve on Utah Children's Polygamy Study Group subcommittee, which was helping service providers reach out to polygamous families. My assignment was to help state workers understand the Fundamentalist Mormon man's perspective. My ultimate goal, though, was to change *their* perspective so no other polygamous family would have to experience what we did when Kyra died. I found I liked working behind the scenes with agency directors and caseworkers. For the first time in my life, I introduced myself by saying, "Hi, I'm Joe, and I'm a polygamist," which drew either stunned silence or nervous laughter. I even met with the director of the state's child welfare division and shared my experience with his agency. In addition, with other committee members I visited editorial boards of several Utah newspapers to urge them to stop painting Fundamentalist Mormons with a broad brush.

The subcommittee was the precursor to a very different organization, one that I've mentioned earlier: Principle Voices, which advocates for Fundamentalist Mormons. Anne Wilde, Mary Batchelor, Linda Kelsch, and Marianne Watson, who are all part of the culture, founded the organization in 2003. Wilde also was a driving force behind *Mormon Focus,* the magazine that featured my wives on its inaugural cover. Principle Voices' twofold mission is to help the public understand our culture and to educate fundamentalists about laws and social services available to them. It has taken an unwavering stand against underage marriage and abuse of any kind and advocates for the decriminalization of the bigamy laws that make polygamy a felony.

Principle Voices also took the lead in organizing the Polygamy Action Committee, an unprecedented gathering of the major Fundamentalist Mormon groups (except the FLDS). Because of doctrinal and leadership differences, the various factions had had little interaction—in some cases, a divide that extended back decades. The Fundamentalist Mormon movement is so big and diverse, so mistrustful of government and, sometimes, each other, that it is difficult to get everyone under the same tent. It was a real feat to bring people together to discuss common concerns and ways we might join forces to promote understanding of our culture and defend our rights, despite our differences. The committee, which continues to meet monthly, is now known as the Principle Rights Coalition, and I have presided as its chairman since the end of 2007. In recent years, we've sponsored educational seminars, given public presentations, taken an active lobbying role when appropriate, and engaged in service projects, public awareness rallies, and charity fund-raisers. In 2010, for example, the coalition organized a talent show and raised $1,800 for Utah's domestic violence hotline.

The coalition also is helping government agencies understand the barriers our criminal status creates, how it pushes us underground and into difficult decisions, and why decriminalization would benefit the government and Fundamentalist Mormons who practice polygamy. Here's an example from my own life. With most of our children, I was able to list myself as the father on their birth certificate applications. Changes to Utah law now require an unmarried father to file a paternity declaration before he can be listed on a birth certificate. I can assure you that I am not the only polygamist who has concerns about filing such paperwork with the government! As a result, my name is not listed on my daughter Tori's birth certificate.

Years ago, Utah Children wanted to make sure polygamous families had access to services designed to protect the health and well-being of children, such as the food stamp and low-income health insurance programs. I pointed out the difficulty plural families had trusting that the information they disclosed would not be shared with law enforcement agencies. I also pointed out the challenges plural families have filling out aid applications completely and honestly. For example, is it fraud to apply under the status "single mother" given that the state does not recognize polygamous unions? When listing members of one's household, is the entire plural family counted? Does it make a difference if the plural family lives in one home or in separate residences?

By the way, plural wives who are not legally married to their husbands may apply as single mothers for food stamps and government-funded children's health insurance programs provided they fully disclose household income, including any support they receive from their children's fathers. Those programs are available to assist children from fundamentalist families, just as they are children of unmarried moms or impoverished families in every state. But the point is, from health insurance applications to tax returns, Fundamentalist Mormons are often relegated to "none of the above" choices.

There are all sorts of calculations that I run through when someone asks me about my "wife" or children. The question I hate most is "How many children do you have?" The minute I answer truthfully and say, "Twenty-four," I've given myself away. So I do a quick assessment: What does this person already know about my family, and which other family members might he or she know? Our answers have to match up, after all. When a dentist recently asked me how many children I had, I decided that since Alina also had an appointment with him, I would give the answer that fit her: seven. My words are always chosen carefully—in that case, "My wife Alina and I have seven children."

The Principle Rights Coalition has accomplished much over the past decade, successfully making our voice heard in legislative debates that directly and indirectly affect us, such as bills on midwifery, marriage, homeschooling, and parents' right to shape the religious education of their children. And individually, a growing number of Fundamentalist Mormons also are speaking up in defense of the lifestyle and their civil rights. Two fathers, one in Utah and one who formerly lived in Pennsylvania, have successfully waged court battles when a divorce threatened to cut them off from associating with their children because of their Fundamentalist views and belief in polygamy. Kody Brown and his four wives also have stepped forward to showcase the polygamous lifestyle in a reality show on TLC, a cable television network. But there are consequences to going public, as the Browns found. A county prosecutor launched an investigation into the family on possible bigamy charges after the first episodes of the show aired in 2010. One wife lost her job and Kody, an advertising salesman, noted that his business suffered as well. Under financial and legal pressure, the family was forced to move from Utah to Nevada. We undertook this book knowing we might face similar repercussions.

So there is more to do, particularly in regard to the laws targeting polygamy. As numerous legal experts have pointed out, the reasoning in the 1879 U.S. Supreme Court's decision in *Reynolds v. United States,* which upholds bigamy statutes that target polygamy, is racist, outdated, and unfounded given today's mores. But the decision stands. Utah and Arizona authorities have, to date, not been willing to take on the kind of case most likely to trigger a review—one involving consenting adults like us who have committed no other crimes and whose religious beliefs are at the heart of our plural marriage.

Legal experts see a precedent for what might happen were such a case to be put forth in the high court's 2003 ruling in *Lawrence v. Texas*. The case involved two homosexual men charged with sodomy. The sodomy laws, the court noted, were aimed at controlling a personal relationship that, while not recognized by law, is "within the liberty of the persons to choose without being punished as criminals." In its ruling, the court found that the Fourteenth Amendment protects liberty rights that involve "the most intimate and personal choices a person may make in a lifetime." The court said Texas's sodomy laws touched on "the most private human conduct, sexual behavior, and in the most private of places, the home."

The *Lawrence* decision also held that a law that brands "one class of persons as criminal solely based on the State's moral disapproval of that class and the conduct associated with that class runs contrary to the values of the Constitution and the Equal Protection Clause, under any standard of review." That's the effect bigamy laws have on consenting adult polygamists like me: we are branded as criminals and subjected to discrimination.*

The truth is, the fallibility of human nature that leads to terrible abuse can be found in every culture and segment of society, including my own culture and our extended families. But there are adequate laws to root out those problems without trampling on civil liberties. Part of the mission of Principle Voices is to ensure that resources are available when plural families need help and that problems are addressed in a healthy, proactive manner.

Critics often claim that polygamy is inherently abusive. A more true statement would be to say that *monogamy* inherently breeds abuse. One example: in 2010 alone, seven women in my home state of Utah who were in monogamous dating, cohabiting, or married relationships were killed by their intimate partners. In more than 170 years of Mormon polygamy, I am unaware of *any* woman murdered by her husband. (I am speaking here only about polygamy among early Mormons and current Fundamentalist Mormons.)

Far more children are sexually and physically abused—and even killed—by boyfriends and fathers who are in monogamous dating, cohabiting, and married relationships with their mothers.

---

* The chief justice of the Utah Supreme Court has taken a similar view, arguing in a dissenting opinion in one polygamy-related case that the state cannot "constitutionally criminalize private, religiously motivated consensual relationships between adults." There is no justification, the justice noted, for "the broad criminalization of [a] religious practice itself as a means of attacking other criminal behavior." *State v. Holm,* 137 P.3d 726 (Utah 2006).

Likewise, across the United States tens of thousands of adolescents run away from their homes or are permanently abandoned by their parents each year, yet it is often a media event when a child leaves a polygamous family.

Yet there have been terrible events involving one group of fundamentalists in recent years. I am horrified by the allegations that FLDS leader Warren Jeffs manipulated numerous families into handing over their underage daughters, some as young as twelve, to be spiritually married and then sexually abused by him. In my opinion, he has taken advantage of his followers' fear of the government and of prosecution to shield his actions. Decriminalization would decrease the likelihood that someone like Jeffs could use the law as a tool to keep people silent and compliant.

Utah was required to add language to its state constitution, adopted in 1895, banning polygamy as a condition of statehood (Arizona's constitution contains a similar ban). In 1935, the Utah legislature increased the criminal status of bigamy from a misdemeanor to a third-degree felony, punishable by up to five years in prison—which led to some of our ancestors' lengthy imprisonments in "crowbar college," as my Grandpa Dave used to call it. He was sent to prison in the mid-1940s, along with my other grandfather, Albert E. Barlow, and some of my wives' forebears.

In Utah, that bigamy law is rarely enforced. In fact, the state attorney general has said, given current limited resources, he will go after only polygamists who have committed other crimes, such as child abuse (to which bigamy charges are often added). Like the founders of Principle Voices, I want to see bigamy returned to its misdemeanor status and the law changed to read as follows: "A person is guilty of bigamy when he or she is civilly married and undertakes to secure a second or additional civil marriage." That articulates the fraud against the state that was originally the intent of bigamy laws.

Like most Fundamentalist Mormon polygamous men, I have remained largely and sometimes literally in the shadows because of a very real fear of economic repercussions and of being prosecuted for bigamy. I am not seeking state sanction for my marriages, but I should not be at risk of criminal prosecution when the religiously motivated way I have structured my family is paralleled by commonplace, secular lifestyle choices. Hugh Hefner's lifestyle is celebrated in popular culture and featured on television shows, but how is his living with three girlfriends at a time more acceptable than our choice to build a family together?

The current bigamy laws are not stopping the religiously based practice of polygamy; all they do, as is evident from the past, is force believers underground, into isolation and secretive behavior. Such laws will continue to make abusive behavior, when it does occur, more difficult to detect and give cover to men and group leaders who are unscrupulous.

The debate about polygamy often overlooks personal choice and constitutional liberty rights. I want the right to structure my family and my personal relationships with other consenting adults as I see fit. I want tolerance for unions like mine, entered into freely and willingly by consenting adults who are motivated by religious belief and whose conduct cannot be shown to pose any substantial harm to the state or to those under its protection.

We are nothing more than a family, one that experiences the same challenges but also the same joys as any other family. For me, that's watching my children make a circle of giant pumpkins in the front yard and use them as seats for a game of Duck Duck Goose. It's helping put on a Sunday brunch for a father-in-law's seventieth birthday, a gathering that brought out close to one hundred relatives. And it's what happened just last summer.

We'd pulled a hose across the back lawn, dividing the grassy area into sides for a crazy game of dodgeball. Vicki was on one side and I was on the other, and all my children were divvied up between us. As seven dodgeballs flew back and forth, so did the laughs. Up on the deck, Val visited with her parents. Across the lawn, Alina prepped hamburger patties for the grill. I couldn't stop grinning as I looked around, and I saw that each of my wives had the same smile on her face. This is just the way we always hoped our lives would be.

That is where it all comes home for me: my family. I am so proud of the courage and character my wives and some of my children have shown in speaking up for the right to live the way they choose despite the strong opposition determined to silence our voices. Like them, I am no longer willing to let our family and our beliefs be defined and defiled by detractors, the uninformed, and those who fled unhappy plural marriages and broken families. I hope telling our story increases public understanding of our lifestyle so that our children, whether they choose to follow our example or not, will be spared the prejudices, misconceptions, and fears we have endured. This is, after all, a country founded on religious freedom, a country that proclaims respect for personal choice when it comes to life, liberty, and the pursuit of happiness.

A BRIEF OVERVIEW OF
FUNDAMENTALIST MORMONISM AND
THE PRACTICE OF POLYGAMY

ALINA, VICKI, VAL, AND I have cultural, family, and religious reasons for deciding to live plural marriage. It was a personal choice each of us made, as adults, after giving the matter prayerful consideration and much thought. As Independents, our family believes that the only church authorized by Joseph Smith is the Church of Jesus Christ of Latter-day Saints, which serves as a teaching institution to spread the gospel throughout the world. The church may not claim us, but we claim it, even though we believe there is more to the gospel than the church currently sanctions.

While plural marriage was introduced by Joseph Smith earlier in the church's history, it wasn't until August 29, 1852, that the LDS Church publicly acknowledged polygamy—specifically, polygyny—as a key tenet of the faith. Newspapers of the day quoted church president Brigham Young, who characterized celestial marriage as "one of the best doctrines ever proclaimed to any people." At the time, there were no federal laws barring polygamy.

But Congress, led by the Republican Party and its campaign against the "twin relics of barbarism" (slavery and polygamy), soon took measures to shut down the practice in the United States and its territories. First came the Morrill Anti-Bigamy Act of 1862, which banned bigamy and "spiritual marriages" and capped the LDS Church's property holdings at $50,000. In 1874, Brigham Young enlisted George Reynolds, secretary to the church's first presidency, as a cooperative defendant to test the constitutionality of the Morrill Act. Reynolds was convicted in 1875. The Utah Supreme Court upheld the decision, which was then appealed to the U.S. Supreme Court, the first freedom of religion case to go before the high court. In January 1879, the court unanimously rejected the claim that the First Amendment protected polygamy, which it described as an "odious" practice common among "Asiatic and African people." The Constitution barred attempts to limit belief, but not practice, the court said. Reynolds served four and a half years in prison before being released in 1881. Four years later, he married his third wife. Reynolds was named as a church apostle in 1890.

The Edmunds-Tucker Act of 1887 finally put the church in a corner. The act called for the church's disincorporation and, with the exception of houses of worship, confiscation of holdings over $50,000. The act also repealed the right of women in the Utah territory to vote (which they had held since 1870), replaced local judges with federally appointed judges, required civil marriage licenses, annulled inheritance rights of illegitimate children, required wives to testify against husbands charged with polygamy or cohabitation, and gave federal appointees control of school textbook selection.

In May 1890, the U.S. Supreme Court rejected the denomination's challenge to the $50,000 property cap and the property seizures, calling plural marriage "contrary to the spirit of Christianity." Four months later, LDS president Wilford Woodruff issued an "official declaration"—addressed "To Whom It May Concern"—denying that the church taught or authorized plural marriages and pledging to follow the law. Known as the Woodruff Manifesto, it read in part as follows:

INASMUCH AS LAWS HAVE BEEN ENACTED BY CONGRESS FORBIDDING PLURAL MARRIAGES, WHICH LAWS HAVE BEEN PRONOUNCED CONSTITUTIONAL BY THE COURT OF THE LAST RESORT, I HEREBY DECLARE MY INTENTION TO SUBMIT TO THOSE LAWS, AND TO USE MY INFLUENCE WITH THE MEMBERS OF THE CHURCH OVER WHICH I PRESIDE TO HAVE THEM DO LIKEWISE. . . . AND I NOW PUBLICLY DECLARE THAT MY ADVICE TO THE LATTER-DAY SAINTS IS TO REFRAIN FROM CONTRACTING ANY MARRIAGE FORBIDDEN BY THE LAW OF THE LAND.

Despite the 1890 Manifesto, many church members, leaders, and patriarchs continued to live in and enter new plural marriages. According to historians, including B. Carmon Hardy and D. Michael Quinn, the LDS Church solemnized more than two hundred plural marriages between 1890 and 1904.* The LDS Church reiterated the prohibition in 1904 and 1933.

* See, for example, D. Michael Quinn, "LDS Church Authority and New Plural Marriages, 1890–1904," *Dialogue: A Journal of Mormon Thought* 18, (Spring 1985): 9–105; B. Carmon Hardy, *Solemn Covenant: The Mormon Polygamous Passage*, Urbana and Chicago: Univ. of Illinois Press, 1992.

Most Fundamentalist Mormons believe that John Taylor, the church's third president, was given divine instructions in anticipation of the 1890 Manifesto. In 1886, he received a revelation directing him to ensure that plural marriage continued as a law of the priesthood, a line of authority operating separately and distinctly from that of the church. President Taylor subsequently appointed five men to join him in the Priesthood Council (also referred to as the Council of Friends), and placed them under oath to ensure that no year passed without children being born in the celestial law of plural marriage. He also authorized the men—Samuel Bateman, Charles H. Wilkins, George Q. Cannon, John W. Woolley, and Lorin C. Woolley—to ordain others to carry on the work. Taylor later added Joseph F. Smith as the council's seventh member; Smith eventually became the church's sixth president.* Operating under the law of the priesthood, plural marriage continued.

Since the 1930s, the fundamentalist movement has splintered into different factions with unique cultures and practices. Most of the fractures in the fundamentalist movement occurred because of leadership disputes, which are now reflected in how each group is governed. A council guides some of the groups, while others have a single leader who is assisted by a priesthood council. The largest groups have lay ecclesiastical leaders, such as bishops, who preside over specific congregations. They also have meetinghouses where members gather for religious services.

* Lynn L. Bishop and Steven L. Bishop refer to Smith's appointment to the Priesthood Council in their book, *The Keys of the Priesthood Illustrated* (Draper, UT: Review and Preview Publishers, 1971), 154.

As in any segment of society, there are occasional instances of individuals who run afoul of the law and engage in abusive behavior. Through Principle Voices and the Principle Rights Coalition, we have strongly condemned such acts.

In recent years, all of the groups have taken a strong, public stand against underage marriage and abuse; in 2008, the FLDS were the last to step forward and publicly say the church would no longer approve underage marriages. With Warren Jeffs still in charge, it is unclear whether that edict stands, though authorities say they are unaware of any such marriages occurring since his arrest in 2006. The FLDS are the only group that practice placement (arranged) marriage, though members of other groups sometimes seek counsel from leaders about suitable marriage partners.

In 2010, Principle Voices estimated there were 38,000 Fundamentalist Mormons (a count that includes men, women, and children) in the United States, Canada, and Mexico. Most are in Utah, Arizona, and nearby states, with scatterings of fundamentalists throughout the country. All fundamentalists consider polygamy a religious tenet, but probably fewer than half are living in plural families, according to Anne Wilde, cofounder of Principle Voices. Here is a brief overview of each community:

Independents

There are approximately 15,000 Fundamentalist Mormons who consider themselves Independents, which means they do not follow a leader, belong to any organized group, or have membership in a church. Some Independents, like our family, trace their practice of plural marriage to the original Priesthood Council. There also are Independents who've come to their beliefs through study of early LDS Church teachings. Independents believe that their primary charge, along with abiding by the gospel, is to perpetuate plural marriage, which is why they avoid organized communities, churches, and groups.

Fundamentalist Church of Jesus Christ of Latter-Day Saints

Referred to as the FLDS Church, this group has about 10,000 members. The sect's name has caused endless confusion for other Fundamentalist Mormons as well as the LDS Church, both of which are often erroneously associated with the group.

Known originally as "The Work," the sect has been based since the 1930s in what are now the twin towns of Hildale, Utah, and Colorado City, Arizona. The FLDS Church was not incorporated until 1991, however. The FLDS also has sizable communities in British Columbia, Colorado, South Dakota, Nevada, and Texas, and there are members living in many other states as well.

Members of the FLDS are distinguished by their conservative clothing and, for women, unique hairstyles, but not all members dress in the prescribed style, particularly those living outside Utah, Arizona, and Texas. Believers practice the Law of Consecration and Stewardship (United Order), an early tenet of Mormonism revealed to Joseph Smith. As part of that, the group holds property in common and relies on joint efforts in community building. The FLDS community in Eldorado, Texas, which features a gleaming limestone temple as a centerpiece, is a testament to the community's remarkable ability to pool money and to its members' industriousness and construction skills.

In 2005, a Utah court assumed control of the FLDS Church's United Effort Plan Trust, which holds virtually all property in Hildale and Colorado City, after finding mismanagement by trustees. The trust was embroiled in state and federal lawsuits as this book was being completed.

The group practices placement (arranged) marriage and believes those unions are inspired by God, who delivers that information to the prophet. Women, but not men, may also pray for inspiration about whom to marry and then share that answer with the prophet.

The FLDS Church, led by Warren Jeffs since 2002, has gained notoriety because of the group's former refusal to stop conducting underage marriages, drawing the attention of law enforcement in Utah, Arizona, Texas, and Canada. In 2007, Jeffs was convicted in Utah of accomplice to rape for a marriage he conducted years earlier between a fourteen-year-old girl and her nineteen-year-old cousin. He was sentenced to two consecutive five-to-life prison terms. He appealed, and in July 2010, the Utah Supreme Court overturned Jeffs's verdict after finding the jury had not been properly instructed before its deliberations. The court ordered that the case be reheard. Utah officials opted to postpone a second trial so Jeffs could face more serious charges in Texas.

On December 1, 2010, Jeffs was transferred from Utah to Texas, where he is charged with bigamy and sexual assault based on alleged spiritual marriages to two minors. As this book went to press, two trial dates—one in July and one in October—had been set for Jeffs. Allegations that Jeffs spiritually married minor girls from Canada have also surfaced. Despite his incarceration, Jeffs apparently continues to lead the FLDS Church, though another FLDS member raised a challenge to his leadership in March 2011.

Apostolic United Brethren
(also known as the Allred Group)

The Apostolic United Brethren (AUB) has an estimated 7,500 members. Many members live in various communities in Utah, but the AUB also has communities in Pinesdale, Montana, and Ozumba, Mexico. The AUB has an endowment house where marriage and other ordinances are performed, as well as a temple, completed in 1983, in Ozumba. Its leaders have taken a strong, public position against underage marriage and abuse of any kind, and several members participate on the Utah Safety Net Committee, an educational/social services outreach group set up by the Utah attorney general's office in 2003.

Centennial Park
(also known as the Work of Jesus Christ)

In 1984, prior to the incorporation of the FLDS Church in 1991, a simmering disagreement among leaders over authority and property fractured the polygamous community that spans Hildale, Utah, and Colorado City, Arizona. The rift led to the creation of Centennial Park, which is located about two miles south of the Utah state line in Arizona.

Centennial Park has about 2,000 members. For the past several years, the Centennial Park Action Committee has actively defended polygamists' civil rights and advocated for the decriminalization

OVERVIEW OF FUNDAMENTALIST MORMONISM AND POLYGAMY

of polygamy. Some Centennial Park members also participate in the Utah Safety Net Committee. The community's private and public schools are highly regarded and Centennial Park has taken a strong stance against underage marriage and abuse of any kind.

Davis County Cooperative Society
(also known as the Kingston Group)

The Davis County Cooperative has about 2,000 members who live mostly in the Salt Lake Valley. The society was founded in 1935, during the depths of the Great Depression, as a United Order effort to benefit members. Its primary operating principle is the Golden Rule—"Do unto others as you would have others do unto you." In 1977, some members formed the Latter-Day Church of Christ. Like Centennial Park, the Kingston Group places a priority on education and is active in the Utah Safety Net Committee.

Smaller Groups

Another 1,500 or so people belong to smaller Fundamentalist Mormon factions, such as the Nielsen/Naylor group (300 people); the Winston Blackmore group (400) in Canada; the True and Living Church of Saints of the Latter Days (200) in Utah; and the Missouri communities, a "melting pot" of some 600 Fundamentalist Mormons.

ACKNOWLEDGMENTS

The Dargers

We would like to thank our parents, whose examples first inspired us. Also, our children, who have sacrificed during the creation of this project and whose future remains our inspiration. We thank AJ Hunt, Stephen Clark, Ryan and Rachel, Zach and Trav and their families for their feedback and support, and Ellen, who was the "other mother" while we wrote this book. A special acknowledgment to Brooke Adams, whose professionalism and dedication made writing this book possible. Thanks to everyone at HarperOne for being so enthusiastic about our story. Finally, Anne Wilde and Mary and Gary Batchelor: we thank you for your tireless work in and contributions to Principle Voices. For more information, please visit us at www.lovetimesthree.com or www.Principlevoices.org.

Brooke Adams

I would like to thank the Dargers for trusting me with their remarkable story. Thanks also to: David Patterson, Foundry Literary+Media, for his first-class guidance; Cindy DiTiberio for asking all the right questions; Suzanne Quist for getting us to the finish line; Kathy Reigstad, whose fine, detailed edit improved the book; Anne Wilde and Mary and Gary Batchelor for opening the door; historians Ken Driggs and Marianne Watson, who always share; Linda Fantin, Anna Cekola, Elaine Jarvik, Amy Donaldson, Mary McDonald, Charlie Ward, Sunny Smith, and Sarah Bruck for their encouragement; ALL my wonderful children for their love and support; and Tom, who spent too many nights and weekends with Lulu. For my dad, who will always be my favorite storyteller.